SCOTTISH
COVENANTER
STORIES

MARGARET,

AGNES.

SCOTTISH COVENANTER STORIES

TALES FROM
THE KILLING TIMES

DANE LOVE

NEIL WILSON PUBLISHING • GLASGOW • SCOTLAND

First published by
Neil Wilson Publishing
303 The Pentagon Centre
36 Washington Street
GLASGOW
G3 8AZ
Tel: 0141-221-1117
Fax: 0141-221-5363
E-mail: info@nwp.co.uk
www.nwp.co.uk

© Dane Love, 2005

First published May 2000
Reprinted April 2002, April 2005

The author has asserted his moral right
under the Copyright, Design and Patents Act, 1988
to be identified as the Author of this Work.

A catalogue record for this book is
available from the British Library.

ISBN 1-897784-98-8
Typeset in Baskerville and Copperplate
Designed by Mark Blackadder
Printed by WS Bookwell Finland

Contents

INTRODUCTION

Throughout south-west Scotland, and in a few places within the central belt and Fife, there survive a large number of 'martyrs' graves'. Many are located on remote moors, marking the spot where the government soldiers killed supporters of the Covenant. Many more are to be found in parish kirkyards, in a number of cases erected by Robert Paterson, the 'Old Mortality' of Sir Walter Scott's novel of the same name, but often replaced by more modern memorials. Almost every corner of southern Scotland has a tale to tell of the years of persecution, from remote and ruinous shepherds' houses where the Covenanters held their secret meetings, to castles and country houses commandeered by the government troops in their quest to capture and punish those who refused to adhere to the king's religious demands.

King Charles I was crowned in 1625 at which time he proposed bringing the Scots church into line with that of England. He was an opponent of Presbyterianism, and thought it would be simpler if the whole country would adopt Episcopacy. He met with Archbishop Laud of Canterbury and planned the introduction of the *Book of Common Prayer* into the Scottish church service. This took some time, and it was not until 23 July 1637 that the Dean read from this new liturgy in the High Kirk of Edinburgh. Traditionally it is said that it was on that occasion

Jenny Geddes stood up in the congregation and threw her stool at the minister, shouting out, 'Wha daur say mass in ma lug?'. The congregation erupted and the service had to be abandoned.

On 28 February 1638 the National Covenant was produced by Rev Alexander Henderson of Leuchars and Lord Johnston of Wariston on behalf of the nobility, landowners and the Church of Scotland. It was placed on public display in Greyfriars' Church and over 60,000 folk gathered there and signed the documents supporting Presbyterianism, while also swearing their loyalty to the crown. The actual document measures approximately 45 inches square and is probably made from deerskin. It was claimed that many of the signatures were written with the subscriber's own blood, but of this there is no proof. Other copies were taken throughout the country for further signatures, such as that from Borgue in Galloway, dated 22 April 1638.[1]

In 1643 the English Civil War ousted Charles from the throne and Oliver Cromwell was installed as Lord Protector. One of his first tasks was to execute the king. The Scots people were against this and fought for his son, whom they recognised as Charles II. However, the English Parliamentarians agreed with the Solemn League and Covenant and agreed that Presbyterianism be adopted as the national religion throughout the rest of Great Britain, resulting in the Covenanters siding with Cromwell. His campaigning brought him into Scotland where a number of battles took place. The Parliamentarians were later to renege on their deal.

The Earl (later 1st Marquis) of Montrose changed his allegiance from the Covenanters (whom he felt were too extreme in many cases) to support the king, waging war on his behalf from 1644-5. He won at Tibbermore in 1644 but was defeated at Philiphaugh in 1645 by David Leslie. After a period in Norway he landed in Orkney and commenced a campaign from the north. He was defeated at Carbisdale by Alexander Strachan and subsequently hanged in Edinburgh on 21 May 1650. Cromwell defeated Leslie at Dunbar in September 1650. Garrisons of soldiers were established throughout the country and a few skirmishes took place between them and the Covenanters, such as the Battle of Hieton near Hamilton, where in October 1650, the kirk records state, 'This dayes was no session keepit, because the enemie was in the Kingdom'.

Although there were thousands killed in the campaigns of Montrose, not many are commemorated by memorials. One of the few was Thomas Small, 'ane vertous husbandman', who died on 1 September 1645 aged 58. He is buried in Ecclesmagirdle kirkyard, south of Perth. Nothing else is known about him.[2] Similarly, Andrew Smith in Huntlie, who died in 1643 aged 63, is noted on his gravestone at Longforgan in Perthshire as 'ane trve Covenanter'.[3]

On 23 June 1650 Charles II landed at Garmouth in Moray where he signed the Solemn League and Covenant, much to the delight of the Scots.[4] He was crowned at Scone in 1651 but suffered defeat at the Battle of Worcester the following year. Eight commissioners were appointed by the English parliament to look after Scotland's affairs, changing to a council of state of nine members. Cromwell established forts throughout the country at Ayr, Leith, Perth, Inverlochy and Inverness to ensure his control of the country.

When Cromwell died in 1658 the country fell into a state of unrest, Cromwell's son being weaker than his father and in 1660 Charles II was fully restored to the throne of Great Britain. Having achieved his goal he abandoned his support for Presbyterianism and the Covenant and set out to claim superiority over the church. The Recissory Act repealed all those acts which had been passed by the Covenanting parliaments. He established Prelacy, whereby the church was governed by bishops, but the anti-Erastians, who could not agree to the control of the church by the state, could not accept this. The period from 1660 until the Glorious Revolution in 1688 was the period of greatest persecution, when thousands were killed in the fields, executed in the towns, banished abroad as slaves, or were fined.

Bishops and 'curates' were appointed to the church in 1662. The so-called 'Drunken Parliament' passed the Middleton Act which ejected non-conforming ministers from their churches. There were around 400 such ministers forced from their parishes. At first the authorities tolerated them preaching in their congregation's houses, or in barns, but it was soon realised that the people's resolve was such that they would not attend the curate's, or government-appointed Episcopal minister's, services. The first attempts at limiting attendance at these Conventicles was made in 1663 and by 1670 attendance became treasonable and preaching at them, a capital offence.

By 1666 the persecution by soldiers, who were given lists of names of non-attendees by the curates, was so bad that the country became restless. When the villagers of Dalry in Galloway witnessed an old man being roasted with branding irons by the soldiers, the rebellion commenced. It had not been planned, but numbers flocked to the cause and a march towards Edinburgh took place. Being spontaneous, the Covenanters were not prepared for the journey and they were ultimately defeated in battle by the soldiers of General Tam Dalyell of the Binns at Rullion Green in the Pentland Hills.

In 1669 the Duke of Lauderdale introduced what were termed 'Indulgences', whereby ousted ministers could accept certain conditions and return to their churches. Although over 100 did, most refused. Around the same time a period of calm, known as 'The Blink' took place. A second declaration of indulgence was made in 1672.

In 1674 the government decreed that conventicles, or meetings in the fields, were illegal and that it was a capital offence to attend these. 'The Bond' was drawn up which stated that landowners and heritors were responsible for making sure that their tenants adhered to Episcopacy. At first the landowners treated this lightly, but soon they were forced into adherence. In 1678 parties of highland soldiers, known as the 'Highland Host', were quartered on suspected Covenanters in the south-west of Scotland. The highlanders were responsible for many atrocities, robbing their hosts of all belongings and livestock, rape, pillage, and destruction. Thousands of pounds worth of damage and theft were done in the few months they were in residence.

What became known as the 'Second Resistance' commenced with the Rutherglen Declaration in 1679. A large conventicle near Drumclog was attacked by the soldiers under Graham of Claverhouse. The Covenanters managed to use the ground to their advantage and were the victors. Thinking that their hour had come, they proposed a march on Glasgow but discovered that the residents had placed barricades across the streets to prevent them from entering the city. The Covenanters turned about and at Bothwell Bridge were to take part in another battle. This time they were soundly defeated, with perhaps 400 killed on the field, and in the subsequent pursuit, 1,200 taken prisoner. Most of these were marched to Edinburgh where they were locked up in an enclosure off Greyfriars' kirkyard. Five months later, after many had escaped, some had died, and others succumbed to signing a declaration of governmental support, 257 Covenanters remained. They were sentenced to banishment and placed on board a ship at Leith, which was to founder off Orkney with most of the Covenanters being drowned.

The period from 1680, after the signing of the Sanquhar Declaration and the Battle of Airds Moss, until 1685 was one of the fiercest in terms of persecution; a few months during 1684-5 becoming forever known as the 'Killing Time'. Most of the well-known martyrdoms took place at this time, including the murder of John Brown at his own front door, in view of his wife and children, and the drowning of two women in the rising Solway tide.

Thousands of Covenanters suffered for their adherence to the cause. Many were persecuted for years but survived and have not been celebrated for their martyrdom. Thousands lie buried in old churchyards, but only a few stones actually comment on their adherence. Robert Laurie lies buried at Dalserf in Lanarkshire.[5] and the 'Godly shoemaker' Robert Nairn is buried at Bonhill in Dunbartonshire.[6]

Many Covenanters managed to break out of prison on a number of occasions. On 16 September 1683, 25 prisoners escaped from the Canongate tolbooth in Edinburgh. A file had been smuggled in and the Covenanters spent hours working on the bars on the window, high above the street. They found that removing one bar left insufficient room to escape, so the rest had to be cut. When a bar fell from the window onto the street below they thought their ploy had been rumbled, but no-one noticed. Of the 25 who escaped, only three were Covenanters – George Aitken, John Dick and Adam Philip. Dick had been active at Bothwell Bridge. He was recaptured in the spring of the following year and executed at Edinburgh on 5 March.

In 1688 the preacher James Renwick was captured and executed at the scaffold in Edinburgh's Grassmarket, the last Covenanter to suffer a public execution. He would also have been the last Covenanting martyr but for the 16-year-old George Wood, who was shot a few days later at his home, near the Ayrshire village of Sorn.

Charles II had died in February 1685 and his brother James VII and II succeeded. He was a believer in the Divine Right of Kings and a supporter of the Roman Catholic faith. The people were against this and a rebellion took place which tried to replace him as monarch with the Protestant Duke of Monmouth, Charles II's illegitimate son. The 9th Earl of Argyll was a main player in this, but his attempt at rebellion was defeated and he was beheaded. In December 1688 James VII fled first to Ireland, then France. This paved the way for William and Mary (James's daughter) to accept the throne. James and his son Charles tried to reclaim the throne in the Jacobite risings of 1689, 1715 and 1745, but were unsuccessful. The Glorious Revolution had taken place, and the king's councillor, William Carstairs, persuaded him to accept Presbyterianism as the established church in Scotland.

Although most of the Covenanters rejoined the established church, there were a good number throughout the country who wished to remain apart. They established the Reformed Presbyterian Church. Similarly, the followers of Rev Richard Cameron formed the 26th Regiment of Foot in May 1689, better known as the Cameronians. They served with distinction until 14

May 1968 when the regiment was disbanded at a special conventicle held at Douglas in Lanarkshire, where they had been raised 279 years earlier.

AUTHOR'S NOTE

The headings of many of the following chapters have been taken from the epitaphs which appear on the original gravestones of the martyrs, hence the poor spelling in some cases! The footnotes give the National Grid Reference of monuments or gravestones associated with the Covenanters, as well as one or two important places associated with them. I wish to acknowledge the part played by my wife Hazel for her support and in checking the manuscript. Acknowledgements are also due to George Scott, past Honorary Secretary of the Scottish Covenanter Memorials Association.

Dane Love
Auchinleck, April 2002

1. Borgue's National Covenant is now in Register House, Edinburgh.
2. NO 107163. Headstone in Ecclesmagirdle churchyard.
3. NO 309299. Original stone slab now in vestibule of Longforgan church.
4. NJ 339644. Plaque on gable of house.
5. NS 799507.
6. NS 395796. Gravestone in Bonhill churchyard.

1

EARLY MARTYRS

On Monday 27 May 1661 the guillotine known as the 'Maiden' was erected in Edinburgh's Grassmarket. It was a fairly common occurrence, for this was the site of public executions in the city. However, the person to be hanged that day was unique. He was not only from the upper classes, being a Marquis and head of a great highland clan, but he was the first to die for his adherence to the Covenant.

Archibald Campbell, 8th Earl and 1st Marquis of Argyll (created 1641), was born around 1607, the son of Archibald, the 7th Earl, who had converted to Catholicism after marrying his second wife. He fled to western Flanders in 1618 after being outlawed but Charles I reversed the sentence in 1677 after which the old man spent his last ten years in London in reduced circumstances. While his son Archibald was still a child, the estates had been passed down to him.

Argyll took part in many battles. On 2 February 1645 he was active against Montrose at the Battle of Inverlochy. His men were severely defeated, so much so that it was said that the waves on the shores of the loch lapped red with blood. He fled from the scene in his boat, bringing about claims that he was a timorous and feeble person.

Argyll was a royal favourite for many years. In 1651, when

Charles was crowned at Scone, it was Argyll who had the honour of placing the crown on the monarch's head. Charles at that time had accepted the Covenants and had promised to maintain true religious freedom for his subjects, having signed the Covenant at Garmouth in Moray.

After the Restoration, Argyll travelled to London where he tried to gain an audience with the king. He was arrested by Sir William Fleming and sent to the Tower, on a dubious political charge, where he remained for around nine months before being transferred to a cell in Edinburgh.

From the scaffold the Marquis told the crowd assembled below, 'I had the honour to place the crown upon the king's brow; now he hastens me away to a better crown than his own.' His head was then placed on the block and the blade hoisted. Its quick descent left the crowd silent. Argyll's body was gifted to his friends. They took it to the Magdalen Chapel in the Cowgate where it lay for some time. It was then moved to the Lothian burial vault at Newbattle before being transferred to the kirk of Kilmun, in Argyll, where it was finally laid to rest.[1] His severed head was taken by the hangman and displayed on a pike on top of the Heart of Midlothian. It was to remain there until 8 June 1664.

There were two other men in gaol awaiting the same fate as Argyll. Rev James Guthrie and Lieutenant William Govan were led out to the scaffold five days later. Guthrie was the minister of Stirling's Holy Rude church; little is known of his life before he became famous as 'the little man who could not bow', – this being an allusion to the fact that he would not succumb to the authorities over the church. Born into an Episcopalian family, Guthrie was probably being brought up to enter the ministry of that denomination. He was sent to St Andrews to study, but there he met Rev Samuel Rutherford.

Guthrie attended many of Rutherford's prayer meetings and theology discussions, which were to influence him considerably. According to what he wrote late in life, 'until the year 1638 I was treading other steps: and the Lord did then recover me out of the snare of Prelacy, Ceremonies and the Service Book.' In 1638 Guthrie was ordained as minister of the small town of Lauder, in Berwickshire, remaining until 1649.

A call to Stirling's Holy Rude church was answered in 1650. His time there was not without trouble, for not all the residents of the town agreed with his strong Protestant views. In 1656 the church was split in two, both figuratively and physically, for a wall was erected dividing the building. One half was ministered to by Guthrie, the other by Rev Matthew Simpson, his former assistant.

Whilst at Stirling, Guthrie wrote a book entitled *The Causes of the Lord's Wrath Against Scotland.* This volume was later considered treasonable, and copies of it were burned by the public hangmen. Anyone found with a copy in their possession could be charged with treason against the crown and government.

Guthrie was arrested a number of times for his failure to accept Charles as head of the church, but on each accasion he was later released. Eventually, in 1657 the General Assembly deposed him from his charge.

When Cromwell was abroad in Scotland Guthrie conversed with him, making him aware of the position of the Church of Scotland. It was Cromwell who referred to Guthrie as the 'short man'. In 1657 Guthrie journeyed to London where he defended the king's right against Cromwell. Guthrie was noted for his royalist views, but these only went so far and he could not accept the king's interference in the work of the kirk.

On 23 August 1660 Guthrie and a number of others met in Edinburgh to draw up a supplication to the restored king. In it they pledged their allegiance to the crown, but desired that the king kept the reformed faith in Scotland. A party of soldiers were sent to the meeting house by the Earl of Middleton. They arrested Guthrie and 10 others, one of their number managing to escape. Guthrie was gaoled in Edinburgh Castle for a short time before being moved on to Stirling Castle. He was to remain imprisoned there for six months.

Guthrie was tried before the Privy Council on two occasions, in February and April 1661. He was charged with treason, but Guthrie, who was defending himself, managed to baffle the lawyers with his knowledge of legal and ecclesiastical matters. The trials lasted for some time, until at length Guthrie himself requested that they be brought to a speedy conclusion. He told the court, 'having now suffered eight months' imprisonment, your Lordships would put no other burden upon me. I shall conclude with the words of Jeremiah, "Behold I am in your hands, do to me what seemeth good to you". If you put me to death you shall bring innocent blood upon yourselves and upon the inhabitants of the city.'

The judges considered Guthrie's plea for some time. Some of them were keen to banish him to the plantations, but Middleton would accept nothing less than the death penalty. Accordingly he was sentenced to die at the Cross. The sentence shocked many throughout the nation. Appeals were sent to the authorities to release him, or else try and persuade him to accept their authority by granting him a bishopric.

Guthrie was hanged on Saturday, 1 June 1661. As he climbed the scaffold steps he addressed the crowds, 'I take God to record upon my soul, I would not exchange this scaffold for the palace and mitre of the greatest prelate in the land.' Once his body was lifeless, Guthrie's head was chopped off and displayed on the Netherbow Port for the next 27 years. Tradition asserts that one day when Middleton was driving his coach through the gateway drops of blood fell from Guthrie's head onto the coachwork. Despite regular scrubbing and polishing, the stains of the martyr were never to be removed, constantly reminding Middleton of his actions.[2]

On the same day Guthrie was executed, Lieutenant (or Captain) William Govan (b. 1623) was also hanged from the scaffold. He was a member of the Remonstrant army but had defected to the ranks of Cromwell's troops. In 1651 a decree of forfeiture was issued against him. Govan had taken a small part in the execution of Charles I, for which he was tried and executed. Before he suffered death, he looked up at the gibbet on which

Guthrie's corpse now hung and declared, 'It is sweet; otherwise how durst I look upon the corpse of him who hangs there, and smile upon these sticks and that gibbet as the gates of heaven.' His head was removed and displayed on the West Bow.

Archibald Johnston was also tried for his treasonable beliefs at the same time. Born a son of the Johnstons of Annandale, he was related to a number of law-lords. He inherited a house in Edinburgh's High Street where the Supplicants, the group who compiled the Supplication which was a forerunner of the National Covenant, met.

He had been Clerk to the General Assembly in 1638 and was instrumental in making sure that the pro-Episcopal members were defeated in their attempt at changing the direction of the kirk by compiling a list of Acts of Parliament which suppressed Roman Catholicism while establishing Protestantism as the religion of Scotland. This was to become the second part of the National Covenant. The first part contained the King's Confession of 1580-1, the third part was compiled by Alexander Henderson. At a meeting held in Greyfriars' Church in Edinburgh on Wednesday 28 February 1638 Johnston read this out to the large assembled crowd and when the Glasgow Assembly finally ended he was appointed Procurator of the church.

In 1641 Johnston was knighted and made a Lord of Session taking the title Lord Wariston, later becoming MP for Edinburgh. Wariston had a knack of being able to unearth old parliamentary papers which he used to support the case against the Episcopalians. It was thought that the church records of 1560-90 had been lost, and the supporters of the Covenant regretted this, but Wariston was able to unearth them, thus adding strength to the Presbyterian voice. In April 1641 Wariston referred to the Records of Parliament, which had been given to Hay of Dunfermline to destroy. The king, knowing this, claimed that they did not exist and therefore could not be used as evidence, but Wariston had somehow managed to save them, and produced them in parliament.

In 1646 Johnston was appointed Lord Advocate and in 1649 Lord Clerk Register.

At the Restoration Wariston knew that the king would not allow him to live long. He fled abroad to the Netherlands, Germany and France. The trial went on in his absence, and he was found guilty of treason and sentenced to death, the proclamation being read out at the Cross of Edinburgh on 13 May 1661.

Wariston was apprehended by one of Charles' detectives at Rouen as he prayed. He was taken back across the Channel to London where he spent six months imprisoned in the Tower. He was then brought back to Scotland and executed on 22 July 1663, 26 months after he had been sentenced. Like Guthrie, his head was removed from his body and displayed on the Netherbow Port.

1. NS 166821. Mausoleum in Kilmun churchyard.
2. NS 792937. Memorial in Holy Rude churchyard, Stirling.

2

FOUGHT WITH GREAT RENOWN

On 13 November 1666 the soldiers from the garrison at Dalry in Galloway were out and about exacting fines from those who had failed to attend church. Corporal George Deanes and three other soldiers from Sir Alexander Thomson's guards had claimed the corn of an old farmer by the name of Grier in lieu of his fine, which he had been unable to pay. Grier had fled his home, but the soldiers caught up with him and brought him back to the village. The soldiers tied his hands and feet together and intended carrying him trussed below a pole 'like a beast'. They were then about to strip him of his clothes and lower him onto a red-hot gridiron.

Four Covenanters who had spent some of the previous months hiding amidst the hills had risked coming into the village that day in order to eat a hearty breakfast at the local inn. One of the men was John MacLellan of Barscobe Castle, a local laird who had fled his home. As they left the inn they witnessed the cruel treatment meted out to old Grier.

'Why do you use the honest man so?' Barscobe asked.

The soldiers, incensed, drew their swords, intending to capture the men and try them. Barscobe took out his pistol (into the barrel of which, having no shot to spare, he had previously rammed fragments of his pipe) and fired. The clay blasted into

Deanes's leg, wounding him. It was recorded that a surgeon later removed ten pieces of the pipe from his body. The other soldiers quickly surrendered.

The Covenanters moved to the nearby village of Balmaclellan, where Alexander Robertson was preaching at a conventicle. The larger group decided that they were strong enough to attack the local garrison, which had 16 soldiers in residence. In the scuffle one of the soldiers was killed. The Covenanters then moved on to Irongray kirkyard, near Dumfries, where they formed themselves into an army of volunteers.

The Covenanters realised that things were now getting serious. They decided that they should kidnap the local commander, Sir James Turner, known as 'Bloody Bite-the-sheep', and hold him whilst negotiations went on with the king. Turner was stationed in Dumfries. Accordingly 54 Covenanters on horseback rode towards the town, followed by around 150 on foot. The weather was wet and wild, resulting in the journey taking longer than expected. They arrived at around nine o'clock on the Thursday morning, 15 November.

A Covenanter by the name of Andrew Gray seems to have taken charge. He led the Covenanters into Dumfries by crossing Devorgilla's Bridge and made their way to Bailie Finnie's house, where Turner was staying at the time, and called out to him to surrender. Turner appeared at the window and asked for quarter, which John Neilson of Corsock duly granted. Gray was ready to shoot Turner, but Neilson intervened, telling him that he had promised Turner that he would be held prisoner. In revenge, Gray searched through the house, taking papers from Turner's chest as well as 6,000 merks. The Covenanters then marched to the burgh cross, where they toasted the king's health and pledged their allegiance to the Covenant, before heading to the Sands beside the River Nith where they held a council of war. Turner was taken with them, at first dressed in his night-clothes, but later allowed to wear everyday clothing.

The Covenanters gathered as many arms as they could find in the town before deciding to make their way to the north-west again. They travelled up the side of Cluden and Cairn waters to Glencairn church, where they rested for a short while. During the hours of darkness they marched back to Dalry, a total of 32 miles. Word came that some soldiers were in the vicinity, so during the following night they made their way north to the wilder countryside around Carsphairn. It was around this time that Andrew Gray, who had claimed to be a captain, mysteriously disappeared. He had already sent on Turner's money 'for safe keeping', and apart from a claimed sighting in Newcastle, he was never to be seen again.

From Dumfries Steven Irvine, bailie in the town, rode to Edinburgh to raise the alarm with the authorities. Lieutenant-General Thomas Dalyell was sent to the west with 2,500 foot soldiers and six troop of horse, marching by way of Glasgow and Kilmarnock to Mauchline in Ayrshire. At the same time the authorities issued a proclamation declaring that the uprising was to be classed as rebellion and all who refused to lay down their arms would be tried as traitors and thus be incapable of pardon.

The Covenanters decided that they should gather as much support as they could muster and march on Edinburgh, where they would lay their demands before the authorities. Thus they headed at first across Glen Muck to Dalmellington and into Ayrshire. At Dalmellington they were joined by the ousted minister of Irongray, John Welsh, who preached at a large conventicle in their midst. He also prayed that Turner would be converted to their beliefs and that he could be forgiven for his sins. The route then led on to Tarbolton and Ayr, near where Colonel James Wallace of Auchans joined them and was appointed commander. Turner's memoirs noted with admiration the leadership qualities Wallace displayed. By this time the force numbered around 700.

Whilst the Covenanting force was in the middle of Kyle, two men were sent on to scout and drum up support. They were John Ross, who came from Mauchline, and John Shields, tenant of Titwood farm in the parish of Mearns in Renfrewshire. Some of the soldiers marching from Edinburgh, under the command of the Duke of Hamilton, captured them near Kilmarnock and they were taken back to the town and held prisoner. They were later moved to Edinburgh where they were tried and hanged on 7 December 1666. Their heads were cut off and sent back to Kilmarnock where they were publicly displayed for a while before being interred in the Laigh kirkyard.[1]

The Covenanters then headed inland, passing through Coylton to Ochiltree, where they rested for the night. On 23 November they continued to Cumnock where they were warned that Dalyell was advancing on Kilmarnock. The weather closed in on them, and they were all soaked to the skin as they made their way across Airds Moss towards Muirkirk. James Turner noted that:

The way to that church [Muirkirk] was exceeding bad, a very hie wind, with a grievous raine in our faces. The night fell dark before we could reach the place where the foot were quartered, with no meate or drink, and with very little fire. I doe confesse, I never saw lustier fellows than these foote were, or better marchers.

The Covenanters rested as best they could in the parish church but many of them became disheartened at this point, and a number began to drift away. Wallace, however, pushed them onward, and when they reached Douglas they rested again in the old kirk of St Bride before marching to Lanark where it was decided to renew the Solemn League and Covenant.

On Monday 26 November Rev John Guthrie, evicted minister of Tarbolton, stood on the forestairs of Lanark tolbooth and addressed the 500 infantry. At the burgh's Townhead Gabriel Semple preached to the 500 riders. A bond was compiled, explaining the origin of the rising, and setting out what their intentions were.

The Covenanters then left Lanark and made their way northwards over the moors to Bathgate in West Lothian, but Dalyell's forces entered Lanark just after the Covenanters had left, and were able to follow them close behind. The Covenanters were forced towards Newbridge, to the west of Edinburgh, from where they moved into Colinton. They had expected to be joined by a number of allies from the Lothians, but these failed to materialise and as they tried to rest in the kirkyard they became increasingly dejected once more.

On the night of 27 November the Covenanters camped at Redford Road, east of Colinton.[2] Their sleep was disturbed early in the morning by the sound of guns as a number of Edinburgh Fencibles had heard of their overnight camp and had come to attack them. A few of the Covenanters were injured in the affray.

Colonel Wallace ordered his men to march towards the Pentland Hills. They made their way past Dreghorn Castle, Fulford and Flotterstone to Rullion Green, the site of an ancient cattle market. Dalyell's soldiers were in hot pursuit, making their way by a drove road from Currie to Kirkstown and onto the Green. The two armies met on 28 November. The Covenanting force was reckoned to be 900 strong; poorly equipped, with only 60 muskets, 40 pistols and 20 pounds of powder between them. It is true to say that they were not really expecting to fight, even then, for they had hoped that the Privy Council would listen to their pleas and suggest a peaceable outcome. The government troops numbered 3,000 regular soldiers, all armed and ready to fight.

The king's soldiers, under the command of Major Joseph Learmont of Newholm, started the fight by firing into the opposition. The Covenanters responded, and the foot-soldiers engaged in fighting with swords in which John Paton of Meadowhead and Captain Andrew Arnot displayed their skill. The pikemen, armed with scythes and other blades tied to poles, charged into the midst of the soldiers, pushing them backward in fear. The Duke of Hamilton was lucky to escape, as was Dean Ramsay. Dalyell's horsemen rode at speed across the grass into the midst of the battle, slaying many in the process. They were followed by Linlithgow's infantry who slaughtered many in their wake. The battle was over. A few small fights continued, but soon the victory was Dalyell's. His soldiers stripped the dead of their valuables and on the following day some women from Edinburgh buried them in shrouds.

Sir James Turner, who had still been held hostage as far as

the field, had agreed with his captors that if the royalist force won then he would ensure that his guardsmen would be released, so long as they did not ill-treat him. At the hour of victory he made his way with the guards to the government soldiers, but the Privy Council refused to honour the bargain.

Many Covenanters fled westward after they realised that the battle was lost. Some were successful in escaping the clutches of the enemy, such as Colonel Wallace, who managed to flee to the Netherlands. John Gordon of Largmore, in the parish of Kells, was wounded in the battle but returned home. He survived only for a short time, and died on 6 January 1667. His brother-in-law, William Gordon of Roberton, was killed in the battle. A son of John, Roger, escaped from Bothwell and survived long after the Killing Times. He presented communion cups and a bell to Kells church in Galloway.[3]

An unknown Covenanter who had been wounded in battle limped slowly westward along the Pentland Hills as far as Blacklaw. There he knocked on the door of Adam Sanderson, a shepherd, but he was too scared to allow him into the house for fear of reprisals. He allowed him to stay in an outhouse, though. The Covenanter, who seems to have known that his time was nearly over, asked Sanderson that if he should find him dead could he bury him within sight of the Ayrshire hills. Next morning, sure enough, Sanderson found the Covenanter lying dead within an oak thicket. He took him to the Black Law, which affords distant views of Ayrshire, and there laid him to rest.[4]

Other Covenanters were shot as they fled for safety. A number are said to have been killed by country-folk in Midlothian, and their bodies buried in the kirkyards of Penicuik and Glencorse. The session minutes of Penicuik for 9 December record, 'Disbursed to John Brown, belman, for making Westlandman's graves, 3s 4d.' William Smith of Moremellen in the parish of Shotts was active in battle but was murdered at a neighbour's home.[5]

The number killed in the battle cannot be accurately determined. According to Charles Maitland of Hatton, who was with Dalyell, 100 Covenanters were left for dead on the battlefield, and another 300 as they fled home. The gravestone on the battlefield commemorates 'about fifty other true covenanted Presbyterians who were killed here in their own Innocent self defence.' Names of those who died include Rev John Cruikshank, an Irish minister who had preached at Lanark, and Rev Andrew MacCormick, another Irish non-conformist who had fled to Scotland after being charged with a plot to capture the Lord Lieutenant in Dublin Castle.[6] According to Robert Mein, postmaster in Edinburgh, no government soldiers were killed, but this is thought to be untrue. There were 120 Covenanters taken prisoner who marched into Edinburgh, where they were crowded into part of the High Kirk of Edinburgh known as 'Haddock's Hole'. The better class of prisoner was locked up in the tolbooth.

On 5 December 1666 the Justiciary Court sat in Edinburgh, Lord Advocate Nisbet in the chair. Many Covenanters were brought before it and charged with treason and rebellion. All were found guilty and sentenced to be hanged on 7 December at the mercat cross of Edinburgh. On that day Captain Andrew Arnot, Major John MacCulloch, Gavin Hamilton in Maudslie (Carluke), John Gordon of Knockbreck, his brother Robert, Cristall or Christopher Strang, portioner of Lickpravick, East Kilbride, John Parker, waulker in Busby Waulkmill, John Ross in Mauchline, James Hamilton, tenant in Kithemoor, and John Shields in Titwood (Mearns) all suffered execution by hanging. According to the Book of Adjournal, 'after they are dead, their heads and right arms to be cutt off and disposed upon as the Lords of his Majesties Privy Council shall think fitt, and all their lands, heretages, goods and gear to be forfault and escheat to his Majesties use for the treasonable crimes forsaids which was pronounced for Doom.' Accordingly the heads of the two Gordons and MacCulloch were sent to Kirkcudbright for display. The two Hamiltons, Parker and Strang's heads were sent to Hamilton.[7] Arnot's head went to the Watergate. Ross and Shields's heads went to Kilmarnock as previously noted. All 10 martyrs' right hands were sent to the tolbooth in Lanark, the spot where they had re-sworn the Covenant.

On 14 December five other Covenanters were hanged in Edinburgh. They were John Neilson of Corsock, John Lindsay, Alexander Robertson, George Crauford in Cumnock, and John Gordon in Irongray.

On Wednesday 19 December four Covenanters were hanged in Glasgow as a warning to the Covenanters from the west. They had been tried two days previously, when the defence claimed that as they had been given quarter on the field of battle, they should not be sentenced to death. The judges ignored this plea, however, and had them hanged. They were Robert Buntine (or Bunton) of Fenwick (Ayrshire),[8] John Hart of Glassford (Lanarkshire), Robert Scott of Dalserf (Lanarkshire) and Matthew Paton, a shoemaker from Newmilns (Ayrshire).[9]

A further trial took place and nine Covenanters were found guilty of rebellion. They were to be hanged on 22 December, but three of them had their sentences deferred. The remaining six suffered martyrdom at the mercat cross in Edinburgh. These were Hugh MacKail, Humphrey Colquhoun, Mungo Knaip in Evandale, Ralph Shiells, collier in Ayr, John Wodrow, merchant in Glasgow and John Wilson in Kilmaurs.

William Mure, the laird of Castle Caldwell in north Ayrshire, had supported the Covenanters on their march to Edinburgh. He was forced to flee to Holland where he died. In 1670 his estates were granted to General Dalyell of the Binns as a thank-you for his victory in battle. The lands were restored to the Mures in 1690. Another landowner who supported the Covenanters was John Maxwell, younger of Monreith. He is thought to have been present in the rising from Dalry. From Rullion Green, Maxwell fled on his grey horse, and tradition states that he did not rest until he reached Monreith Castle, over 110 miles away in Wigtownshire. The laird rewarded the horse with never having to carry a passenger again, and 'As guid as a Pentland horse' became a local saying. Maxwell himself was pursued by the authorities, on one occasion evading capture by hiding in an

Edinburgh lady's meal girnal. He escaped to Ireland, where he died, his Scottish estates being forfeit.

1. NS 427380. Headstone in Laigh kirkyard, Kilmarnock.
2. NT 227686. Tall memorial marks site of camp.
3. NX 631783. Gravestone in Kells churchyard.
4. NT 078522. Gravestone on Black Law. Original gravestone now in Dunsyre church (NT 071481).
5. NS 843630. Gravestone in Kirk of Shotts kirkyard.
6. NT 219524. Gravestone on site of battle.
7. NS 723555. Gravestone in Hamilton old churchyard.
8. NS 464435. Memorial in Fenwick churchyard.
9. NS 537373. Memorial in Newmilns churchyard.

3

A FAT CHRISTMAS- PIE TO THE PRELATES

Hugh MacKail (born 1640) was the son of Rev Matthew MacKail, the minister of Bothwell Church, until he was forced out by the Middleton Act in 1662. Hugh was sent to Edinburgh University for an education, where he lodged with his uncle, also Hugh MacKail, and it was soon realised that he was a youth of great ability. Such was his talent that he was brought to the attention of one of the former Lord Provosts of Edinburgh, Sir James Stewart of Kirkfield and Coltness, who employed him as a tutor to his family, as well as a chaplain.

In 1661 MacKail applied to the presbytery for a licence to preach, which was freely granted. He gained considerable respect in the churches of the city but, like his father, found himself disagreeing with the authorities who were trying to impose Episcopacy on the country. His last sermon, at the beginning of September 1662 was given in the High Kirk of St Giles and was a thinly veiled swipe at those in authority. Although he referred to a 'Pharaoh on a throne, a Haman in the state, and a Judas in the church', these references were easily deciphered. He knew that he was now a wanted man.

Supporters of the king made their way to Goodtrees House, the home of Sir James Stewart, where they intended to apprehend MacKail. They missed him by just a few minutes, for he had decided to flee to Holland. Stewart and his second son, Walter, were charged with being present at this sermon, and also for entertaining MacKail at their home. This charge was later dropped, however.

MacKail remained in the Netherlands for three years. What he did there is not known, but it has been surmised that he stayed in Rotterdam and probably came into contact with Robert MacWard and John Brown of Wamphray, who were also in the city at that time.

Hugh MacKail returned to Scotland in 1665. He had expected the country to have settled in the intervening years but instead found that the land was now a hotbed of rebellion. When the western Covenanters commenced their rising in Galloway which ultimately ended at Rullion Green, MacKail was influenced to join them. He made his way to Ayr where he met up with the growing number of supporters. MacKail was not a fighting man, for his body was small and his stature weak. At one point he fainted and lay for a time as if he was dead. In William Veitch's record of the rising he noted that MacKail 'would have fallen off his horse, if one had not laid hold of him and held him up.' Nevertheless, he was able to keep going until the Covenanters reached the outskirts of Edinburgh.

It was near to Cramond Water that MacKail realised it was futile for him to continue. He left the Covenanters behind and made his way towards the south side of the city where his father had a temporary home. At Braid's Craig, near to Liberton, a party of dragoons came across and arrested him. They searched him for any clues on the actions of the Covenanters and many questions were put to him as to their whereabouts and names of the leaders taking part. but MacKail refused to reveal any information to the dragoons. MacKail in fact had a small sword on him but he made no resistance. The soldiers decided to take him to the old tolbooth and placed him in a cell.

The authorities appointed the Earl of Rothes to interrogate MacKail. He was not only charged with being present with the rebels before Rullion Green, he was also charged with seditious words spoken in St Giles. As MacKail refused to betray any of his associates, Rothes ordered that the 'boot' be placed round his legs. This instrument of torture involved a box or tube to be placed round the leg. Wedges were then placed around the knee and blows to the wedges made by a hammer. Still MacKail refused to release any information. Eleven blows of the hammer were given in total, which smashed the bones in his knee. MacKail responded, 'I protest solemnly in the sight of God, I can say no more though all the joints in my body were in such great anguish as my knee.'

Realising that they could torture him no further, and that he was unwilling to give up any information, the authorities returned MacKail to his cell. He was left in agony, unable to walk from the injuries received and his torture also brought on an 'inflammatory fever'.

On 18 December a second trial took place. MacKail confirmed that he had been with Covenanters as they marched from Ayr to Edinburgh, and he admitted he was in the possession of a sword when he had been captured. The authorities thus gained their reason to try and execute MacKail. He was sentenced to die at the market cross of Edinburgh at 2 o'clock on 22 December 1666 and he was only 26 years old. A number of influential people, including the Duchess of Hamilton and Marchioness of Douglas, appealed for MacKail's life to be spared, but to no avail.

MacKail was hanged as sentenced. He faced death with considerable courage and some regard his final testimony as one of the finest amongst the many recorded during the years of killing. His cousin, Dr Matthew MacKail, had arranged with the hangman to receive the corpse from the gallows and he took MacKail's black coat and wore it as a sign of mourning, until it fell to pieces. The corpse was taken to the Magdalen Chapel where it was dressed before being taken to the Greyfriars' kirkyard for burial. From the day of MacKail's execution until 1678 there were no more Covenanters executed in Edinburgh.

Five other Covenanters taken at the Battle of Rullion Green

also suffered death on the same day – Humphrey Colquhoun, Mungo Knaip in Evandale, Ralph Shiells, a collier from Ayr, John Wilson of Kilmaurs and John Wodrow, a Glasgow merchant.

4
GIBBETS WERE
IN FASHION THEN

A Royal Commission was published on 5 December 1666 which created a number of trials of the prisoners taken at the Battle of Rullion Green. A selection of noblemen and other gentlemen were appointed in different parts of the country who were given the power to hold courts, cite witnesses and use other methods in order to establish the guilt or otherwise of those who had appeared in arms that day on the Pentland foothills. Each area had a minimum of three men appointed in charge of these courts, and in order to facilitate a speedy response to the rising, they were given the power to hold their own assizes and pass whatever sentence they saw fit.

One of these courts was located at Ayr. The four men assigned were the Earl of Kellie, Lieutenant-General William Drummond of Cromlix, Charles Maitland of Hatton (later created Earl of Lauderdale), and James Crichton, Sheriff of Nithsdale and brother to the Earl of Dumfries. They established their court on 22 December that year, and 12 prisoners taken at the battlefield were summoned before the court two days later. Not surprisingly, the dozen men were found guilty, and all were sentenced to be executed. To widen the effects of the punishment on the people of the south-west of Scotland, it was decided to split up the group, with eight to be hanged in Ayr, two in Irvine, and two in Dumfries, so that the residents would see the punishment inflicted on those who appeared in arms and defied the king's authority.

The eight men due to be hanged at Ayr however caused the authorities considerable problems, as the local hangman refused to perform the deed, and absconded from the district.

A message was then sent to Irvine, where a highlander from Strathnaver, William Sutherland, was the burgh hangman, asking him to carry out the executions. Sutherland was illiterate, and had come to the south of Scotland to learn to read. At first he settled in Paisley, where he is noted for hanging a few witches, but he moved to Irvine where he obtained a more steady job. There he learned to read, studying the Bible in great detail, and supporting the Covenant. The provost of Irvine called on him to go to Ayr, but Sutherland refused. He was arrested and taken to the tolbooth. A guard was sent to escort him to Ayr, where again he was held in the tolbooth.

The curate of Ayr parish, George White, told him of Jewish examples of executions to try and persuade him that it was morally right to hang the Covenanters, but Sutherland responded by quoting the Scriptures. White eventually gave in, and claimed that Sutherland had the the devil in him. The judges tried to persuade Sutherland to carry out the act, with Dalyell and Drummond threatening him with the boot, but they failed to convince him. The Earl of Kellie then ordered him to be locked up in the stocks where he remained for some time. Drummond ordered his men to aim their guns at him. He was blindfolded and his chest bared, but when it was realised that he was more willing to die than carry out the executions, he was sent to the town gaol where he languished for many weeks before being freed. During his time in the cells he wrote a declaration on his life which was later published in Wodrow's *History of the Sufferings of the Church of Scotland,* as well as in other pamphlets.

The Ayr authorities now had something of a predicament on their hands. At length they came up with the idea that they would allow one of the eight prisoners to go free if he would agree to hang the other seven. At first the men doggedly refused, but after some time thinking about the possibility of saving his life, one of them acquiesced. This was Cornelius Anderson, a tailor from Ayr, and according to the traditional tale it is said that he would only agree to carry out the task if the other seven men would forgive him.

On the appointed day, 27 December, the seven men were led out of the tolbooth to the town gibbet, which was affixed to its exterior wall. A large crowd gathered to watch. Cornelius Anderson was so distressed by the thought of carrying out seven murders that the provost of Ayr had to ply him with brandy in order to calm his nerves and make him sufficiently drunk that he knew little of what he was doing. It was he who pulled the lever which caused the trapdoor to open, leaving the men hanging from the gibbet. After each was pronounced dead, the body was lowered down and the next Covenanter prepared.

The seven martyrs were later taken from the tolbooth and buried in the churchyard, overlooking the River Ayr. They were James Smith of the Old Clachan of Dalry, Alexander MacMillan or MacCulloch of Carsphairn, James MacMillan in Marduchat, John Short of St John's Town of Dalry, George MacCartney in Blairkennie, John Graham of the Midtoun of Old Clachan, and John Muirhead of Irongray.[1]

The two Covenanters who had been sentenced to die at Irvine lay in their prison cells for another four days. Rev Alexander Nisbet, minister of the parish, paid them a visit during this time. According to an old account, 'he found them ignorant, and very much discouraged and damped with the near views of death and eternity.' Nisbet spoke long with the men, and after he had left it is said that their spirits were greatly lifted. On 31 December James Blackwood of Fenwick and John MacCall of Carsphairn were brought out to the gibbet in Irvine, where once again Cornelius Anderson was instructed to carry out the executions. The two men are said to have died full of joy and courage, and the crowds who had gathered to watch admired their spirit. The bodies were later laid to rest in Irvine kirkyard.[2]

Cornelius Anderson was later so overcome with remorse that he suffered from depression from and misery. He was treated with contempt in the county, and so emigrated to Ireland. Somehow word travelled just as fast, for he could find no work nor lodgings, even as far south as Dublin. He was forced to build himself a crude shelter on the outskirts of the city. Within a few days this structure caught fire, burning Anderson within it.

The town council in Dumfries met on 30 December in order to prepare for the command to deal with the two men taken at Pentland and who had surrendered themselves as prisoners at the battle. It was requested of them that they:

sie their sentence for hanging the persounes, and affixing of the heides and right armes of Jon Grier in Ffourmerkland, and William Welsch in Carsfairne, upon the eminenest pairts of this Burgh.

The provost, Thomas Irving, and his magistrates, 'condescendit that the Bridge-port is the fittest place quere upon the heids and armes should be affixed, and therefoir appointed them to be affixed to that place.' The name of the first Covenanter is often given as William Grierson; William Welsh is sometimes described as being from Kirkpatrick Irongray. The death sentence was carried out on 2 January 1667. After they were executed their heads and right hands were cut from their bodies and taken to the bridge port as intimated, where they were displayed on spikes as a warning to the inhabitants. However a rumour sprang up that supporters of the Covenant were planning to rescue the severed parts of the two bodies from the Bridge-port, and so the council met again to discuss how to prevent this. They sent an appeal to the Earl of Lauderdale and asked that they be allowed to move the heads and hands to the top of the tolbooth, which was more secure, and thus frustrate the 'disloyal personnes who might take them away under the clouds of the night, to the prejudice of the Burgh.' The corpses of the two martyrs were later buried in St Michael's kirkyard.[3]

Four other Covenanters were taken to Glasgow for execution at the same time. Robert Bunton or Buntine of

Fenwick,[4] John Hart of West Quarter, parish of Glassford, Robert Scott of Shavock farm, Dalserf, and Matthew Paton, a shoemaker from Newmilns,[5] were captured on the field of Rullion Green and held in prison for a time. They had surrendered as prisoners of war and had been given quarter. On 17 December 1666 they were placed on trial before the Justiciary Commission in Glasgow where it was pleaded that as quarter had been given they could not be executed, but the plea was ignored. The judges were the Marquis of Linlithgow, Earl of Wigtown, Earl of Eglinton, and Mungo Murray, who ordered the execution to take place on 19 December at the cross of Glasgow. When the men tried to address the crowds from the scaffold the soldiers drowned out their voices with the beating of thier drums. The martyrs were later interred in the cathedral burial ground.[6]

1. NS 339219. Gravestone in St John's churchyard, Ayr.
2. NS 322387. Gravestone in Irvine churchyard. Blackwood also commemorated on memorial in Fenwick churchyard. (NS 465434).
3. NX 975757. Gravestone in St Michael's churchyard, Dumfries.
4. Also commemorated on memorial in Fenwick churchyard (NS 465434).
5. Also commemorated on memorial in Newmilns churchyard (NS 537373).
6. NS 602656. Gravestone in Glasgow Cathedral.

5

CONVENTICLES

On 13 August 1670 an 'Act against Conventicles' was issued by the
Scots parliament. A 'Coventicle' was a 'field meeting' organised
by ministers who had been thrown out of their churches and
manses and they were growing in number. Attendance could be
enormous, and the government was concerned that they were
becoming a hot-bed of revolutionary ideas. The act declared that
any minister who organised such a meeting was liable to be
executed – if someone captured one and handed him over to the
authorities he would receive 500 merks – should the minister be
killed then the person responsible would be indemnified. Those
who attended the conventicles could expect to be fined or locked
up in gaol indefinitely. If a conventicle was held in a house or
barn, as many were in the early days, the owner of the property
could be fined, and should the meeting take place within a
burgh, then the magistrates could expect a fine.

Conventicles had taken place for some time before this act
was passed. In the 1660s a number of meetings had taken place
throughout Ayrshire, such as Galston Muir in July 1665. A
warrant was issued on 25 January 1666 against a number of
ministers who had officiated at these services. The first
conventicle to take place in the Borders occurred in 1672 at
Pilmuir, near Lauder in Berwickshire.

Rev Gabriel Semple was probably the first minister to organise field meetings. He was ousted from his church of Kirkpatrick Durham in Kirkcudbrightshire in 1662. Forced to leave his manse also, he moved in with John Neilson, the local laird at Corsock Castle. Semple held meetings at first in the great hall of the castle, but soon it was too small for the numbers attending. He moved into the castle garden and then into the surrounding woods and fields. Neilson was reported to Sir James Turner by the local curate, and he was fined £100. He was later imprisoned in Kirkcudbright tolbooth. When he was released soldiers were billeted in his castle. Neilson was expected to pay for their keep. His wife, Mary MacLellan (d. 1697), and six children were forced to leave the castle, and the soldiers plundered from both Neilson and his tenants. Neilson took part in the Pentland Rising and was tortured by the boots, and even though he screamed fearfully, he told the authorities nothing. Neilson was finally executed at Edinburgh on 14 December 1666.

In 1672 a reward of £400 was offered for Semple's arrest. He even travelled as far south as Cumberland and Northumberland in 1677 to hold meetings. In July 1681 he was apprehended at Oldhamstocks in East Lothian and cruelly treated on his march to the Canongate tolbooth. He was released due to his ill health, and he fled to England. He died in August 1706.

Followers of the Covenant were willing to risk the fines and sentences in order to hear the preachers. Thousands of Covenanters' children were taken to these meetings where they were baptized by these ministers. At the Holy Linn, on the Garple Burn near Balmaclellan in Galloway, Rev Thomas Verner baptized 36 children at one service.

Communion was also dispensed at a number of conventicles and these services were some of the most popular. The first conventicles to dispense communion appear to have taken place in 1674. One was held that year at Allanbank, near Edrom in the Borders. John Blackader and John Welsh preached to around 3,200, many of whom took part in communion. At Gateshaw, near Morebattle in Roxburghshire, a large meeting took place in

1677 at which Welsh, Archibald Riddell, Andrew Morton, Patrick Warner and George Barclay dispensed communion. A large communion conventicle was held in August 1678 at Craigdow Hill, four miles from Maybole in Ayrshire, at which Welsh, Warner, Richard Cameron, Archibald Riddell and John Kid took part. This service lasted two days and 7,000 are said to have attended. 600 armed men were posted around the site to warn of attack from government soldiers. Another large conventicle took place at East Nisbet in Berwickshire in 1678, at which 1,600 were able to be seated, 3,200 taking part in total.

Rev William Veitch was a noted field-preacher. At one of his conventicles held at the Blue Cairn on Lauder Moor, Berwickshire, in 1676 almost 4,000 turned up to hear him preach. The Covenanters' Well is in the vicinity. Although imprisoned on the Bass Rock, Veitch survived the Killing Times and was appointed minister of St Michael's Church, Dumfries, in 1694. He retired in 1715 and died in 1722, aged 81.[1]

The first conventicle to be attended by armed Covenanters appears to be one held at Hill of Beath in the parish of Dunfermline, Fife, on 18 June 1670. Rev John Blackader and Rev John Dickson, minister of Rutherglen, officiated. During the sermon armed soldiers came upon the Covenanters. A few Covenanters had come with arms and when the lieutenant of the soldiers withdrew his staff the armed Covenanters advanced on him with pistols. Blackader intervened, and the soldiers felt it was prudent to withdraw and make a report. They compiled a list of those attending and many Covenanters were fined or even banished for taking part. On 5 May 1678 an armed conventicle was held at Whitekirk in East Lothian, to which over 1,000 followers attended. Soldiers arrived on the site, but they were disarmed and sent away. In a scuffle John Hogg, one of the soldiers, was killed. James Learmont was later arrested and executed in Edinburgh on 27 September, not for killing the soldier, but simply for being there. Another skirmish took place at a conventicle held at Cumberhead, near Lesmahagow in Lanarkshire, on 30 March 1679. A party of soldiers who came upon the meeting were easily outnumbered and repelled.

A massive conventicle took place on Skeoch Hill in Kirkcudbrightshire in 1679. There were 6,000 Covenanters in attendance to hear John Welsh, John Blackader, Samuel Arnot and John Dickson, of which 3,000 were allowed to take part in communion. In the centre of the congregation a series of large boulders were arranged in four parallel rows for the communicants, perhaps around 300 in number, to sit on. These stones, known as the Communion Stones, are still there.[2]

Some conventicles were carried off without any problems. Welsh was the ousted minister of Irongray, in which parish Skeoch Hill is located. He had been asked by many to hold a communion service. Blackader, ousted minister of the nearby parish of Troqueer, was invited to take part, and he had to journey from Culross in Fife to the site. The night before the service he stayed at the house of Caitloch, in Glencairn, home of William Fergusson. Welsh preached on the first day at a place known as Meiklewood Cross and intimated that communion would take place on the following day, not naming the place, but details of its location were passed to adherents.

Arnot, the ousted minister of Tongland in Galloway, opened the service, followed by Welsh. Blackader and Dickson assisted in dispensing communion to those in attendance. Covenanters took it in turn to be seated on the communion stones, returning to hear the main preachers after they had drank wine and eaten bread.

The conventicle had been infiltrated by a few non-adherents, servants in the employ of the Earl of Nithsdale and Sir Robert Dalziel of Glenae. They slipped off early to inform of the conventicle. Word of this came to the Covenanters, who formed themselves up in defensive lines, William Gordon of Earlstoun, and a Nithsdale laird taking charge. Sentries were posted to keep a look out, but after three hours they stood down. The Covenanters then dispersed, spending the night in local barns and houses. A further meeting was held on the Monday at a spot three miles from the Communion Stones, and it too passed without any disturbance.

Not all conventicles were held in the open moors. City and town dwellers often organised meetings within their homes to which friends and acquaintances were invited. The magistrates of Glasgow were requested to suppress meetings in the city on 22 February 1672. On 3 April 1678 Patrick Anderson was summoned before the Privy Council for holding a number of meetings in his home at Potterrow in Edinburgh between the years 1674-8.

Covenanters were most likely to be captured or executed-usually on their way to and from conventicles. The fact that they were away from home and probably had a Bible in their possession was enough for the authorities to justify fining or executing them, often killing them where they were found.

In April 1673 James Davie and a number of friends met at his farm of Blackdub, near to Bathgate in West Lothian, in order to hear Rev Archibald Riddell preach. During the service word reached them that a party of dragoons from Mid Calder garrison, under the command of Lieutenant Heron, was approaching. The meeting was brought to an untimely end, and the congregation fled over a wet moss which so hampered the soldiers' horses that they were unable to follow. The dragoons, however, drew their pistols and fired across the peat moss. Only one person suffered in the gunfire, James Davie, who was later interred at Bathgate. A number of others were imprisoned, with their clothes, Bibles and other belongings taken by the soldiers.[3]

1. NX 975757. Memorial in St Michael's churchyard, Dumfries.
2. NX 859790. Monument on site.
3. NS 990681. Gravestone in Bathgate churchyard.

6

THE HIGHLAND HOST

One of the methods employed by the authorities in attempting to quell the Covenanters was the quartering of highland soldiers on the residents of the south-west of Scotland. The commission was issued on 26 December 1677 and by the following January the highland troops were making their way south. It is reckoned that 8,000 highlanders were brought south from Stirling to Glasgow and the south-west. The Ayrshire heritors wrote to Lauderdale requesting him not to send so 'inhumane and barbarous a crew of spoilers' into that county. The appeal fell on deaf ears. Those who failed to adhere to the government's laws concerning worship were subject to becoming the 'host' for these soldiers, who would eat the householder out of house and home, and when they moved on they often stole the contents of the house. Around 20 or 30 highlanders were billeted in Mearns parish, but many parishes are known to have put up a lot more.

The soldiers were infamous for their exploits and poor treatment of their hosts, and the threat of them being quartered upon parish heritors was enough to persuade many to adhere to the king's laws. Indeed, in most areas the highlanders were withdrawn in February 1678. The session minutes of Muirkirk in Ayrshire for 15 April 1678 note that, 'We had no sessonne for som moneths before this because of the hielanders lying amongst us.'

In south-west Scotland the Covenanters were less willing to accept the king's authority over the church, and many accounts detail the actions of the highlanders.

A decree of 29 January 1678 stated that everyone should give up their arms. This was an attempt to disarm the public and make it less likely that they would rise against the government. A typical record is that from Largs in Ayrshire, which ordered 'the Largs heretours, lyferenters, conjunct fiars, tenants, cotters and others to disarm in 13th February at the Kirk of Largs.'

In Kilmarnock a full company of soldiers arrived at the home of William Taylor, a merchant in the town. He was obliged to feed them and keep them for nothing. Another local was James Aird, who lived at Milton. He had 24 soldiers living under his roof for three weeks, during which time he too had to supply food and drink to them. Nine highland soldiers were quartered on William Dickie for six weeks. Likewise he was required to feed the men, and when they eventually left his house, they stole bags full of ornaments, cutlery, plates and a sock full of money, to a total value of around 1,000 merks. The soldiers also maltreated him and his family. His wife was pregnant, yet one of the soldiers stuck his dirk into her side; she died soon after. Dickie himself was struck on a number of occasions for not supplying all the soldiers' needs and one of the beatings resulted in two broken ribs.

The minister of Kilmarnock, Rev Alexander Wedderburn, was so appalled by the actions of the highlanders in the town that he condemned them in one of his sermons. The highlanders heard this and caught up with him as he walked through the streets. In a scuffle one of the soldiers lunged at the minister with the butt of his gun, winding him and causing him to fall to his knees. He died of a respiratory disease later.

Sir Hew Campbell of Cessnock Castle was a known supporter of the Covenant. When the highlanders came into Ayrshire a garrison of 50 foot and ten horse were quartered in his home. Sir Hew was tried in 1684 on a charge of berating the Covenanters who had failed to fight at Bothwell five years earlier. He was also active in the Argyll conspiracy of 1684-5. He was sent to the Bass Rock and his estates forfeited on 13 June 1685. Campbell was held prisoner on the island until his health began to fail. He was allowed back to Edinburgh where he died in September 1686.

In the village of Mauchline four different memorials of various ages commemorate the same five martyrs, all of whom were hanged there on 6 May 1685. They were not local men, but Covenanters picked up by the highland soldiers on a march from Falkirk. Peter Gillies was a noted Covenanter who was a native of Skirling, in the county of Peebles. He worked as a waulk-miller, but for allowing a Covenanting minister to take a service at the mill in 1674 he was thrown out of his home by the landowner, who had been informed of the service by the curate. He seems to have travelled north and settled in the parish of Muiravonside on the southern extremity of Stirlingshire. His religious beliefs remained as strong as ever, for in 1682 the curate of that parish sent soldiers to his home but he managed to escape. The list of fugitives issued on 5 May 1684 names Peter Gillies in the Walkmill of Woodside as a wanted man, and he had to flee his home. His wife was pregnant at the time, and Peter came home regularly to visit her. Shortly after she gave birth the soldiers watched the millhouse more regularly, and spotted Gillies paying one of his night-time visits. He was easily apprehended, and his wife had to watch as they threatened to kill him. As the soldiers took him away they carried with them a considerable amount of plunder.

At Peter Gillies's house was John Bryce, a weaver from West Calder, who had been at the mill to collect cloth which had been dressed for him. He too was apprehended by the soldiers and tied to Gillies. The men were forced to march in front of the soldiers for a few miles before being told to kneel in front of the musketeers. The men thought that they were about to be shot, but the soldiers then seem to have changed their minds, and allowed the men to rise up. The soldiers took them westward instead, towards Carluke.

At Carluke William Fiddieson and Thomas Young were captured by the foot soldiers under the command of Cromwell

Lockhart of Lee Castle, which stands nearby. The highlanders then marched further west, arriving at Mauchline on 4 May 1685. Already held in Mauchline Castle was John Browning, the nephew of John Brown of Priesthill. On the following day a trial was set up before Lieutenant-General William Drummond. A jury of 15 soldiers was appointed, and not surprisingly they were found guilty of refusing to pray for the king. The five men were hanged on Mauchline Loan the following day. At the execution they were refused Bibles, and when their corpses were taken from the scaffold they were buried at its foot, without the use of grave-clothes or coffins.[1]

Some of the 'Highland Host' were quartered at Cunning Park House, near Ayr, which was at that time a property of the kirk session. The Earl of Cassillis, who was a supporter of the Covenant, also had highlanders quartered on him. They ate and stole goods to the value of £32,000 Scots from him.

A party of highlanders came to Falla Hill, the home of Thomas and Robert Russell, and took six horses from them. The Russell family were known Covenanters, and in 1679 Rev John Blackader preached at a conventicle here. A year later Donald Cargill did likewise. The Russells were called before Mr Honeyman, curate at Livingston, who requested them to take the Oath of Abjuration, but they refused. The brothers were let off at the time, and seem to have thought that they held some sway over the curate, so they asked him if he could help in getting their horses back. Negotiations went on for a time until the curate eventually gave them a letter which he told them to take personally to the garrison at Lanark, where the horses had been taken. The Russells set off on their journey, but at Carluke their curiosity got the better of them, so they opened the letter. It read, 'Sir, I have sent you two rebels. Grip them fast. All you have taken from them is too little.'

Although most of the highlanders had left the south west by March 1678, there were some who remained. A party of them were quartered in Annandale and as late as June 1685 a detachment was still based in Leadhills. The monument on the summit of Carsgailoch Hill, south of Cumnock, notes that the martyrs were shot 'by a party of highlanders' in 1685.[2]

Many parishes have records which detail the cost to the inhabitants of putting up the soldiers, sums of money which were long in recouping. Men from Caithness were quartered within the parish of Cumnock, and an account was made later of the losses sustained in the parish.

The parishes of Cumnock, Old and New, sustained of loss by quartering two hundred and fifty Caithness men, fifteen nights, with some officers	*£1093 6s 8d*
Exacted by their Officers and cleared off their quarters as appears from their notes	*£ 200*
Item, dry quarters to some officers	*£ 64*
Free quarters to them	*£ 60*
Plunder by these soldiers	*£ 958 17s 4d*
By quartering ninety-five of Caithness men six nights	*£ 171*
By quartering three hundred and twenty Caithness men one night	*£ 96*
Dry quarters and plunder by these	*£ 372 2s 4d*
Extendeth to	*£3015 6s 4d*

The total for Ayrshire was reckoned to be around £138,000 Scots.

The total for Avondale parish in Lanarkshire was reckoned to be £1,700, though it has been surmised that this figure was only one third of the real total.

The highland soldiers were responsible for many killings, virtually being mercenaries who balked at nothing. The 'Highland Host', according to Wodrow, 'committed the most notorious outrages, wounded and dismembered some persons without the least show of provocation.'

1. NS 501273. Memorials on Mauchline Loan.
2. See Chapter 40.

7
PEACE TO EACH NOBLE MARTYR'S HONOUR'D SHADE

It was shortly after the Covenanters had risen and marched on Edinburgh, only to be defeated at the Battle of Rullion Green, that General Thomas Dalyell of the Binns decided to move his headquarters to Ayrshire. He and his men took over Dean Castle and began to throw their weight about. The castle remained a headquarters of the soldiers until the Glorious Revolution. Among those in charge of the garrison over the years were Major Andrew White and Captain John Inglis, responsible for a number of martyrdoms mentioned in other chapters. Dalyell, who was somewhat illiterate, noted of the Covenanters that 'ther was noe mor to be doune bot tak them out and hang them.' It was said that they lived a lifestyle as though they were living in an enemy's lands. They robbed the town of food and goods, took valuables from individuals and committed atrocities by the score. The folk of Kilmarnock reckoned that within a few months they had sustained losses amounting to over 50,000 merks, or around £3,000 Sterling, which was a considerable figure in the 17th century.

Every local person was treated as a possible rebel, for the greatest number of men who marched on Edinburgh had come from the south west. Any hint of adherence to the Covenant would result in Dalyell summoning you, and if you did not report to his garrison then his soldiers were be sent out to track you down. One man whom Dalyell wished to interrogate was David Findlay of Newmilns. It was known that he had been in Lanark on the same day that the insurgents had passed through the town, reading out their declaration at the cross.

The soldiers captured Findlay at his home and dragged him to the old castle of Newmilns, which was also used as a garrison for the soldiers and a gaol for the Covenanters. Brought before Dalyell, he was asked many questions about why he was in Lanark that day. Findlay seems to have been able to persuade Dalyell that he had been there purely by chance, and had not gone as part of the marching army. Dalyell then asked what Covenanters he had seen in Lanark, but Findlay, being a stranger to the burgh, was unsure of any of their names. Dalyell was angry at this, for he had hoped to receive a long list of names whom he would track down.

In a rage Dalyell then ordered the soldiers to shoot Findlay at the village's gallows. This came as much as a surprise to them as it did to Findlay. An officer was instructed to carry out the deed, but he thought that Dalyell was only pretending – trying to force more information from Findlay. Soon it was realised that this was not the case. Findlay was taken from the castle and tied to the base of the gallows.

David Findlay pleaded with the lieutenant to allow him at least one more night of life in order to prepare for death. The lieutenant instructed to carry out the execution was so moved by his pleas that he returned to Dalyell to try and have the execution held back, but to no avail. Dalyell was adamant, responding, 'I'll teach you to obey without scruple – go and despatch him.'

The gun was raised and Findlay was shot where he stood. The soldiers then stripped him of his clothes, and the mutilated body was left lying on the ground.[1]

In the centre of Kilmarnock, off what is now King Street, stood an old burgh gaol, known to the locals as the Thieves' Hole. Dalyell used this to lock up many Covenanters during his time in the town. At one time there were so many Covenanters forced into the cell that they were unable to lie down and had to stand all day and night. As might be expected, the lack of sanitary conditions resulted in disease, and many fell ill. One of the prisoners was so ill that the remainder pleaded with the soldiers to allow him out. They returned later with the word from Dalyell that he could be released, so long as his body was returned later, either dead or alive. As it turned out, the prisoner did die at the home of his friends, and his relatives were forced to return the corpse. The body lay outside the prison door for some time before Dalyell allowed it to be taken away for burial.

On another occasion the soldiers left Dean Castle to pursue a Covenanter known to them. He managed to effect his escape in the town by entering the front door of a house and escaping out the back. When the soldiers came to the house they found that it was empty, apart from the woman who lived there. She was able to confirm that a man had come into the house, but where he went or who he was she could not tell. The soldiers felt that she was hiding something, so took her back with them to Dean Castle. She was locked up in an underground vault, remaining there for some time. The vault was so damp that it was home to toads and frogs, and the conditions were so unsavoury that rats had infested it. The woman remained incarcerated until she died.

One day Dalyell was the worse for drink when the soldiers brought him a young boy, son of one of the known fugitives. Questions were put to the frightened lad, but he was unwilling to tell Dalyell anything about his father. The order was then given to hang the boy. On another occasion one of the soldiers under Dalyell, named Mungo Murray, ordered that two farm-workers should be hanged from a tree by their thumbs. They had been suspected of giving shelter to two Covenanters who were being pursued. After Murray left, two of the soldiers felt so sorry for them that they cut the ropes which tied up the thumbs.

One day in October 1682 a travelling packman arrived in Kilmarnock. He was James Robertson, who belonged to Stonehouse in Lanarkshire. Whilst in the town he went to visit one of his acquaintances, John Finlay of Muirside, who was held prisoner by Major Andrew White in Dean Castle at the time.

Finlay had admitted being at Drumclog, but without arms, and refused to admit whether or not he had spoken to Rev Donald Cargill. During Robertson's visit the soldiers grabbed a hold of him, took his pack from him, and locked him up. Accusations were made that he had nailed a proclamation against the Test Act on the door of the kirk. He was kept in the cell for around 10 to 12 days during which time he was treated cruelly. The authorities then transported the two men to Edinburgh where they were questioned by the Committee for Public Affairs. Robertson was asked his opinions of the king, and though his answers were fairly non-committal, he was found guilty of treason. Both he and Finlay were taken to the Grassmarket on 15 December 1682 where they were executed. Robertson tried to address the crowd, but as was typical of the time the drummer caused so much noise that he could not be heard. Robertson complained about this whereupon he was severely beaten by the town-major. Also hanged that day was William Cochrane of Carnduff, Avondale parish.

1. NS 537373. Memorial in Newmilns churchyard.

8

BLUIDY CLAVERS

One of the most infamous persecutors of the Covenanters was John Graham of Claverhouse, created Viscount Dundee in 1688. He was abhorred by the Covenanters for the part he played in ordering the execution of many of their friends and supporters. Many Covenanters were martyred at his command, and not a few were actually killed by his own hands. One of the most infamous examples of his killing was the martyrdom of John Brown of Priesthill, which is covered in chapter 37.

John Graham was born in 1648 in Glen Ogilvy, near Dundee. He was educated at St Andrews and served in the French and Dutch armies for a number of years. In 1677 he returned to Scotland where he was appointed commander of an Independent Troop of Horse. He was given the task of suppressing the Covenanters by the Privy Council. On 28 December 1678 he wrote to his commander-in-chief, the Earl of Linlithgow, from the Black Bull Inn in Moffat[1], where he based himself for a time:

> My Lord, I came here last night with the troop, and am just going to march for Dumfries, where I resolve to quarter the whole troop. I have not heard anything of the dragoons, though it is now about nine o'clock, and they should have been here last night, according to your lordship's orders. I suppose they must have taken some other route. I am informed since I came that this county has been

*very loose. On Tuesday was eight days, and Sunday, there were
great field conventicles just by here, with great contempt of the
regular clergy; who complain extremely that I have no orders to
aprehend anybody for past demeanours. And besides that, all the
particular orders I have being contained in that order of
quartering, every place where we quarter we must see them, which
makes them fear the less. I am informed that the most convenient
posts for quartering the dragoons will be Moffat, Lochmaben and
Annan; whereby the whole county will be kept in awe. Besides that,
my lord, they tell me that the end of the bridge of Dumfries is in
Galloway, and that they may hold conventicles at our nose, we
dare not dissipate them, seeing our orders confine us to Dumfries
and Annandale. Such an insult as that would not please me;
and, on the other hand, I am unwilling to exceed orders, so that I
expect from your lordship orders how to carry in such cases.*

A conventicle did take place on the Galloway side of the
Nith, and Claverhouse, receiving orders that he could act in that
province, decided to demolish the building where the meeting
had taken place. The Covenanters had tried to pass off the hall as
a byre, by placing a few hayracks within it, but to no avail. The
walls were flattened and the timbers burned. 'So perished the
charity of many ladies,' recorded Claverhouse.

In the kirkyard of Galston in Ayrshire is a headstone
commemorating Andrew Richmond, 'who was killed by bloody
Graham of Claver-House, June 1679'. His father was the farmer at
Parkieston. The stone is distinguished by a carving which depicts
the actual shooting of Richmond. He is shown to one side
pointing at the Bible, and to the left is a figure of a soldier taking
aim at him with a gun. Basically no more is known of the story of
Andrew Richmond.[2]

On 31 January 1682 Graham was given a commission to
pursue and punish:

*...several persons of disaffected and seditious principles in the
shires of Wigtown and Dumfries, and the Stewartries of
Kirkcudbright and Annandale, who have for disquiet and
disturbance of the peace for divers years past deserted the public*

ordinances in their parish churches, haunted and frequented
rebellious field conventicles, and committed divers other disorders
of that nature.

He took the place of Sir Andrew Agnew of Lochnaw, the
10th hereditary Sheriff of Galloway, who was deemed to be too
soft in administering the acts. Graham travelled to Stranraer
where he made the old castle which stands in the centre of the
town his headquarters for a time. In March 1682 he wrote a letter
from there in which he details some of his recent exploits:

> I am just beginning to send out many parties, finding the rebels
> become secure, and the country so quiet in all appearance. I sent
> out a party with my brother Dave three nights ago. The first night
> he took Drumbui and one Maclellan, and the great villain
> MacClorg, the smith at Minnigaff that made all the clikys, and
> after whom the forces have trotted so often. It cost me both pains
> and money to know how to find him: I am resolved to hang him;
> for it is necessary I make some example of severity, lest rebellion be
> thought cheap here. There cannot be alive a more wicked fellow.

MacClurg was to be lucky yet again, for he escaped the
clutches of Claverhouse and must have been alive in 1684 when
his name is listed in a roll of fugitives.

Claverhouse was to take over other buildings for his
occupancy whilst in the south west. He commandeered a house
in Kirkcudbright owned by Sir Robert Maxwell and later based
himself in Kenmure Castle. Lady Kenmure told Claverhouse that
'if the King would bestow two or three hundred pounds to repair
the house, she would be very well pleased his soldiers came to live
in it.'

A tailor, William Graham, was visiting the home of his
mother at Crossmichael in Kirkcudbrightshire in December 1682
when a party of Claverhouse's soldiers came upon the house.
William tried to make a getaway, but as he fled from the house he
was spotted by the soldiers. Claverhouse ordered them to pursue
him, and when they caught up with Graham they instantly shot
him dead.[3]

Claverhouse's troops were in the Tweedsmuir Hills in July

1683, having set out in search of the Covenanters from their base in Moffat. Near to the farm of Hartfell, they came across one William Moffat, a known fugitive, who resided there. He fled as fast as he could over Greenhillstairs into Evan Dale, where he expected to elude his pursuers. He arrived at Raecleugh where he hid himself in a hollow by the burn. The soldiers missed him, and continued on some way. The laird of Raecleugh, William Johnstone, who had watched Moffat elude the soldiers, then came to the spot to let him know that it was now safe to come out. As they stood talking the soldiers, who had stopped to decide where to look next, spotted them and came back. Moffat set off again, crossing over Beattock summit and dropping down to Elvanfoot. There he eventually lost the soldiers. The laird of Raecleugh was not so lucky. The soldiers returned to his castle at a later date and took him prisoner. He was tried for his support for the Covenant, and in particular for his hiding Covenanters who had been active at Enterkin Pass.

In the parish of Colmonell, in southern Ayrshire, is a memorial stone located on the south side of the parish church, commemorating Matthew MacIlwraith, or Micklewrath, as his name is sometimes spelled. Matthew was a farmer's son, living at Blair, near to Barrhill. He was in love with a Miss MacEwan, daughter of the farmer at Barbour farm, and it is said that they were engaged to be married. However, Matthew was never to see the happy day. A troop of soldiers appeared at Blair farm and surprised the family whilst they were conducting family worship. Matthew, who had been listed as a fugitive in May 1684, tried to escape from the house, but as he made his way across the farmyard a bullet from a soldier's gun wounded him. He was still fit enough to run five miles to Dangart Glen, but the pain was such that he could journey no further. Consequently, he tried to find somewhere to hide. The way was too rough for the horses to follow, but four soldiers had pursued him on foot, and it was not long before they came upon his panting body. As MacIlwraith scrambled up the side of the gully one of his pursuers threw his dirk which severed his achilles tendon. Unable to run any further, the other persecutors soon caught up with him and stabbed him in the stomach. 'By bloody Claverhouse I fell, who did command that I should die,' states the memorial stone. MacIlwraith was then shot without any trial or chance to swear the Oath of Allegiance.

The body of MacIlwraith was left to lie where he fell. His family were too frightened to go and collect it for burial, just in case the soldiers heard of this and came for revenge. However, on the following day, as night began to fall, two women came to the glen, wrapped the corpse up in a grey plaid, and secretly transported it to the kirkyard. Many years later a Janet Carson revealed that she had been one of these ladies. The name of the other woman was never revealed, but tradition avers that it was none other than MacIlwraith's fiancée who helped to bury her lover.[4]

In May 1685 Claverhouse moved his headquarters to Selkirk, in the Borders, from where he continued his persecution of the Covenanters. A number of incidents took place among the hills at the head of the Ettrick and Yarrow valleys. The curate of St Mary's, one named Binram, was murdered by Halbert Dobson. A troop of 20 men from Traquair House, under the command of Coupland, went in search of Dobson. They spent a few nights in the vicinity of St Mary's Loch, interviewing the locals and gathering evidence. A party of highlanders came upon a young boy who was so ill that he was unable to respond to their questions. In cold blood, he was shot by a highlander from Braemar. The corpse was thrown into a bog.

Five of the soldiers, having been separated from the main party, failed to turn up at the rendezvous. A search was made for them and five murdered bodies were discovered in a narrow pass at Chapelhope. Coupland returned to Traquair with the report, whereupon Claverhouse set out with 50 men in hot pursuit. One Covenanter was shot as he tried to escape and was buried on the summit of Watch Knowe, above the Grey Mare's Tail. The soldiers chased another four, who ran along the ridge to the north. They were captured and taken prisoner, but back at Birkhill pass it was decided to shoot them. They were later interred at Ettrick kirkyard.

In Dumfriesshire's Dryfesdale lived Andrew Hislop, his younger brother, two sisters and widowed mother. Their cottage stood at Windshiels, about one mile north of Gillesbie, in the parish of Hutton and Corrie. They had sheltered a Covenanter who was so ill that he died whilst living in their house. During the night the sons dug a grave in a field which lay next to their home and there laid the Covenanter to rest.[5] Somehow word reached Sir James Johnstone of Westerhall that this had taken place, and he ordered the body to be exhumed, in order that it may be identified. The widow was punished by having her cottage razed to the ground and her belongings confiscated, in all a loss of some £650 Scots.

Claverhouse caught Andrew Hislop at the beginning of May 1685, either the 1st or 10th, depending which account is read. It is reported that he spotted Claverhouse approaching, and that Hislop had tried to mount one of his own horses which for some reason shied away. Hislop was forced to run for cover in a thicket nearby. According to tradition, Hislop's barking dog led the soldiers to where he was concealed. Johnstone asked the locals for the use of a rope, with which to tie up Hislop, but none would give one. At length a man 'without scruples' announced that he would 'give you ropes to hang all the Whigs in Dryfe.' Hislop was taken prisoner and transported to Craighaugh, at Eskdalemuir, where Johnstone was at the time. Johnstone, whose commission allowing him to decide whether the Covenanter was guilty or not had expired on 21st April, still pronounced him guilty. He was ordered to be shot by Claverhouse, who at first tried to delegate this to the commander of the highland soldiers under his command. He refused, swearing that 'he would fight Claverhouse and his dragoons before he did it.'

Still unwilling to carry out the deed, Claverhouse announced, 'The blood of this poor man be upon you, Westerhall, I am free of it.'

Andrew Hislop refused to wear a blindfold; instead he

stood, Bible in hand, facing his three executioners. He sang some
verses from the 118th Psalm and before the shots were fired he
told the dragoons that they would have to answer for their crimes
on judgement day. His mother was told that her son was dead,
whereupon she asked, 'Which one?' Being told that it was
Andrew she announced, 'It is well, he is best prepared to die.'[6]

In 1689 Bonnie Dundee, as he became known, raised an
army of highland men on behalf of James VII, and marched on
Killiecrankie, where a battle took place on 27 July. Although his
forces numbered between 1,800-2,000 men, he was outnumbered
by almost two to one. Nevertheless, his men were victorious in the
battle against the soldiers under General Mackay, who retreated
across the River Garry, one of them famously leaping the rocky
chasm. Claverhouse was mortally wounded and his body was
stripped of its armour and clothing. A soldier found the corpse
on the following day and, wrapping it in a plaid, had it taken to
the kirk at Old Blair, near to Blair Atholl, where it was buried.[7]

1. NT 085051. Plaque on wall of inn.
2. NS 500367. Gravestone in Galston churchyard.
3. NX 729670. Gravestone in Crossmichael churchyard.
4. NX 145857. Gravestone in Colmonell churchyard.
5. NX 157930. Gravestone near Windshiels.
6. NY 250984. Gravestone at Craighaugh, Eskdalemuir.
7. NN 867665. Memorial in vault at Old Blair church.

9

BLOODY BRUCE
DID MURDER ME

Earlshall Castle is a rather grand Scots baronial tower house which stands to the east of Leuchars in Fife, six miles from St Andrews.[1] Construction of the tower commenced in 1546 by Sir William Bruce and was completed in 1617 by his great-grandson, William. In the 17th century the owner of the castle was the second William's grandson, Andrew Bruce, who became infamous as one of the most notorious persecutors of the Covenanters. According to tradition he paid one of his soldiers one guinea to give him the right of cutting off the head and hands of Richard Cameron, who fell on Airds Moss. Perhaps this was a shrewd move, however, for he was able to later claim the bounty of £500 Sterling which had been placed on Cameron's head. More of this will be recounted in the chapter on Airds Moss (see chapter 16).

In September 1678, when Graham of Claverhouse's troop was commissioned, Bruce was appointed lieutenant under him. Shortly afterwards, in February 1679 he was appointed Sheriff-Depute of Dumfries, Kirkcudbright and Wigtown shires. In February 1680 Bruce was promoted to Captain of Claverhouse's troops, when Claverhouse went to England to join the court of James VII and II.

Bruce was involved in a number of major executions and

skirmishes. These include the Battle of Airds Moss, Lochenkit martyrs and Auchencloy, all mentioned in chapters of their own.

Andrew Bruce was active in traversing the South-west of Scotland in pursuit of the Covenanters. One of his informers was named James Wright, who knew the whereabouts of James Kirk, a wanted man. Kirk lived at Sundaywell Tower, in the parish of Dunscore, and thus was a man of considerable standing. However, for his attendance at the Battle of Rullion Green in 1666, his name was added to the roll of wanted men. Being a landowner, Kirk was at first let off with fines, but those exacted by the Earl of Middleton and Sir James Turner were so severe that for three years he and his family had to live abroad. Kirk later returned, and moved to the nearby parish of Holywood, where he created a hideout for himself and managed to survive for almost 20 years. One day he was to meet John Blackader who was returning from a large conventicle held near Culross. Kirk invited him to preach at a large communion service which had been planned for the parish of Irongray.

It was at Holywood that James Wright professed to be a friend, and advised Kirk to move to a hiding-place he knew about which was not too far from Wright's home. Kirk took this advice, but on the first night of his residence in May 1685 he was seized by a party of dragoons under the command of Bruce.

'Will you take the Abjuration Oath?' Bruce inquired.

Kirk is said to have 'modestly refused' the offer, whereupon Bruce informed him to prepare for death. Kirk sang from the Psalms and prayed, and all the while the soldiers tried to persuade him to reveal the hideouts used by his associates, 'for then we could spare your life.' Kirk refused to tell them anything. Thinking that there might still be a chance of him supplying information, Bruce ordered his men to tie him up and take him back to Dumfries.

Kirk spent the night in the prison cell in the county town. On the following morning (13 May 1685) he was taken to the Whitesands, where again Bruce placed some questions before him. Kirk still refused to answer, and despite some women pleading for his release, the order was given for him to be shot.

Kirk begged that his life be spared for one more day, but Bruce replied, 'No, no. No more time; the devil a peace you can now get made up.'

'Sir, you mistake it,' replied Kirk. 'You cannot mar my peace with God.'

Flying into a rage, Bruce ordered his men to fire. Two or three shots resounded at the one time, one of these coming from the gun of Dalyell of the Binns' second son.[2]

Bruce did not limit his actions to the lands of Dumfries and Galloway. An Ayrshire man was martyred by him. Thomas MacHaffie was the son of John MacHaffie, farmer at Largs farm, in the parish of Straiton. He was named as one of the many fugitives in a list compiled on 5 May 1684 and as such had to flee from his home. He was to spend the next two years in hiding, on one occasion making an escape near to Maybole, where he had been planning to attend a conventicle. One of the places used by him was a cave known as the Aughty of the Starr, located near to Loch Macaterick in the Galloway hills. Here MacHaffie and two friends spent most of their time in hiding, far from habitation. However, in the winter of 1685-6 he was suffering from influenza, a result of the privations endured, and he dared to move nearer to home.

MacHaffie found a place of concealment on the farm of Linfern (or Linfairn), about three miles south of Straiton. There, by the Palmullan Burn, he had built himself a semi-subterranean hideout in a cleuch between two waterfalls. In January 1686 he became aware of someone approaching. Discovering that it was the soldiers under Bruce he managed to drag himself from his bed and try to make a run for it. He did not get far, however, and made an entry into the farmhouse of Linfern where he threw himself down onto a bed, weak and exhausted. The soldiers were not far behind, and realised that he must have gone into the building. The house was searched, and it was an easy task to find MacHaffie. The Oath of Abjuration was offered to him, but MacHaffie refused it. Bruce then ordered his men to take the

Covenanter outside where he was to be shot. A large boulder in the field next to the farm marks the site where the execution took place.[3] MacHaffie's body was later taken to Straiton where two headstones mark his grave.[4]

In 1687 Bruce was one of five persecutors who had gathered in Miss Rome's tavern in Dumfries. Whilst they planned their next move to capture Covenanters they drank wine and smoked tobacco. The five men did not pay for their fare, and Miss Rome had to submit an account to the town council:

> *Spent with Lieutenant Colonell Windram, Captaine Strauchane, Captain Bruce, Leivetenant Lauder, Leivetenant Livingstone, six pynts of wine, with tobacco and pypes, £6 9s 4d.*

1. NO 465211.
2. NX 971759. Memorial stone on Whitesands marks the spot where he was executed. Gravestone is located in St Michael's churchyard (NX 976757).
3. NS 379013. Boulder on site of martyrdom.
4. NS 380049. Gravestone in Straiton churchyard.

10

FLYING THITHER FOR HIS LIFE

The village of Forgandenny and its parish of around 6800 acres lies in the pleasant and wide vale of Strathearn, a few miles south of Perth. The village is little more than a collection of houses surrounding the old parish church, the countryside around being home to many of the rich estates of Perthshire.

In the late 17th century the lands of Freeland were the property of Lord Ruthven, his tower house standing east of Forgandenny village (now much expanded and known as Strathallan School). At the castle's gate, on the Green of Freeland, was a cottage occupied by Andrew Brodie. Brodie was a wright to trade, and spent most of his time making country furniture and repairing carts. He and his wife had four young children.

In October 1678 word reached the supporters of the Covenant that a hill-preacher was coming to the district. A conventicle was proposed for a Sunday, and it was to be held on the summit of Culteuchar Hill (as it is spelled on modern maps – Wodrow names it as 'Caltenacher'). This was the highest point of the parish, 1017 feet above the level of the sea, the northernmost summit of the Ochil Hills. From the top a wide panorama is visible, making it easy to see anyone approaching.[1]

That Sunday morning Brodie and his wife left their home

and set out to walk the two miles or so to the conventicle site. The first mile was easy, crossing flat countryside, but the second was steep, climbing quickly to the lower summit of Westhall Hill. They were glad to take an odd rest, gazing back over the strath to the winding River Earn beyond their home. Soon, though, they came upon the summit of the hill, where they were pleased to see a good turnout for the sermon.

Who led the praise that day has been forgotten, but the Covenanters in attendance sang their psalms fervently. Prayers were offered to the Lord, and the sermon preached was listened to avidly. During a moment's quiet reflection a sound was heard from the near distance. A look-out who had been placed to watch the surrounding countryside had spotted something in the valley below. It was soon realised that a party of soldiers were in the area, and as they seemed to be heading directly towards the site of the conventicle it was quickly surmised that they had somehow received word of the field meeting. The order was given to disperse and the crowd ran away in all directions, as quickly as they were able.

The searchers were none other than the Stewart laird of Ballechin (near Logierait in Perthshire) and a party of highland soldiers. (Stewart later took part in the Battle of Killiecrankie. He put so much effort into fighting that his hand swelled greatly and the basket hilt of his sword needed to be cut off.) When the soldiers discovered the Covenanters the command was given to the highlanders to fire shots into the totally unarmed crowd. By a considerable stroke of luck there were no casualties at that point in time. One man was not so lucky, however. Andrew Brodie made his way towards a cave on the hillside which he had known since his youth. It was not much of a cave, to be sure, and some folk claim that it was little more than a natural hollow in the hillside, perhaps the source of a tributary of the Kelty Burn. Brodie's plan was to take his wife thither and hide until the soldiers had gone away. However, as he was making his way to the mouth of the cavern a highland soldier spotted him and took aim with his gun. The shot sounded across the heath-covered slopes of the Ochil Hills and Brodie's body slumped to the ground, just 200 yards from the conventicle site.

Brodie's wife was devastated, and began to tend her dead husband's body. She took off a scarlet cloak which she had been wearing and placed it over his corpse. As she kneeled by his side a soldier is said to have come up beside her and asked what she now thought of her husband. Her reply, which is also attributed to the wife of John Brown of Priesthill, was that she now thought more of him than ever.

At some later time, probably under the cover of darkness, a group of Brodie's friends made their way to the cave, following the instructions given by his widow. They came across his corpse and dragged it down the steep hillside to the kirkyard of Forgandenny, where it was secretly laid to rest.[2]

1. NO 096152.
2. NO 088183. Headstone now located in porch of church.

11
A FOLLOWER
OF THE LAMB

John Welwood was born around 1649, one of three sons of James Welwood. His brothers were Andrew, author of *Meditations representing a Glimpse of Glory*, and James, doctor in London. When John was nine years of age his father was appointed the parish minister at Tundergarth in Dumfriesshire. Three years later, at the publication of the Act of Council, he was deprived of his charge.

John Welwood became a minister like his father, but because of the troubles did not settle in any parish. He is known to have preached in many private homes, in places like Falkland in Fife and in Moray, as well as in Northumberland in England. A number of his letters survive. He wrote to Catherine Ross on 25 January 1677:

> There is more universal persecution than heretofore. The Lord, as I think, intends to bring his people very low before the deliverance. How low they shall be brought I cannot guess. . . . It is three Sabbaths since I came from Hatton. And coming through the Merse and East Lothian I was refreshed to see that, notwithstanding all the persecution, the people are ever drawn more and more from the curates in the Merse. The curates gave up a list of 3,500, all which (a few excepted) were fined and forced to pay their fines. If I had time I would tell you of their rigour. But guess

it by this. They took from some poor people 20 pence and 10 pence from others, blankets, coal sacks, from others, and yet the people came out abundantly to the meetings.

In 1679 John Welwood was banished to Perth, where he lived with 'an honest man,' John Barclay. He continued to preach, but only to small groups, and usually to one family at a time. These were invited to Barclay's home where Welwood held service for them.

Welwood was noted for his apparent ability to prophesy things. However, many of these prophecies were described as being of an evil nature. One Sunday he preached at a place known as Boulter Hall, in the parish of Forgan, near to St Andrews. In the congregation he spotted a lad wearing a uniform which indicated that he worked in the palace of Archbishop Sharp of St Andrews. Once the sermon was over he spoke to the lad, telling him to return to his master with a message. 'Tell him from me that his wicked life is now near an end, and that his death shall be sudden, surprising and bloody.' Sharp's murder is recounted in the following chapter.

In April 1679 he predicted the death of Andrew Ayton of Inchdarnie. Welwood told this lad that Archbishop Sharp was about to be murdered and that he himself would shortly die:

You'll shortly be quit of him, and he'll get a sudden sharp offgoing, and ye will be the first that will take the good news of his death to heaven.

This turned out to be true, for within hours of Sharp's murder soldiers under the command of the Justice-General and the laird of Lundy caught up with Ayton as he rode towards Cupar. A shot was fired and he was mortally wounded, dying on 3 April. Ayton's body was searched and papers concerning Sharp's death were found. Another man, Hendry Shaw, was also taken at this time.

Four of Welwood's sermons have been preserved by John Howie in his *Collection of Lectures and Sermons*. These have been described as having 'a fiery earnestness' through them. Written in short sentences, they seem to be like proverbs.

John Welwood survived in Perth for just three months, dying in April 1679. He seems also to have been able to predict when he would die, for on the morning of his last day he said, 'Now, eternal light, no more night nor darkness to me.' He died soon after.

The magistrates of Perth soon discovered that an intercommuned minister had died in their town and sent a man to arrest the corpse. He took with him the command that Welwood could not be buried within the bounds of the burgh, but that his friends had permission to inter the corpse anywhere else they pleased.

On the morning of the funeral the magistrates of Perth were out to see who attended to the coffin and bore it along the road. Soldiers were sent to apprehend these people, and they were taken to the town gaol where they were locked up.

Two other mourners were able to avoid imprisonment and journey five miles south to Dron kirkyard, where they intended to dig the grave. The minister, Rev Pitcairn, was at the kirkyard gate to meet them, but refused to allow them the keys to the burial ground. Instead the two men had to climb the kirkyard wall and dig the grave in the south-east corner. Welwood's corpse was later brought here and interred.[1]

1. NO 141159. Gravestone in Dron churchyard.

12

HEADS AND HANDS
OF MARTYRS OFF

The Archbishop of St Andrews, James Sharp, was originally ordained as the presbyterian minister of Crail in Fife and was so trusted that he was selected for the job of going to London to negotiate the survival of the Church of Scotland at the Restoration in 1660. However, he changed his allegiance and on 16 December 1661 he was consecrated as Archbishop of St Andrews. His swapping sides from Presbyterianism to Episcopacy was only one reason why he was detested by the Covenanters. He was renowned for his strong beliefs, and after the Battle of Rullion Green he was one of the most vociferous in demanding the execution of the Covenanters who had been taken prisoner. When the king sent a letter demanding that no more lives be taken, Sharp held on to the document long enough to cause the death of hundreds more.

In his home county of Fife, Sharp was a zealous persecutor of the Covenanters. He appointed William Carmichael as the county's Sheriff-Depute and set him the task of tracking down the Presbyterians who failed to attend the curate's churches. Carmichael took to this task with vigour, for he was able to take the Covenanters' possessions and thus extend his fortune. He was noted for drinking and squandering money, and had lost a family fortune already. Carmichael tortured thousands of people; he beat information out of women and children, and looted their homes.

The Covenanters of Fife were so annoyed with Carmichael's actions that they decided something had to be done about him. Any time he had been reported for his cruelty resulted in further torture. A number of Covenanters who were hiding from him decided that they would 'scarr him from his cruel courses.' On Saturday 3 May 1679 twelve Covenanters hid themselves in the countryside where Carmichael was due to spend the day hunting. Although they spent the day scouring the countryside in search of him, they were unable to find him. The reason was simple – Carmichael had been warned that there were men making inquiries about him, and he felt it was wise to keep himself locked up indoors.

The 12 Covenanters eventually came to Ceres village, where three of them left the party. This left David Hackston of Rathillet, George Balfour of Gilston, John Balfour of Kinloch (known as 'Burly'), William Dingwall of Cadden, James Russell of Kingskettle, Andrew Guillane of Balmerino, Alexander and Andrew Henderson of Kilbrachmont and George Fleming of Balboathy. Their patience paid off, for it was near Ceres that they received word that Archbishop Sharp's coach and six was making its way along the road from Kennoway towards St Andrews and at once they determined to ambush him. Hackston had to be persuaded, however, for he had a civil matter against the bishop to clear up, and he felt this would prejudice his case. At a small clachan known as Magus[1] the nine Covenanters began to pursue the coach. Russell rode out in front, coming alongside the carriage to check that the archbishop was in fact within. When Sharp spotted the man he yelled to his coachman to speed up, for he feared that his life was in danger. One of the archbishop's servants, who was riding on the outside of the coach, turned round and took aim with a small gun. However, he was unable to fire it, for one of the Covenanters managed to pull him from the coach and take his gun. A few shots were fired at the carriage, but with no effect.

One of the Covenanters struck out with his sword and hit the postillion on his head, causing him to fall from his position. The rest soon brought the coach to a halt and forced open the doors. Sharp and Isabella, his daughter, were cowering within. One of the men ordered the archbishop to come out, but he refused.

Russell addressed the archbishop. 'I take God to witness, whose cause I desire to own in adhering to the persecute Gospel, that it is not out of any hatred of your person, nor from any prejudice you have done or could do to me, that I intend now to take your life, but because you have been, and still continue to be, an avowed opponent of the flourishing of Christ's kingdom, and a murderer of His saints.'

The archbishop pleaded with Russell to save his life, and he promised that he would make sure that Russell and his companions' lives would be spared also. But Russell refused, and told the archbishop some of the reasons why his life must be taken. He reminded him of his part in bringing about the execution of James Mitchell on 18 January 1678 in Edinburgh. Mitchell had been responsible for an earlier attempt on the life of Sharp on 11 July 1668. He was apprehended but managed to escape. Caught a second time, he was tortured with the boot and imprisoned on the Bass Rock until his date of execution. Russell then mentioned James Learmont, who had taken part in the killing of a soldier, John Hogg, at the Whitekirk conventicle in May 1678. He was later executed in Edinburgh on 27 September 1678.

The archbishop then offered the Covenanters money if they would spare his life. They would have none of it, and forced him to come out of the carriage and prepare for death. He fell to his knees and crawled towards Hackston's horse, beseeching him to protect him. Hackston responded by telling that he would never lay a finger on the archbishop, and rode away.

Turning his attention to the other Covenanters, he pleaded for his life. According to a superstition which had been popular in Fife at the time, the archbishop could not be killed by a bullet.

The Covenanters drew their swords and together struck out at the figure on the ground. Despite Hackston's pleas to 'Spare the grey hairs,' and Guillane's demands that the archbishop be spared, the remainder of the party killed him. His body was covered with sixteen stab wounds. The Covenanters looked in his pockets and took a few papers which belonged to him. The servants and Sharp's daughter were not touched at all and were left to deal with the aftermath. His corpse was taken to St Andrews, from where a runner was sent to Edinburgh to notify the authorities of what had happened.

From Magus the Covenanters rode three miles to what is known as the Covenanter's Cave, located in a sandstone cliff in Dura Den, near Kemback.[3] On the way they came across another of the archbishop's servants, whom they forced to dismount, and disarmed him. At their hiding place the Covenanters sat down to pray, and afterwards to read the papers which they had found in the carriage. It is said that the contents of these documents left them feeling that what they had done was justified. The Covenanters then fled to the west of the country, where they joined Robert Hamilton in nailing a declaration to the market cross of Rutherglen on the day appointed for celebrating the king's birthday.

A fortnight after his murder, Archbishop Sharp's funeral took place in St Andrews. The authorities used his belongings to great effect – the coach in which he had been travelling across Magus Moor was drawn through the crowd, with the men on it dressed in mourning robes. The gown which Sharp had worn at the time, and which was spattered with patches of dried blood, was draped over the coffin and carried in the procession. His body was laid to rest in Holy Trinity Church, where Bishop Paterson (infamously remembered as the inventor of thumbscrews) preached the funeral sermon.[2]

The authorities were quick to react. A proclamation was issued which denounced the men as 'assassinates'. As they were known to be residents of the kingdom of Fife, the landowners in the county were ordered to take all their tenants and cottars to the burghs of Cupar, Dunfermline, Kirkcaldy or St Andrews, where they were questioned by the sheriffs-depute. Any who failed to appear were to be regarded as supporters of the Covenant. Rewards of 10,000 merks were offered to anyone who supplied information leading to the capture of those responsible. Even a complete indemnity from justice was offered to any of those who had taken part if he would bring his accomplices to justice.

No-one was willing to betray the Covenanters, and none of those responsible was captured on a charge of taking part in the murder. David Hackston was taken on the battlefield of Airds Moss and subsequently hanged in Edinburgh on 30 September 1680. William Dingwall was wounded at Bothwell Bridge and died soon after. A young man, Andrew Ayton of Inchdarnie, was captured in a dragnet operation which took place on the day of the murder and the arresting soldiers were led by the Justice-General and the Laird of Lundy. Ayton was shot and wounded, dying soon after. Although he had taken no part in the murder, the soldiers discovered letters on his person which indicated that Sharp's murder had been preconceived. Hendry Shaw was captured at the same time, and more documents were discovered in his home. What happened to him after is not known.

Andrew Guillane was caught four years after the murder. He had been a weaver in Balmerino, Fife, but was now working as a labourer on a farm in the parish of Cockpen. He was reported by the curate for not attending the church and on 11 June 1683 the soldiers apprehended him. He refused to toast the king, so the soldiers took him to the tolbooth in Dalkeith, Midlothian. From there he was transferred to Edinburgh tolbooth. He was chained to a large iron bar, one which was 12 feet long and $2\frac{1}{2}$ inches in diameter, which prevented his escape. It was still not known that he had taken part in Sharp's death. One day, however, whilst questioning him, the examiner mentioned that Sharp had been killed whilst in the act of prayer, which was regarded as most unchristian. Without realising it, Guillane responded by saying that, 'He would not pray one word, for all that could be said to him.' It was enough to seal his fate.

Guillane was executed at the Gallowlee, which lay midway between Edinburgh and Leith, on 13 July 1683. Before he breathed his last the hangman cut off his hands and then severed his head. This was no simple task – the hangman was drunk and it required nine strokes to break the spine. The head and hands were displayed on Edinburgh's Netherbow Port. Guillane's body was then taken from the scaffold and transported to Fife, where it was hung from a tall pole on Magus Muir, the site of Sharp's execution. The body swung from its chain for around 10 months, until some locals took it down and buried it on the spot. The Privy Council was displeased at this, and on 27 May 1684 issued a commission to the Earl of Balcarres ordering him to banish abroad anyone found guilty of this deed.[4]

Two Covenanters who were thought to be connected with Sharp's murder were Laurence Hay and Andrew Pitulloch. Hay was a weaver from Fife and Pitulloch was a farm worker from Largo, in the same county. They were apprehended by the authorities and taken to Edinburgh where they were held in gaol for some time. They were taken before the Justiciary court on 11 July 1681 where they were tried and found to be members of a praying society. This society had produced *A Testimony Against the Evils of the Times* and both men had subscribed to it. They were hanged at the Grassmarket on 13 July 1681 and their heads subsequently removed. These were ordered to be displayed on the tolbooth at Cupar, where they remained on public view until the Glorious Revolution. They were then buried in the parish kirkyard along with one of Hackston's hands.[5]

1. NO 456152.
2. NO 509166. Monument in Holy Trinity church, St Andrews. Also cairn on site of murder at Magus Muir.
3. NO 416146.
4. NO 458145. Gravestone near Claremont farm.
5. NO 373146. Gravestone in Cupar churchyard.

13

A RENCOUNTER AT DRUMCLOG

A large conventicle was planned for Sunday 1 June 1679. It was to take place at Hairlawhill, which lies two miles from Darvel in Ayrshire. The preachers included Thomas Douglas, who was later outlawed with a price of 3,000 merks on his head. Many folk attended, travelling from miles around.

The number of people making their way across country alerted the authorities, and John Graham of Claverhouse was sent with a party of dragoons to arrest and disperse them. Claverhouse was in Glasgow at the time, and he set out through Rutherglen, arriving in Hamilton on the evening of Saturday 31 May. Here Claverhouse's men carried out a search of a number of houses and captured Rev John King and 14 of his followers, all of whom were heading for the conventicle. These men were bound together, and one old account states that they were driven in front of the soldiers like beasts.

The government soldiers arrived in Strathaven at six o' clock on the Sunday morning. There they were able to discover the location of the conventicle. Claverhouse is said to have been rather hot-headed at this time, and rode at speed towards the site. Accounts of his men vary – Claverhouse said that they were keen to fight the Covenanters, but it was also noted that he threatened to court-martial any who failed to take part in the conflict.

The Covenanters had been informed of the approaching soldiers – a lookout fired a shot to warn the congregation. He probably saw them approaching as the site of the conventicle was on the summit of a low hill known as Glaister Law. The preacher, Thomas Douglas, ended his sermon with the famous statement, 'You have got the theory, now for the practice.'

Robert Hamilton was appointed to be their leader, even although he had no military training, but he was keen to engage in battle. The son of Sir Thomas Hamilton, Robert was 29 years old at the time. Hamilton issued the command that no quarter was to be given. From Hairlawhill the Covenanters marched towards Drumclog, where at length they came face to face with the soldiers. The women and children and any unarmed men in their number were left at the rear.

Claverhouse's men crossed the moors westwards from Strathaven. When they reached Drumclog they were surprised to find that the Covenanters were not actually engaged in prayer or worship, but were lined up ready for battle. King and the other prisoners were left tied up to the side whilst the soldiers lined up facing the Covenanters. It is said that both armies arranged themselves on good grassland, separated by a deep but narrow bog, as narrow as a few yards wide in places.[1]

Claverhouse's soldiers numbered around 150, all of whom were mounted on horseback.

The armed Covenanters numbered around 300, of which only 50 were mounted. Their weaponry was basic. Some had swords and guns, but the majority had home-made weapons or farm implements, such as pikes, cleeks or pitchforks. Robert Hamilton's officers were David Hackston of Rathillet, John Balfour of Burleigh, Henry Hall of Haughhead, Robert Flemming, John Loudoun, John Brown of Priestshiel, and William Cleland. Other names of folk who fought on the Covenanter's side have been passed down in their families. They include a Lambie from Ladybrow, who was wounded, Hugh and George Woodburn of Loudoun Mains, Hugh being their standard bearer.

George Woodburn was only 18 years old that day. He was

sent back to Darvel where he was to go to the home of John Nisbet of Hardhill, which farm stood at the west end of the village. On their return they picked up John Morton of Broomhill, blacksmith in the village.

Claverhouse surveyed the opposition as they lined up to the west and decided that his chances of winning were slim. Accordingly he sent out a flag of truce, but the Covenanters refused to accept this. The two forces moved closer to each other, separated by the deep ditch. Claverhouse ordered 12 of his men to advance and shoot at the opposition. Hamilton copied this command, and 12 Covenanters went forward and fired. No casualties occurred. The same tactic took place three times, until the Covenanters sent forth 12 on horseback and six on foot. In the cross-fire one of the soldiers was wounded and he fell from his horse.

The loss of one of his men drove Claverhouse to increase the number of soldiers sent forward. Around 30 dragoons were sent to advance, whereupon Cleland retaliated. Another of the soldiers fell, this time dead. It was said that it was Cleland himself who killed the first man on the battlefield. A second group of dragoons then advanced, taking aim at the foot-soldiers under Cleland. He ordered his men to lie low, which they did, taking shelter behind a peat bank. The bullets whirred over their heads, and had John Morton not raised his head above the bank to see what was happening, no Covenanter would have been killed. When Morton did this a bullet hit him in the neck, pierced his windpipe, and passed right through to the other side.[2]

Claverhouse's horsemen then came up to the edge of the bog, but the ground was sodden and the horses began to struggle, sinking into the wet peat. The Covenanters cheered at the sight of the soldiers struggling in the bog. Cleland led his men forward on the left flank, and Balfour took up the rear with his horsemen. They forced a way across the bog and lunged into the midst of the soldiers. The greater number of them and their willingness to fight was enough to instil fear in the dragoons. The advance was successful, with more soldiers falling to the ground. Among these were the officers, Cornet Crawford and Captain Blyth.

Taken aback, the government troops decided to turn and flee, and when the rest noticed this they followed suit. The Covenanters were surprised to see the dragoons running away, and with renewed energy chased them with vigour. They managed to kill about 30-40 of the soldiers, John Nisbet of Hardhill killing seven of these. The horses killed in battle were buried beneath a mound, and when this was later levelled it was reckoned that it contained the bones of 28 horses.

The Covenanters under Balfour chased the soldiers as far as their farm-horses were able to carry them. Thomas Weir of North Cumberhead (or Waterside) farm managed to take the standard, but the bridle on his horse broke, meaning that he was unable to control it properly. He was wounded to the head and died three days after the battle. William Cleland managed to catch hold of the bridle of Claverhouse's horse, but support did not arrive quick enough to allow him to take Claverhouse himself. Thomas Finlay, a farmer from Southfield, stabbed Claverhouse's horse with his pike, injuring it. Claverhouse forced it onward, and at a spot since known as the Trumpeter's Well at Caldermill he mounted another horse which had belonged to his trumpeter. The trumpeter was a lad of around 14 years of age. He was killed and tradition states that his body was disposed of in the well.

In Strathaven the local men attacked Claverhouse and the retreating soldiers. This took place in a narrow roadway called the 'Hole-closs'. Here 12 dragoons were killed in the skirmish before the soldiers managed to get away. They scurried towards Glasgow. On the way the dragoons met an old farmer, Gideon MacNaughton of Greenloan, East Kilbride. For some reason the soldiers exacted their revenge on him and killed him.

Claverhouse had ordered his guardsmen to kill the prisoners from Hamilton in the event of his men being defeated. However, they were left behind as their guardsmen fled, and John King began to enjoy himself, shouting at Claverhouse, 'Are you no' waiting for the efternune sermon?'

Hamilton had asked his men to give no quarter, but a number of dragoons were taken prisoner by the Covenanters.

Hamilton had wished to kill them all, but a number of Covenanters persuaded him to spare them. These men were disarmed, after which they were allowed to go free. One, however, was killed by Hamilton. He was later accused of cruelty in putting this prisoner to death, whereupon he responded in a letter:

...there was 5 more that without knowledge gote quarters, quhom notwithstanding I desired might have been sent the same way that their neighbours were, and its not being doon I reckoned ever amongst our first stepping aside.

The Covenanters only lost one man of their number on the battlefield, but five others were mortally wounded. William Dingwall was wounded when his horse was killed. However, it is said that even in this state he was filled with joy at the thought of the victory and his impending arrival in Heaven. He spoke his final testimony which was so meaningful and profound that for many years after visitors to his grave in Strathaven were moved to tears.[3] Thomas Flemming of Loudounhill was buried at Loudoun.[4] John Gebbie of Feoch is buried at Newmilns.[5] James Thomson lies in the old kirkyard at Stonehouse[6] and Thomas Weir of Waterside at Lesmahagow.[7]

When Claverhouse managed to return to Glasgow that evening he was suffering from fatigue, but he still managed to write a letter to his Commander-in-Chief:

I thought that we might make a little tour to see if we could fall upon a conventicle; which we did, little to our advantage; for when we came in sight of them, we found them drawn up in batell, upon a most advantageous ground, to which there was no coming but through mosses and lakes. They wer not preaching, and had got away all there women and shildring. They consisted of four battaillons of foot, and all well armed with fusils and pitchforks, and three squadrons of horse. We sent both partys to skirmish, they of foot and we of dragoons; they run for it, and sent down a battaillon of foot against them; we sent threescore of dragoons, who made them run again shamfully; but in the end they percaiving that we had the better of them in skirmish, they resolved a generall engadgment and imediatly advanced with there foot, the horse folowing; they came throght the lotche; the greatest body of all made up against my troupe; we keeped our fyre till they wer within ten pace of us: they recaived our fyr, and advanced to shok; the first they gave us broght down the Coronet Mr Crafford and Captain Bleith, besides that with a pitchfork they made such an openeing in my rone horse's belly, that his guts hung out half an elle, and yet he caryed me aff an myl; which so discoraged our men, that they sustained not the shok, but fell in disorder. There horse took the occasion of this, and purseued us so hotly that we had no tym to rayly. I saved the standarts, but lost on the place about aight or ten men, besides wounded; but the dragoons lost many mor. They ar not com easily af on the other side, for I sawe severall of them fall befor we cam to the shok. I mad the best retrate the confusion of our people would suffer, and I am now laying with my Lord Rosse. The toun of Streven drew up as wer was making our retrait, and thoght of a pass to sut us off, but we took courage and fell to them, made them run, leaving a dousain on the place. What these rogues will dou yet I know not, but the country was flocking to them from all hands. This may be counted the beginning of the rebellion, in my opinion.

On the following day a number of Covenanters decided to march into Glasgow. The city was ready for the attack, however, with Lord Ross constructing barricades at the roads into the centre of the town and placing armed guards at these. The Covenanters, under Hamilton, Balfour and Hackston, faced up to the soldiers. They split into two groups, one attacking the Gallowgate, the other the top of High Street but, having no artillery and losing seven of their number, decided to retreat and rejoin the rest of their party who were by this time gathered at Bothwell Bridge.

1. NS 626396. Monument on battlefield at High Drumclog. Also memorial on outdoor
   centre wall (NS 625396) and at Ryelandside (NS 650398).
2. NS 537373. Gravestone and monument in Newmilns churchyard.
3. NS 705447. Gravestone in Strathaven cemetery.
4. NS 492374. Gravestone in Loudoun churchyard. Also commemorated on
   monument at Newmilns (NS 537373).
5. NS 537373. Gravestone and monument in Newmilns churchyard.
6. NS 748469. Gravestone in Stonehouse old churchyard.
7. NS 814398. Gravestone in Lesmahagow churchyard.

14

WE AT BOTHWELL DID APPEAR

The Covenanters' victory at Drumclog caused alarm in Edinburgh where the authorities held meetings and planned to quell the rebellion. The Privy Council met and issued a 'Proclamation against rebels in arms in the west.' This classed the Covenanters as insurgents guilty of high treason, and warned that if they did not give themselves up within 24 hours then the authorities would treat them as 'incorrigible and desperate traitors', to whom no pardon could be allowed. On 5 June the militia were ordered to be ready, and on 7 June the heritors and freeholders in 19 of Scotland's counties were ordered to gather as many servants and followers on horseback as they could raise. A note was sent to the king in England who replied that he was in agreement with the plans, but that nothing should be done until troops could be sent from England and Ireland.

The Duke of Monmouth travelled up from England to take command. He caught up with the army, now around 10,000 strong, near to Kirk of Shotts and marched them to Bothwell Moor, arriving on 22 June.

The Covenanters were camped on Hamilton Moor, having travelled from Drumclog to Glasgow, where they failed to take the city, before returning south. After that fiasco their numbers began to drop, and many of their support deserted. A council of war was called, at which it was decided the army should only be made up of those who were not guilty of any sins. Thomas Weir of Greenridge seems to have become a major sticking point for the Covenanters, for 13 years previously he had been a trooper under Dalyell's command at Rullion Green. A minister and some elders were sent to speak to Weir, with the task of asking him to confess the sins he was guilty of during his time with Dalyell. Weir refused, claiming that he should not be removed from the army for something he had done 13 years earlier, and in any case he argued, had he not shown his allegiance by joining the Covenanters. The Covenanters' council refused to accept this, and after some heated debate Weir decided to leave. His followers decided to join him and the split in ranks caused considerable confusion.

Word reached the Covenanters that the enemy was approaching, having been spotted near Bothwell Bridge. David Hackston and 24 horsemen were sent to spy on the government soldiers. He discovered a detachment of them hidden behind some bushes, awaiting such a reconnoitre. Hackston sent back for support, but the Covenanters, too busy arguing among themselves over the Weir dispute, sent only a dozen horsemen to his assistance. The 36 Covenanters seem to have been enough to repel the ambush, who returned with exaggerated stories of the Covenanters' strength. Consequently further soldiers were sent to Bothwell to assist.

The intervening days were spent by the Covenanters marching back and forth between Glasgow, where they read out a declaration at the tolbooth as well as gathering what arms they could. The Covenanting forces number began to rise slowly, with folk travelling from south-west Scotland to help in the expected battle. James Ure of Shargarton came from Stirlingshire and the north with about 200 others, bringing the total to 5-6,000. Ure was an Episcopal minister who changed to Presbyterianism. After the battle he escaped and was in hiding for nine years. His estate was forfeited for his adherence. In the attempt to capture Ure his mother was found guilty of attending conventicles – she was to die in Glasgow prison.[1]

John Welsh arrived with followers from the south – 140 with horses and 300 on foot. Weir's following of horsemen decided to return with him. However, the discussions again became heated, with the wording of the declaration in Glasgow being disputed by Welsh and Sir Robert Hamilton. Proposals to draw up a new declaration acceptable to both sides lasted a number of days, even to the extent of swords being used in a threatening manner, during which time many Covenanters left to return home. On 14 June, a Saturday, the council decided that Welsh and Hume should preach on the sins of the time at the following morning's service, only to be told by the ministers that they would pick a subject for the sermon themselves. Further wrangling took place, with many of the officers, including Hamilton, Hackston, Hall, Paton, Balfour, Cleland and Cargill, leaving ranks on three occasions before they were persuaded to rejoin.

In the three weeks from Drumclog the government forces had spent their time strengthening their number, improving their skills and drilling ready for action. The Covenanters, in contrast, had moved their camp almost daily, and spent most of their time arguing amongst themselves over matters which should not have divided their ranks, particularly at that time. They had ignored all that is important in getting ready for battle, such as training, preparing arms and ammunition, and setting in provisions.

The battle commenced on the Sunday morning, 22 June. The Covenanters had not expected to fight on a Sunday, but word from Hackston, Henry Hall of Haughhead and Andrew Turnbull, who were guarding the bridge, surprised them with the announcement that the enemy was preparing to fight. The Covenanters moved up towards the banking on the side of the river and placed their single cannon to face the bridge.[2]

A document, or supplication, was drawn up by some Covenanters and it was resolved to send a runner to the Duke of Monmouth to request the right to free exercise in religion and a free parliament. A Galloway laird surnamed Murdoch, and one named Hume took this plea, which Monmouth read. He then listened to their thoughts on the matter, but responded that the king had given him no authority in this field. He did, however, promise to get their wishes granted. In the meantime, he warned them, they would have to lay down their arms. If they did not return within half an hour with this promise, then he had no choice but to engage in battle.

The two men returned to their officers and reported on what Monmouth had to say. When Sir Robert Hamilton heard Monmouth's demand he retorted, 'And hang next.'

Almost exactly on the half hour (some say the government forces did not allow the full time – but the Covenanters did not intend giving up in any case) the king's troops opened fire with the three cannon which they had. Their aim was too high and the balls flew over the Covenanters who responded with gunfire so accurate that a number of royalists were killed. Those in charge of the cannon fled and David Leslie shouted after them. 'Would they fleg for country fellows?'

The battle continued for another three hours and 300 Covenanters bravely defended the bridge. Their ammunition began to run low, and word was sent back to the main force to send more. The reply was that there was insufficient, and that this force should retire from the bridge and rejoin the main force. Though unwilling to leave such a strong position, the troops under Hackston agreed.

The Covenanters then formed up on the moor. They were all in good spirits, and the divisions seem to have been forgotten. Then word spread that Welsh and other leaders had deserted the field and Captain John Paton had to try and find new officers to take their place. Weir's horsemen made a dash forward before retiring behind, passing through the ranks and sending them into disarray. At this the royalists fired their cannon and moved forward. Fifteen Covenanters were killed.

The Covenanters then took fright and panic spread like wildfire throughout their ranks. They turned to flee, and the royalists were astounded at the sudden change in their manner. They rode after them, slaying around 400 as they caught up with them. The biggest percentage are said to have been killed in the narrow glen of the Whistleberry Burn, which flows into the Clyde on the south side of the bridge.

James Reid of Kittochside, East Kilbride, had been in charge of the East Kilbride Covenanters. At the retreat he spotted the Kilbride standard in the hands of the enemy. He was so fired with rage that he ran straight among them with his broadsword flailing and managed to tear the flag from its pole. He wrapped it around his body and was able to dodge all the bullets which fired in his direction as he escaped.

Hundreds of prisoners were taken after the battle. Two of these were ministers, John Kid and John King. They were taken to Edinburgh where they were executed on 14 August. King, who had fought at Drumclog, is said to be the basis of Sir Walter Scott's 'Gabriel Kettledrummle' in Old Mortality.

Many Covenanters later died of their wounds. Robert and Walter Lockhart of Birkhill had fought both at Drumclog and Bothwell. Robert's horse was shot from under him at Bothwell and he fled from the field. To avoid the dragoons he hid up a tree for a time. He was later found lying dead in a bog, a victim of exposure and fatigue. His corpse was taken to Carluke where it was buried.[3]

Soldiers pursued two brothers surnamed Smith and a third Covenanter up the glen of the Wellshaw and Earnock burns towards Little Earnock, near Hamilton. The Smiths lived at Earnockmuir farm. At the upper part of a garden they were caught and killed. Buried on the site, three large pines mark their graves.[4]

Some were more lucky. One Covenanter fled to the north-east but fell to the ground from exhaustion. His fiancée came to the battlefield once the soldiers had gone, searching for what she expected to be the corpse of her lover. At length she discovered him almost two miles from the scene of battle, lying on the ground. He was still alive, but only just. The fiancée, Mary Rae, wanted to give him a drink of water from a local well, but had nothing in which to carry the liquid. He was so severely wounded that he could not move, so she lifted him herself and carried him across the fields to the well. There she washed his wounds, slaked his thirst, and nursed him back to health.[5]

Another 1,200 Covenanters surrendered and were taken to Edinburgh, where they were imprisoned in Greyfriars' kirkyard. Five were tried in Edinburgh on 10 November and were found guilty of rebellion. They were sent to Magus Muir in Fife, where Archbishop Sharp had been murdered, and there 'to be hanged till they be dead, and their bodies to be hung in chains until they rot, and all their lands, goods, and gear to fall in his Majesty's use.' These men were Thomas Brown, James Wood, Andrew Sword, John Waddel and John Clyde. The execution took place on 25 November, the bodies being laid to rest in a cornfield.[6] Of their backgrounds, Brown was a shoemaker in Edinburgh, Wood came from Newmilns in Ayrshire,[7] Sword was a weaver from Barry parish in Kirkcudbright, Waddel was from New Monkland in Lanarkshire and Clyde was just 21 years old.

Immediately after Bothwell Bridge the authorities sent out their soldiers to hunt down any they thought may have taken part in the battle. Claverhouse was reported to have carried out many acts of cruelty at this time, as well as robbing and pillaging at will. On the day after the battle Arthur Inglis of Netherton, a farmer in the fields looking after his cattle, was apprehended at Stockelton Dyke by a party of his soldiers. The only reason they could come up with for shooting him was that he was alone in the fields with a Bible in his possession. They assumed that he had been at the battle, but it is reckoned that he was innocent of this. It is said by some that his son did take part in the fight. The shot only wounded Inglis, but a second dragoon drew his sword and ran it through his body.[8]

Another victim was seventeen-year-old Arthur Tacket, who lived in Hamilton. On the day of Bothwell he left his home with a gun and after the defeat was able to return home. A local laird, proprietor of Raploch, heard of this and had him arrested. Taken to Edinburgh, he somehow managed to be set free, perhaps because he was from a well-to-do family. A few years later, however, he was declared to be a traitor. In 1684 he was caught making his way from a conventicle at which James Renwick had preached. He was tortured by the boot and thumbscrews in an attempt at finding out who else was at the meeting, but he refused to say anything which would incriminate another. Instead the authorities hanged him in the Grassmarket on 30 July 1684 for having been at Bothwell.

John Wilson had been a captain in the Covenanting forces. He was the son of Alexander Wilson, Town Clerk of Lanark. After Bothwell he was captured in the spring of 1681 and held prisoner for two years. He faced the Privy Council on 17 April 1683 who decreed that he should hang at Edinburgh's Grassmarket on 16 May. He left behind a wife, children and some sisters.

Dozens more were martyred for their part in Bothwell. Robert Garnock, a blacksmith from Stirling was executed on 10 October 1681. Thomas Lauchlan lost his life on 16 August 1682. Alexander Home of Humetoun was hanged in the Grassmarket on 29 December 1682 and David MacMillan was killed on 16 May 1683. Arthur Bruce of Dalserf, John Cochran of Lesmahagow and John Whitelaw of Staun farm New Monkland were killed on 30 November that year. James Dick had been sentenced to death but escaped from Edinburgh Tolbooth on 16 September 1683. He was recaptured and executed in 5 March 1684.

1. NS 652949. Gravestone to James Ure in Kippen churchyard.
2. NS 711578. Monument at north end of Bothwell Bridge commemorates battle.
3. NS 847503. Gravestone in Carluke churchyard.
4. NS 701539. Memorial stone which formerly stood here is now in Hamilton old churchyard (NS 723555).
5. NS 725589. Mary Rae's Well was rebuilt in Gordon Place, Orbiston, Bellshill.
6. NO 456151. Gravestone on Magus Muir.
7. NS 537373. Memorial in Newmilns churchyard.
8. NS 769540. Original memorial at Cambusnethan old churchyard. Modern memorial cairn at Wishaw (NS796552).

15

DEERNESS

On 15 November 1679, 257 Covenanters were herded out of the Covenanters' Prison in Edinburgh's Greyfriars' kirkyard, where they had been kept imprisoned since the Battle of Bothwell Bridge in June. They were marched down the road to Leith, without being told where they were headed. At the port a ship was lying at the Roads, and small boats were used to ferry the prisoners to it.

The ship was owned by a merchant in Leith named William Paterson, who had transacted with the provost of Linlithgow, Mr. Milns, laird of Barnton, to take them away to the plantations. Milns had also the distinction of being the first person to burn the Covenant.

The Crown of London was so small that there was little room for the Covenanters on board. Many of those on the ship were so sick that those who were reasonably fit had to spend all their time standing, so that the ill could at least lie down. They remained off the shore of Leith for 12 days thereafter. By this time word had spread in Edinburgh that the Covenanters were no longer locked up in the kirkyard. It was confirmed that they were now on board a ship awaiting deportation to Barbados in the American colonies, where they were to be sold as slaves. The citizens of Edinburgh who were friendly to the cause took a collection and were able to present the Covenanters with £1,000 Sterling, which they hoped would make life in the colonies a bit better for them. One of those on board, James Corsan of Kirkcudbright, managed to get a letter sent to his wife from the ship as it lay in Leith Roads. He writes:

> All the troubles we met since Bothwell were not to be compared to one day in our present circumstances. Our uneasiness is beyond words. Yet the consolations of God overbalance all; and I hope we are near our port, and heaven is open for us.

The ship eventually left the Firth of Forth on 27 November and sailed up the east coast of Scotland. The December storms turned the North Sea into a raging torrent.

By 10 December the vessel had reached Orkney, where the anchor was lowered for the night. During a storm the ship was pushed by the winds and waves, causing the anchor to drag along the sea bed. In the moonlight the watch spotted the high cliff of the Mull Head of Deerness and he raised the alarm. The Covenanters tried to make an escape, but the captain had ordered the hatches to the hold to be locked and would allow none to escape. The crew of the ship headed for the small boat which was tied alongside and managed to make it to safety.

The Covenanters within yelled and screamed for the captain to open the hatches, but he refused. They were left on board the ship as it was driven onto the rocks, all the while the waves battering and breaking the timber hull in two. When the hull was eventually breached by the rocks, many of the Covenanters managed to force their way from the boat, and by clinging to the broken planks managed to float to the island, but as they scaled the cliffs the captain and his crew forced them back over, plunging to their deaths. Only 49 Covenanters are known to have survived.

The 209 Covenanters stuck on board drowned as the ship sank. When the ocean released her victims, the Orkney folk gathered the corpses from the beaches and buried them at Scarva Taing.[1]

The names of most of the Covenanters on board *The Crown*

of London are known. They came from all over the south of
Scotland, from Ayrshire in the west to the Borders in the east, and
from the Lothians south to Galloway. Some of those drowned
were renowned Covenanters, others were only known from their
appearance in arms at Bothwell.

The list of Covenanters on board the vessel is as follows.
Four men were drowned who belonged to Renfrewshire. They
were James Cunningham from Eastwood, John Govan from
Neilston and William Auchincloss and William Buchan from
Paisley.

Ayrshire lost 53 Covenanters in the wreck – another seven
survived. From Kilmarnock in Cunninghame came James
Anderson, Robert Anderson, William Brown, John Cuthbertson
and Thomas Finlay.[2] A sixth man from Kilmarnock was also
present, Patrick Watt, but he was lucky enough to escape.
Nothing is known of their background. Fenwick parish lost David
Bitchet, William Bitchet, Andrew Buckle, David Currie, James
Gray, Robert Tod, John White and John Wylie. A ninth man,
Robert Wallace, escaped. Loudoun parish lost Thomas Wylie.
James Bouston from Dreghorn was also drowned and Stewarton
parish lost Andrew, Robert and Thomas Wylie. David MacCubbin
and William MacCulloch from Dalry perished in the sea.

The middle third of the county, known as Kyle, lost many
men. From Dalmellington parish Walter Humper and Hugh
Simpson were drowned. Humper's son, also Walter, managed to
escape, as did Hugh Cameron and Quintin MacAdam. From
Cumnock parish John Gemil and James Mirrie lost their lives.
Andrew Welch was lost from the neighbouring parish of
Ochiltree; Andrew Richmond from Auchinleck. Mauchline
parish was the home to William Drips and William Reid, both of
whom were drowned. John Campbell and Alexander Paterson
from Muirkirk also suffered. James Young and George Campbell
were lost from Galston,[3] but Andrew Thomson from Dundonald
and George Dunbar from Craigie both survived.

From the southern third, or Carrick, were lost Alexander
Burden from Barr, John MacClellan, Thomas MacClurg and John

MacCornock from Colmonell and William Caldwell from Girvan. Maybole lost six men, Mungo Eccles, Thomas Horn, Robert MacGarron, John MacHarrie, John MacWhirter and William Rodger.[4] Straiton lost George Hutcheson, Alexander Lamb and James MacMurrie. The adjoining parish of Kirkmichael lost five sons, John Brice, Robert Douglas, James MacConnell, John MacTire and Robert Ramsay. Thomas Germont and John White from Kirkoswald also died.

Lanarkshire, or the Shire of Clydesdale as it was known in the 17th century, lost 39 men, another nine escaping. Walter MacKechnie, William Miller, Alexander Pirie and Francis Wodrow were Glaswegians who perished. Francis Wodrow was the second son of John Wodrow, who had previously been imprisoned following Rullion Green and was hanged in Edinburgh on 22 December 1666. John's nephew was Rev Robert Wodrow (1680-1734), who became minister of Eastwood in 1703 and who wrote *The History of the Sufferings of the Church of Scotland from the Restoration to the Revolution*. Andrew Snodgrass was lost from Govan. From East Kilbride five men were drowned – Robert Auld, James Clark, John Clark, William Rodger and John Struthers. Shotts parish also lost five men, John Aitken, Robert Chalmers, John Killen, Peter Learmont and Alexander Walker. A sixth man, John Thomson, escaped. He had been declared a fugitive and was arrested. Although willing to declare the Battle of Bothwell Bridge as rebellion, he denied that the death of Archbishop Sharp was sinful, hence his banishment. Six men from the Monklands were drowned. They were Thomas Barton, William Grinlaw, Thomas Mathie, William Miller, James Waddel and John Wynet. Bothwell lost William Breakenrig.

The parish of Avondale, in which lies the town of Strathaven, lost eight men in the wreck. They were Andrew Aiton, Robert Allison, William Allison, Thomas Brownlee, John Cairnduff, John Cochran, Andrew Torrance and John Watson. Nearby Glassford lost John Craig and John Miller. Thomas Crichton and James Couper (or Cowper) perished from Carnwath.[5] James Thomson and Thomas Wilson died from

Quothquhan. Biggar lost John Rankin. Lesmahagow lost George and Robert Weir. Other Clydesdale survivors were William Scoular from Cambusnethan, John Gardner and William Waddel from Monkland, someone surname More from Bothwell, William Fram from Calder parish, James Penman from Quothquhan, Thomas Swan from Carstairs and George Draffin from Lesmahagow. Draffin was to suffer further ill-luck, for he was subsequently captured and banished a second time, on that occasion reaching America.

Galloway lost relatively few men. They were James Corsan from Kirkcudbright, James Houston from Balmaghie, James Donaldson from Kelton, Samuel Beck, Robert Brown and Samuel Hannay from Kirkmabreck and John MacTaggart from Penninghame. Borgue parish lost four men – John and Robert Brice, Andrew Sprot and William Thomson. Girthon lost Andrew Donaldson; Kirkpatrick Irongray Andrew Wallet. A number of Galloway men managed to escape – John MacCartney, John MacGhie and Andrew MacWhann from Kirkcudbright; Robert Caldow of Balmaghie; Alexander Murray of Penninghame; John Martin and John Richardson of Borgue; John Malcolm and John Smith from Dalry; John Edgar from Balmaclellan and Andrew Clark of Lochrutton.

Dumfriesshire's loss all came from Nithsdale. They were James Colvil, John Ferguson, David Mackervail, Robert Milligan and Thomas Rosper from Glencairn parish and John Kennedy and Thomas Milligan from Closeburn. William Ferguson, John Milligan, John Murdoch and John Smith, all from Glencairn, managed to escape.

From the Border counties were lost John Scot of Ettrick and Robert Young of Galashiels. Robert MacGill of Galashiels managed to break free. From Nenthorn parish was lost Samuel Nisbet; James Aitchison escaping. Cavers parish lost Samuel Douglas, John Greenshields, James Hobkirk and Richard Young – James Leidon, James and William Glasgow and James Young survived. Kelso lost William Hardie; Jedburgh John Mather; Melrose Andrew Cook and John Young. Sprouston parish lost

Thomas Cairns and Walter Waddel. Castleton parish lost John Pringle, William Scot, John Unnes and Alexander Waddel. William Herd of Ashkirk was drowned, as was Andrew Newbigging of Bowden. James Custon and John Ellit of Southdean were lost, William Swanston escaping. John Oliver of Hobkirk was also lost.

East Lothian lost only one Covenanter, James Tod from Dunbar. Mid Lothian lost a dozen. They were Thomas Gilchrist, James Graze, Alexander Russel and James Steel from Calder parish; John Brown and Alexander Murray of Mid Calder; Alexander Bisset from East Calder; Thomas Pringle of Stow; James Tinto from Temple; James Fork from Crichton; Thomas Williamson from Cranstoun and William Reid of Musselburgh. David Samuel of East Calder and Thomas Mackenzie of Liberton survived the wreck.

The county of Linlithgow, or West Lothian, lost 20 men. Torphichen was one of the worst affected parishes, losing John Addie, John Allan, Alexander Bishop, Andrew Easton, James Easton and John Thomson. A seventh Covenanter survived, John Pender. John Thomson of Dalmannie was lost, as was John Govan of Kirkliston. Livingston parish, which had a garrison, sent seven Covenanters to their deaths – John Bell, Patrick Hamilton, William Henderson, Thomas Ingles, John Steven, Patrick Wilson and William Younger. Bathgate lost David Ralston; Abercorn James and John Gib. Thomas Borthwick of Linlithgow and Andrew Murdoch of Kinneil also perished.

From Fife five drowned – James Beal of Newburn, James Kirk and Andrew Prie (or Pirie) from Largo and Kilconquhar, John Kirk of Ceres and Robert Boog of Strathmiglo. Thomas Miller of Ceres survived. James Lilburn of Kinross was drowned but Robert Kirk and Robert Sands of Orwell survived. Perthshire lost five men – John Christison of Kilmadock, John Donaldson and Patrick Keir of Kincardine, and Andrew and John Muire of Glendevon.

Daniel Cunningham of Drummond parish in Stirlingshire was killed, as was James Galbraith of Kippen. Gargunnock lost

Thomas Brown, James Buchanan, Patrick Gilchrist and Thomas Miller; James Sands escaping. St Ninians parish lost John MacNure and John Neilson; Andrew and Thomas Thomson escaping. James MacKie of Denny perished. Robert Hendrie, John Morison and Andrew Young from Airth were lost, as was Thomas Phalp of Muiravonside. Hugh Montgomerie of Falkirk survived. The sole person lost from Dunbartonshire was James Finlayson of New Kilpatrick.

1. HY 570086. Monument at Scarva Taing on Deerness.
2. NS 427380. Monument in Laigh Kirkyard, Kilmarnock.
3. NS 500367. Memorial stone in Galston churchyard.
4. NS 295110. Monument near Cargilston farm, Maybole.
5. NS 975464. Gravestone in Carnwath churchyard.

16

AN ENCOUNTER WITH THE BLOODY ENEMIES OF TRUTH

On 22 June 1680, the first anniversary of the Battle of Bothwell Bridge, Rev Richard Cameron and around 20 of his followers marched into the Nithsdale town of Sanquhar and gathered at the burgh's market cross. Michael Cameron, his brother, read out the document, which was entitled 'The Declaration and Testimony of the true Presbyterian, anti-Prelatic, anti-Erastian persecuted party in Scotland', commonly called the 'Sanquhar Declaration'. This was then affixed to the wooden market cross. The Declaration disowned Charles II and his brother the Duke of York, and declared 'war with such a tyrant and usurper and the men of his practices, as enemies to our Lord Jesus Christ, and his cause and covenants.'

After the publication of the Sanquhar Declaration the Covenanters involved were wanted men. Prices were placed on their heads, ranging from 5000 merks for Richard Cameron, dead or alive and decreasing for other members. It was only a matter of time before the authorities caught up with them.

A month passed during which Cameron and his followers kept themselves distant from any centre of great population. Cameron hid amongst the Threeshire Hills, on the borders of Ayrshire, Dumfriesshire and Lanarkshire. His last sermon was delivered on 18 July at Kype Water, a moorland stream which falls into the Avon Water near Strathaven.

On 22 July 1680 a party of soldiers from the garrison at Sorn Castle were out on the road. They travelled along the road from Cumnock towards Muirkirk, intending to turn round at Tarrioch and make their way back to Sorn. They were looking for Covenanters associated with the declaration. The curate of Ochiltree parish had informed the landowner, Sir John Cochrane of Ochiltree, who in turn notified the authorities that the Covenanters were in the area, and for his information Cochrane was rewarded with 1,000 merks. As the soldiers journeyed beyond Boghead farm they spotted a group of Covenanters who had just eaten and were taking a rest out on the moor.

The Covenanters simultaneously noticed the approaching soldiers. Their leader, David Hackston of Rathillet, told them that they would require to fight, which all were willing to do. He formed them up on the peaty moor, ready to face their enemy. The Covenanting force was small, comprising only of Hackston and 23 others mounted on horseback, with 40 footmen in front. He placed 15 horse under him to the left; Robert Dick was placed on the right with eight other horses. Among the number was Rev Richard Cameron, who had spent the previous night at Meadowfoot farm, the home of William Mitchell, which lay by the side of the River Ayr. During the night he had dreamt that he would die on the following day, and when he awoke he washed his hands and face, prophesying, 'This is their last washing; I have need to make them clean, for there are many to see them.'

The government forces, which were reckoned to number 112, approached from the north-east. Their leader was Andrew Bruce of Earlshall. The two groups halted for a short time, during which Cameron said a prayer, asking the Lord to 'spare the green and take the ripe.' At around four o' clock in the afternoon Bruce sent about 20 of his foot dragoons to attack, whereupon Hackston sent a similar number. Both horse platoons then charged, the Covenanters firing the first shots, killing and wounding a few of the enemy.

David Hackston then led a charge through the government

troops, being pursued by a couple of dragoons. However, his horse became stuck in the bog and he had to leave it behind and continue to fight on foot. He then fell into combat with David Ramsay. Both of them fought with small swords. Whilst this took place three mounted dragoons came from behind and struck Hackston, leaving him wounded on the ground. Ramsay, who was known to Hackston, saved his life by taking him prisoner. According to Hackston's account of the battle:

> They searched me and carried me to their rear and laid me down, where I bled much, where were brought severalls of their men sore wounded. They gave us all testimony of brave resolute men. What more of our men were killed I did not see, nor know, but as they told me afterwards, the field was theirs.

The Battle of Airds Moss was still evenly balanced at this point, but the foot Covenanters were inexperienced and began to panic. They fired shots at the horses from a distance, wasting ammunition. One of the Covenanters, James Gray, was regarded as their best man, the official report citing him as 'the one that mauled them most.' Nevertheless, he was to die on the field.

The greater number of the regular troops was soon to overcome the Covenanters. Nine of them were killed, and five, including Hackston, were taken prisoner. During the fighting a dark thundercloud had passed over, sending forth heavy rain and mist which allowed many of the wounded Covenanters to escape. Although defeated, the Covenanters had managed to kill 28 soldiers in battle. It is related that the soldiers described the Covenanters as:

> ...men of the greatest courage they ever saw set their faces to fight, though they had been at battles abroad; and if they had been well trained, and armed and horsed as we were we would have been put to flight, and few of us escaped; their shots and strokes were deadly, and few recovered. Though there were but nine of them killed, there were twenty-eight of us killed dead, or died of their wounds in a few days.

The nine Covenanters who fell on the field were buried there. They were Rev Richard Cameron and his brother Michael,

Captain John Fowler, James Gray of Chryston, John Gemmel, John Hamilton, Robert Dick, Thomas Watson and Robert Paterson of Kirkhill, Cambusnethan parish.[1]

Bruce persuaded one of his soldiers to allow him the pleasure of hacking Cameron's head from his body, taking this trophy and his hands to Edinburgh in order to claim the £500 bounty. A similar fate also befell John Fowler, but the soldier responsible for this had mistaken him for Michael Cameron. Richard Cameron's head was taken to his father who was at that time locked up in the tolbooth. Asked if he recognised him, he took the head and kissed it, saying, 'I know him, I know him. It is my son, my dear son.' The head and hands were then taken to the Netherbow Port where they were publicly displayed on spikes.

The five Covenanters who were arrested were treated as scum. A Mr. Manual who belonged to Shotts and John Vallance of Auchinleck died of the wounds received in battle, the former as he was being placed in Edinburgh Tolbooth, the latter the next day. Archibald Allison of Evandale and John Malcolm of St John's Town of Dalry were both hanged at the Grassmarket in Edinburgh on 13 August, dying 'in great assurance, and comfortable hopes of well-being', according to Wodrow. Allison's final testimony tells of his charges:

> They charged me with rebellion, for joining with those whom they call rebels, and declared enemies to the king, and enemies to all good government. For my part I never called them so. I declare here, where I stand, before Him who will be my Judge within a little, my design in coming forth with arms was to hear the Gospel preached truly and faithfully; and I know it was the design of that poor handful to defend the Gospel, and to keep up a witness and testimony against the abounding corruptions with which this land is filled from end to end.

David Hackston was tied up and taken to Douglas, where the party rested. A local woman, Janet Cleland, brought a surgeon to look at his wounds. Fearing for his own safety, the surgeon only staunched the blood. Next day at Lanark he was questioned by Dalyell and Lord Ross, but as his answers were not to their liking, Dalyell threatened to roast him alive. Instead he was tightly bound and thrown into the tolbooth. A day or so later he was forced to walk some miles barefoot before being placed on a horse and taken to Edinburgh. Found guilty, he was hanged on 30 July. The Privy Council determined that:

> ...his body be drawn backward on a hurdle to the cross of Edinburgh; that there be a high scaffold erected a little above the cross, where, in the first place, his right hand is to be struck off, and, after some time, his left hand; then he is to be hanged up, and cut down alive, his bowels to be taken out, and his heart shown to the people by the hangman; then his heart and his bowels to be burned in a fire prepared for the purpose on the scaffold; that afterwards his head to be cut off, and his body divided into four quarters, with both his hands, to be affixed at St Andrews; another quarter at Glasgow, a third at Leith, a fourth at Burntisland; that none presume to be in mourning for him, or any coffin bought; that no person be suffered to be on the scaffold with him, save the two baillies, the executioner and his two servants; that he be allowed to pray to God Almighty, but not to speak to the people; that the heads of Cameron and John Fowler to be affixed on the Netherbow; that Hackston and Cameron's heads be fixed on higher poles than the rest.

The reason that parts of his body were taken to different areas of the country and publicly displayed was to act as a warning to anyone else thinking of rising against the crown. One of his hands was sent to St Andrews recalling his part in the murder of Archbishop Sharp. This was later taken to Cupar and displayed there, before it found rest in a grave with the severed heads of Laurence Hay and Andrew Pittulloch.[2]

In further searches for men involved in the Battle of Airds Moss, the soldiers captured James Skene, Andrew Stuart of Bo'ness and John Potter of Uphall. They were taken to Edinburgh where they were hanged on 1 December.

1. NS 643259. Monument and gravestone on site of battle.
2. NO 372146. Headstone in Cupar churchyard.

17

THE GALLANT GORDONS

Earlstoun Castle stands on the east side of the Water of Ken, two miles north of St John's Town of Dalry in Galloway.[1] The old tower dates from the late 16th century, and was originally built by the Sinclair family. Alexander Gordon of Airds married the heiress Margaret Sinclair in 1615, obtaining the estate.

Alexander Gordon of Earlstoun was one of the first of the family to come to notice regarding the Covenanters. In 1635 Thomas Sydserf, the Bishop of Galloway, had appointed a minister to the church at Dalry. This man was much disliked by the parishioners, who had not been consulted, and Gordon was one of the main protagonists in campaigning for his removal. As a result he was summoned to appear before the High Commission court, but when he did not appear he was fined and banished to Montrose in Angus. He was later able to return to Galloway, where he was appointed to attend the General Assembly in 1638, became a Commissioner in 1641, and served in the Covenanters' War Committee for the Stewartry. He died in 1654. He had been offered a knighthood, but had turned it down.

Colonel William Gordon succeeded to the estate of Earlstoun. In his youth he had trained for the ministry, but on the outbreak of Civil War he joined the army and commanded a company of soldiers under General Leslie. When the Duke of Monmouth landed in the south of England, Gordon was the Governor of Fort William, and he led the rebellion on the west coast of Scotland. He erected extensions to Earlstoun in 1655, his initials and that of his wife, Mary Hope, being incorporated in the wall. For his loyal adherence Gordon was created a baronet in 1706.

When Episcopal ministers were forced on the folk of Galloway, rioting took place at Kirkcudbright and Irongray. In the latter village the womenfolk, led by Margaret Smith, attacked a party of soldiers who were guarding the curate. At her trial in Edinburgh, Margaret was condemned to transportation to Barbados, but her tale had been told with such innocence that she was reprieved. The authorities came to Kirkcudbright where they tried to persuaded Gordon to introduce an Episcopal minister at Dalry. He refused, and was cited to attend a court in July 1663. At further trials in November and the following March it was said that he had attended conventicles conduced by Gabriel Semple, one of the ousted ministers, at Corsock and Airds woods; he had held meetings in his own home where Thomas Thomson had preached and he had attended others at the home of his mother, Robert Paton preaching. There was sufficient evidence to have Gordon banished abroad, this to take place within one month of passing sentence. During this period of time he was to pay bail of £10,000, or otherwise remain in prison. William Gordon was to pay a total £3,500 in fines for his adherence to the Covenant.

William Gordon's wife was pregnant with child at the time of his banishment. She had to seek refuge with friends, and when the daughter was born in 1665 she had her baptised by Rev John Blackader as no other minister was willing to risk this. The baptism took place at Drumshinnoch.

Earlstoun Castle was seized by the authorities and used as a garrison following the Pentland Rising. Sir William Bannatyne (or Ballantine) used it as a base for one of his party of soldiers. It is reckoned that from 43 families within the parish of Dalry his soldiers extracted no less than £9,577 Scots (£800 Sterling) in fines. Much worse was the torture Bannatyne's men inflicted on the parishioners. It is said that his men came to the home of

David MacGill, but he managed to escape dressed as a woman. Still in the house was his wife, whom the soldiers decided must have been guilty of assisting her husband to escape. Bound with ropes, she was tortured with lighted matches forced under her nails, so much so that she lost one of her hands and died within a few days. Bannatyne's actions were so evil that even the authorities were concerned at what he was doing. He was forced to emigrate and died abroad in misery.

William Gordon was able to return to Scotland sometime after the battle at Rullion Green. He had to lie low however, for he was still a wanted man. As he was making his way to the battle at Bothwell Bridge on 22 June 1679 he was met by a company of dragoons near to the farm of Crookedstone, in the parish of Hamilton. When they called out to him to halt he refused, so they pulled their guns and shot him. He was 65 years old. Permission to inter him at Dalry was refused, so he was laid to rest in the nearby kirkyard of Glassford. A memorial stone was raised over his grave, but such was the risk of adding an inscription that it remained plain until 1772.[2] A sword and Bible which belonged to him were long preserved by the Gordons of Greenlaw.

William's son, Alexander, succeeded to the baronetcy and estates, but not for long. He too was a Covenanter who had fought at Bothwell, having been sent on in front by his father. He was fortunate enough to escape from the battlefield and spent much of his time in hiding, part of this being spent in the Netherlands. Tales recount how he managed to escape capture in Hamilton by disguising himself as a woman caring for a baby. He was able to live near to his home at Earlstoun, where he built himself a hideout deep in the woods. Such was his strength and ability that he was known as the 'Bull of Earlstoun'.

A special meeting of the Justiciary Court was held on 18 February 1680 to deal with those landowners who had supported the rebellion. Dunbar of Machermore, Gordon of Craighlaw, Gordon of Culvennan, MacDowall of Freugh and MacKie of Larg were among those found guilty in their absence, and were sentenced to be executed, should they be found. William Gordon of Earlstoun was also found guilty, even although he was by this time dead, but that was so that his estates could be forfeited.

Alexander Gordon attended a meeting of the Covenanters' Societies at Priesthill on 15 March 1682. It was resolved to send him to the Netherlands where he was to describe to the reformed churches of the persecutions enacted on the church in Scotland. Alexander seems to have travelled back and forth across the North Sea on more than one occasion, his final journey being at the end of May 1683. Just as the ship was about to set sail from Newcastle a party of soldiers embarked. Gordon, who was travelling under the pseudonym of Alexander Pringle, took fright and threw a box containing papers overboard. Unfortunately they floated and were able to be rescued by the soldiers. Gordon and his servant were arrested and sent to Newgate in London.

Alexander was later transported to Edinburgh where he was placed under trial. He had been suspected of having some part in the Rye House Plot, when there was an attempt to assassinate the king and his brother, the Duke of York, and place Monmouth on the throne, but this could not be proved. He already had been sentenced to death following Bothwell Bridge, so the authorities decreed that he should lose his head at the Cross of Edinburgh on 28 August that year. In the intervening time they realised that it might be possible to torture a condemned man, but they had to send to London for clarification. This was agreed to on a technicality, so Gordon underwent trial by torture on 25 September. Still no confession was forthcoming, although he did reveal that Sir John Cochrane had kissed the king's hand one day and had spoken with the conspirators the following day. Cochrane, however, was by this time safe across the water in the Netherlands. On 23 November Charles II sent a letter ordering Gordon to be tortured. He was placed in the centre of the council chamber, surrounded by guards. The boot was about to be applied to his legs, but Gordon's rage was such that he managed to throw off the soldiers restraining him. Such was the loudness of his bellowing that it was thought he was suffering from some form of madness, so he was sent for medical tests.

According to four of the city physicians, Gordon was suffering from *alienatio mentis, furore latente laborans*. Their advice meant that he was transferred from the tolbooth to the castle rock, where he was given plenty of fresh air. He remained there for over four months before being taken back to the tolbooth cell. Gordon petitioned the authorities to return him to the castle rock so that he might get fresh air, but they decided instead to allow him a fortnight in August of sea breezes on the Bass Rock prison.

When Gordon was being brought back to Edinburgh from the rock he tried to make an escape. He was unsuccessful in this, and in order to foil any other attempts he was weighted down with irons tied to his body. He was moved to the prison cells at Blackness Castle, on the shores of the Firth of Forth, where the dampness was unbearable. At length, in January 1689, he was allowed to go free.

His wife, Jean or Janet Hamilton, also suffered many privations. When she was ejected from Earlstoun she had to find shelter in a makeshift building by the side of the Garple Burn. This was long pointed out as 'Jean's Wa's'. During her lonely hours in hiding she scratched a message onto a rock there, recounting the troubles. Part of this reads:

> *The Enemy said I should not get to stay in Galloway gif I went not to their kirk ... The persecution is great. There are many families that are going to leave their houses and go out of the lands ... I have written that Alexander may not venture to come home.*

Janet Gordon spent some time on the Bass Rock with her husband, and whilst there she composed a number of poems, later published as *Lady Earlstoun's Soliloquies*. She died at Earlstoun on 26 February 1696.

In 1690 the estate of Earlstoun was restored to Sir Alexander Gordon. He settled back in Galloway, becoming a leader in the Kirkcudbright Militia and a Commissioner of Supply for the county. He lived until some time after 1726.

1. NX 612840.
2. NS 731470. Gravestone in Glassford old churchyard.

18

NONCOMPLYANCE WITH A WICKED TIME

The authorities established a number of garrisons in Lanarkshire which were used to suppress the Covenanters of the county. One of these was Strathaven, or Avondale Castle, the ruins of which still stand in the midst of that town.[1] The tower was first garrisoned in 1650 and in 1668 the Earl of Linlithgow stationed his troops there. Later, the Earl of Atholl's troop of guards were stationed there until 1673, when they were moved to a new garrison at East Kilbride where the locals were responsible for supplying grass for the soldiers' horses. In 1678 all the lairds and their servants in that parish were ordered to meet in the kirkyard where they were to hand in all weapons belonging to them. In 1685 a local troop of militiamen was raised by a number of East Kilbride landowners to assist in the search for Covenanters.

In 1682 the Privy Council fined the burgh of Lanark 6,000 merks for allowing many Covenanters to escape unpunished. To pay for this, the magistrates 'stented' the burgesses and heritors of the town in the following year. The town was a base for royal troops during the Killing Times, headed by James Irvine of Bonshaw. Thomas Lauchlan was imprisoned in Lanark tolbooth, having been taken after the battle of Bothwell Bridge. On the evening of 15 June 1681 a group of Covenanters came into the burgh and attacked the gaol. In the scuffle one of the magistrates,

Bailie Wight, was overcome, and the town officer, John Shirlaw, was wounded, but Lauchlan was freed. Next day the magistrates of the burgh decreed that the tolbooth should thereafter be guarded through the night. Two of the officers in charge of the troops in Lanark, Lord Ross and Captain Wight, contacted the bailies to find out why Lauchlan was able to escape. It was decided to quarter eight companies of infantry and one of dragoons on the residents of the town, but one James Tennant, maltman in the town, decided to lock up his buildings and leave the town rather than put up the soldiers. He later returned and though summoned before the council, was able to get away with his 'crime' without sentence.[2]

The obelisk at Lanark commemorating the Covenanters gives a list of those who suffered. Apart from those mentioned elsewhere in this book, it lists John Wilson, who took part at Bothwell and was executed in Edinburgh on 16 May 1683. William Tweedale, bailie of Lanark, and Hugh Weir, merchant in the town, were forfeited of their possessions. Listed as fugitives or outlaws were Thomas Henshilwood, Robert and John Alston, James and John Howison, John Semple, mason, John Morrison, Gideon Weir, gunsmith in Lanark, James Chalmers, Archibald Simpson (and fined £240), James Park, Thomas Pillans, Robert Logan, Thomas Inglis, Richard Martin, John Pumphrey, Michael Lamb, William Ferguson (who was ultimately apprehended and banished to Virginia) and William Scott of Holmhead. 'Traitors' were David White, smith in the town, David Gibson, Alexander Anderson, William Padzean, mason, and John Jack of Nemphlar. Michael Somerville, bailie of Lanark was fined £600. Others fined included someone surnamed Ellon (£360), Andrew Tennant (£360), Gabriel Hamilton (£360), Alexander Wilson (£360), Gideon Jack (£1,000), John Pillans (£240), John Fisher (£240), James Cunningham of Bonnyton (£360) and James Gray in Jerviswood (£600). John Bannatyne of Corehouse was imprisoned and outlawed as a rebel. He was later to become minister of Lanark. William Thomson, procurator at the town's sheriff court, was also imprisoned, as were James Muirhead Jr and

Alexander Brown, merchant. James Lawrie, writer in the burgh, was sentenced to be executed in his absence in 1681, but in 1684 this punishment was remitted.

The countryside of southern Lanarkshire was ideal for holding conventicles, for the moors were expansive and the population sparse. A well known conventicle site was at Auchengilloch, five miles due south of Strathaven.[3] Four miles east of here is Cumberhead farm, where a conventicle was held on 30 March 1679. The authorities became aware of this meeting and sent some soldiers from the nearby garrison under Lieutenant Dalyell to disperse it. The Covenanters, however, felt that they had the strength to resist them and captured Dalyell and seven soldiers. The Covenanters had thoughts of killing Dalyell, but a Douglas man, William Cassils, would not allow it. At a later date Cassils received a royal pardon.

Blackwood House in Lanarkshire is an old mansion, having been extended a number of times over the centuries. In the latter part of the 17th century its owner was William Lawrie, who was also factor to the Earl of Douglas. He had married the widow of the owner of the estate, and as he was responsible for her son and heir he was often styled 'the tutor of Blackwood'. He was a friend of the Covenanters, and when the men of the west were planning their march on Edinburgh (which resulted in the Battle of Rullion Green) he tried to persuade them to lay down their arms and adopt a peaceful settlement. In the same uprising he took a letter from the Covenanters to the Privy Council in Edinburgh requesting the right to worship as they pleased. Despite his attempts at mediating, the authorities treated him with contempt, arrested him and placed him in gaol. Lawrie remained in his cell for 12 months before being granted his freedom.

In 1682 a charge of 'assisting and countenancing the rebels' was placed before him, and again he was arrested. It was claimed that he had allowed the Covenanters to take the two guns from Douglas Castle to Bothwell Bridge, and following the battle had allowed them to return to their tenancies on Douglas estate. He was taken to Edinburgh where he remained in prison for some months. On 7 February 1683 he was condemned to death. He was led out from his cell to the market cross, where he was 'to have his head severed from his body – his name, memory, fame and honours to be extinct, and his lands forfeited to his Majesty for ever.'

Within days a letter was received from King Charles II in which he approved the sentence given to Lawrie, but which also held back the execution until March. Again a reprieve was forthcoming, postponing the execution until November. The date of execution came and went once more, and Lawrie was still in prison the following January.

The purpose of Lawrie's long spell in prison was designed to act as a warning to other lairds in the west of the country, letting them see what to expect should they too fail to report Covenanters who lived on their lands.

William Lawrie was finally freed following a petition from the Earl of Douglas who claimed that he was indispensable to the estate, and that he had not completed all the estate's affairs. His sentences were all quashed at the Glorious Revolution, and a special act of parliament was passed in his favour, restoring all his lands and privileges. His convictions were declared null and void.

John Brown was a servant to William Lawrie, remaining at the estate whilst his master was in prison. One day in March 1685 Lieutenant Murray and a party of dragoons came to Blackwood House, and discovered Brown in the fields. He was questioned about his right to be there, and as Brown gave no resistance he was promised quarter. Murray must have decided later that he had no wish to take Brown prisoner. It was easier to simply shoot him than have to take him back to gaol. Thus, with no trial of any form, Murray ordered his men to shoot. Brown was buried where he fell.[4]

Robert Paterson, who died at the Battle of Airds Moss, had a son, William, who was to follow him in achieving the martyr's crown. For his non-conformity to the laws of the time he was driven from his farmhouse at Kirkhill in the parish of Cambusnethan and forced to live rough. The authorities were keen to capture him, and his name appears in the list of 1,900 fugitives issued in 1684. He was caught on one occasion and sent abroad to serve in the armed forces. He was able to effect an escape however, and returned to Scotland. He was caught a second time at a conventicle held at a place known as Charonheugh in April 1685. Fourteen men had gathered to observe the Sabbath when a troop of soldiers came upon the spot. Most of the Covenanters managed to escape, but William Paterson and three others were captured by Captain Bell. The Covenanters were offered the chance to swear the Abjuration Oath, which all but Paterson agreed to do. The other three were let go, but Paterson was taken back to Strathaven Castle where, that afternoon, he was shot. He had not been given any trial. His corpse was later buried in Strathaven burial ground.[5]

Another execution took place in Strathaven in the same month. John Barrie, or Burrie as his surname is sometimes spelled, was out and about in the district. Peter Inglis and his party of dragoons came upon him, and questioned him. According to Wodrow, 'he had his pass in his hand, and had showed him it.' Inglis, however, was unwilling to accept this, and decided that he was one of the fugitives which he had been searching for. Accordingly he shot him dead.[6]

John Smith was caught by the soldiers in February 1685 as he was walking in the fields. The soldiers were led by Colonel Thomas Buchan and the Rt Hon Cromwell Lockhart of Lee Castle. Lockhart was the provost of Lanark from March 1683 until August 1688. The soldiers asked him questions, and Smith seems to have answered these in a way which was unacceptable to the soldiers, so they shot him dead on the spot. Nothing else is known about him. His corpse was taken to Muirkirk kirkyard where it was laid to rest near the northernmost corner.[7]

William Cochrane of Carnduff farm was caught by the soldiers in the parish of Evandale. They asked him whether or not it was lawful for subjects to rise in arms against the king; but he refused to answer. Other questions followed, which Cochrane dismissed as 'kittle', but when he was asked to say 'God save the king', he refused. The soldiers then arrested him and took him to Edinburgh, where he was found guilty of treason, and hanged on 15 December 1682 at the Grassmarket. Also suffering on the scaffold on the same day was James Robertson, a packman from Stonehouse.

William Young was a Covenanter who is described as being 'distempered and much crazed in his judgment.' He was a tailor in Strathaven and was captured by the soldiers and placed in gaol in Strathaven Castle. He was then transferred to Hamilton and thence to the Canongate tolbooth in Edinburgh. On 21 August 1684 he managed to make an escape from his cell, but was caught soon after. On his return to gaol he was treated cruelly, his only solace was that he was tried on the following day and executed on 27 August within a couple of hours of being found guilty. He was hanged at the same time as James Nicol, a merchant burgess from Peebles. He had shouted at the authorities during the earlier execution of the Enterkin rescuers and been arrested. Nicol had fought at Bothwell and regarded Hackston's execution as murder, and thus had been listed in the roll of wanted men.

John Willison of Glengeith was a noted Covenanter who sheltered many threatened ministers at his home.[8] He had a shunamite chamber constructed in which they hid. Willison survived the years of persecution and was interred at Crawford.

1. NS 703444.
2. NS 888432. Obelisk commemorating all Lanark Covenanters in St Kentigern's churchyard.
3. NS713357. Monument on site of conventicle.
4. NS 773432. Monument at Doocot Cottage, Blackwood estate.
5. NS 705446. Gravestone in Strathaven cemetery.
6. NS 705446. Commemorated on same gravestone as Paterson, Strathaven cemetery.
7. NS 700278. Gravestone in Muirkirk churchyard. Also commemorated on
   memorials in Muirkirk cemetery (NS 696278) and Smallburn Road (NS 685265).
8. NS 948167. Commemorated by a memorial window at Crawford church
   (NS 955209). Plaque in Elvanfoot church (NS 955167).

19

DUST SACRIFICED TO TYRANNY

Alexander Smith was a resident of the parish of Cambusnethan, which lies in Clydesdale. Now filled by the large towns of Wishaw and Newmains, in the 17th century the parish was less populated and more rural. Smith was arrested in 1681 on the charge of having fought at Bothwell Bridge, and was transported to Edinburgh, where he was lodged in prison awaiting trial. He was quite a determined fellow, however, and with the assistance of a few others he managed to make an escape from gaol, dressed in women's clothing.

A search party was sent out to look for him, and eventually they came across him near to his home county. He was caught again and this time the authorities imprisoned him in Glasgow. Plans were made to have him transported to Edinburgh once more, to face an even greater trial, but somehow word leaked about the proposals.

A number of Smith's friends made their way to a spot north of Inchbelly Bridge, which lies on the roadway from Kirkintilloch to Kilsyth. This was a rather indirect route from Glasgow to Edinburgh, which would corroborate the leak. The authorities may also have had some inkling that a rescue might be attempted and thus were unwilling to take the direct route. In any case, when the party guarding Smith crossed the bridge over the River Kelvin, which at this point is little more than a large burn, they were suddenly surprised by an ambush. Shots were fired on both sides, and in the ensuing tumult a number of wounds were received on both sides. One person was to die, a soldier in the guard party. Realising that the rescuers meant business, they allowed their charge to go free.

As the soldiers began to gather themselves together again their tempers began to rise. They were determined to bring someone to justice for the murder of the soldier. They set off in the direction the Covenanters had gone. Within a short distance they came across two men, unfortunate enough to be in the wrong place at the wrong time. They were James Smith and John Wharry, or MacWharrie, as his name sometimes appears. Although they were both seated on the ground, and had no arms about them, they were apprehended by the soldiers. Perhaps the same surname was enough for the soldiers to regard them as having some connection with the rescue.

Dragged to Glasgow, they were imprisoned for a few days. During this time they were able to write letters to their family, Smith corresponding with his father and mother and Wharry with his mother, brother and sisters.

The two men were placed under trial on 13 June 1683, and though proclaiming their innocence to the last, witnesses were brought forward who were willing to swear that Smith and Wharry had been involved in the rescue. These witnesses were none other than two of the soldiers involved in the fracas. Consequently, the sentence of death was passed. Within hours the two men were dragged to the scaffold, where John Wharry began to address the crowd which had assembled. It is said that he faced the execution cheerfully and gallantly.

The order had been given that the right hands of the men should be cut from their bodies prior to execution, for having used them in swearing the Covenant. When the hangman came forth with the axe Wharry lay his neck over the block and prepared to die. Major Balfour cursed at him, 'It is not your head, but your hand that we are seeking!'

'Then I heard you wrong,' Wharry replied, 'but I am most willing to lay down my neck, hand and other limbs of my body for the cause of Christ.' Wharry's hand was placed over the block and Balfour swung the axe, severing it from Wharry's body. Wharry then held his arm aloft, the blood pumping from his wrist, and yelled to the crowds, 'This blood now seals our Covenant!'

Major Balfour then carried out the hanging, and within a few silent minutes another two martyrs had paid the ultimate sacrifice. Shortly afterwards the bodies of Smith and Wharry were taken north to the site of the rescue at Inchbelly. A few friends of theirs had managed to acquire two coffins in which they hoped to bury the martyrs, but when Major Balfour spotted them he ordered his men to have them destroyed. A makeshift scaffold was erected in the midst of a field, and from the gibbet the two corpses were suspended by chains. They remained there for some time, until the people of the district were brave enough to remove them and bury them on the same spot.[1]

Another Covenanter who was to suffer death at Glasgow was William Boick. He was executed on 14 June 1683 and subsequently buried in the ancient kirkyard at the Clachan of Campsie, located at the foot of the Campsie Fells.[2] Boick may have been involved with the rescue of Smith, though there is no proof of this. Nevertheless, he was executed at Glasgow at virtually the same time as those involved. According to the records of the city, five Lords of the Justiciary Court sat on 14 June, and Boick's case may have been dealt with by them.

Boick was offered the chance to take the Test Oath but he refused. As he was being prepared for execution he seems to have taken cold feet and offered to swear the Act, but by this time it was too late, and the executioner had to carry out his duty. Boick's hanging was used as an example to other like-minded individuals, as attested in a letter from Graham of Claverhouse to the Earl of Aberdeen:

> *I am as sorry to see a man day [die], even a whigue, as any of them selfs; but when on[e] days [dies] justly for his owen faults, and may saue a hondred to fall in the lyk, I have no scrupull.*

1. NS 669749. Gravestones on site of gallows.
2. NS610797. Gravestone in Campsie old churchyard.

20

WHERE PLEASANT NISBET LIVES

The Nisbet family lived in the Ayrshire parish of Loudoun. They were descended from Murdoch Nisbet, who was one of the Lollards of Kyle, or those who anticipated the Reformation in Scotland and adhered to the Protestant cause. He had to flee Scotland, taking with him his handwritten New Testament in Scots, which had been completed around 1520. It was to be passed down through the family for many generations until in 1909 it was acquired by the British Library.

Three of the Nisbet family were to die for the Covenanting cause, whereas one joined the royalist side and was responsible for not only persecuting many folk, but brought about the execution of his own cousin.

John Nisbet of Hardhill is the most noted Covenanting member of this family. He was born in 1627, the great-grandson of Murdoch, and fought under Gustavus Adolphus in the Thirty Years' War in Germany and Denmark. After the peace of Munster was signed in 1648 he returned to Hardhill where he was to marry Margaret Law. John Nisbet joined the Covenanters on their march towards Edinburgh and he was active at the Battle of Rullion Green in November 1666. In the fighting he was severely wounded and left for dead, but he recovered during the night and was able to escape. His wounds had still not healed a year later. He also fought at Drumclog where he is said to have killed seven soldiers. At Bothwell Bridge he was appointed a captain and tradition claims he stood fighting on the bridge as long as he had a companion beside him.

The Privy Council placed a price on Nisbet's head. His house was searched and, according to his son's memoirs, 'they held a drawn sword to my mother's breast, threatening to run her through unless she would discover her husband. She, weeping, told them that for anything she knew he was killed (for she heard that it was so), and that she had not seen him; so they took what suited them in the house, and went off.' His wife and children were later thrown out of their home, and were left to suffer the privations of homelessness. She died after four years of suffering. John came as soon as he heard this, but by this time she had been buried some days. His daughter also died and both were laid to rest under the cover of darkness in the kirkyard at Stonehouse.

In 1682 the soldiers searching for Nisbet arrived at Allerstocks farm, home of John and William Smith. They had put up Nisbet on occasion and were arrested for this. Taken to Edinburgh tolbooth, they were later released on paying 1,000 merks. Also living at Allerstocks was James Thomson. The arrival of the soldiers at his home so distressed his wife that she died of fright, leaving six young children.

One day soldiers arrived at Hardhill farm, where they found the two Nisbet boys, James and Alexander, at that time aged 14 and 10. (An elder son, Hugh, must have left home by then.) The dragoons were trying to find out the whereabouts of John Nisbet, who had been on the run since the Battle of Bothwell. The younger boy was tortured with drawn swords and pistols were fired next to his head whilst he was blindfolded. He was beaten and kicked, and denounced as 'a vile, ugly, dumb devil.' As he would not reveal any information, the soldiers struck him to the ground where he was left lying in his own blood.

The elder of the two boys, James, was to grow up to face the scaffold five years later. He lived at Highside, near Darvel, and was denounced as a rebel. Nisbet had risked travelling to Glasgow to attend the funeral of his cousin, John Richmond of Knowe, who had been executed on 19 March 1684. At the funeral Lieutenant Robert Nisbet recognised him and he was apprehended. He was taken to the guard-house, where some questions were put to him. Answering these unsatisfactorily, he was transferred to the prison. Whilst in gaol he was cruelly treated, and watched constantly; so much so that he was unable to write a full testimony. For some reason James was not executed at the cross but at a spot on the north side of the town, at the Howgate Head, on 5 June 1684. James had previously written much of his life story, recording that:

> The Lord's watchful providence prevented me losing my life at all the following places – namely, when amongst the hurry of the enemy's cruel searches at my father's house of Hardhill, at the Bennet Hill, at Gelt Hill, at Garclagh Hill, at the Castle of Kyle, at Dornal, at Corsancone Hill, at Greenock Mains, at Cargilloch, at Wallaceton, at Cubb's Craigs, at Barlonochie, at the Heilsh Wood, at Hairstocks, at Carnduff Hill, at Friarmidden Moor, at Spango Glen, at Hoggan Burn, at Cairnscamb, at Leadloch, and Crossford, at Middton, at Burnhouse, and at Loudoun Wood.

James's account, entitled *Private Life of the Persecuted, or Memoirs of the First Years of James Nisbet, One of the Scottish Covenanters*, is now preserved in the Signet Library in Edinburgh.

One Saturday in November 1685 a group of Covenanters met at the farm of Midland, which lies near to Fenwick. John Nisbet was there, as were Peter Gemmel (aged 21), George Woodburn and John Fergushill. They were in the midst of a prayer service when a party of 40 dragoons came to the house. The leader of the soldiers was none other than John's cousin, Lieutenant Robert Nisbet. The soldiers searched the house for an hour but found nothing. As they were journeying back to their base two men met them, one of whom told them that they were 'good seekers, but ill finders.' This spurred them on to return to Midland, where a more thorough search was undertaken. The four Covenanters were discovered this time, hiding in the byre alongside the cattle. Shots were fired from both sides, Nisbet being wounded in six places. He was luckier than his friends, for they were killed in the affray. Gemmel, Woodburn and Fergushill were later buried at Fenwick.[1]

Gemmel's two brothers, David and John, also suffered for the Covenant. David fled to Ireland for three years, during which time his land was confiscated. John was held prisoner in Canongate tolbooth and, refusing to acknowledge the king's superiority over the church, was banished to Barbados in 1685 where he was forced into slavery. He seems to have returned following the Glorious Revolution.

The soldiers took Nisbet of Hardhill firstly to Ayr, where he stood trial, before it was decided that he should be sent to Edinburgh. In his trial there, held before the Lords of Justiciary on 30 November, he admitted to having attended a conventicle in the past two months which took place between Eaglesham and East Kilbride. Nisbet was sentenced to be executed at the Grassmarket on 4 December. Nisbet's 'lands, goods and gear to be forfeited to the king's use.'

Glen farm at Darvel was the home of John Nisbet, called 'the younger' by some to distinguish him from his uncle, Nisbet of Hardhill. He was captured by Major Balfour and his dragoons and taken into Kilmarnock where he was put in prison. He was questioned as to the whereabouts of his uncle, but refused to tell them anything.

The charges placed before Nisbet were that he had been at the battle of Bothwell Bridge, disowned the curates, was a follower of Cameron and refused to pray for the king. Nisbet was proud to reply that he was guilty of all four. A number of questions were put before him, and he was able to answer all these in a calm manner, even although he knew that he faced certain death. It was also noted that his answers were devised such that he would betray none of his friends.

Major White, in his capacity as a justice, pronounced the sentence – he was to hang in Kilmarnock on 4 April 1683.

On the morning of the execution Nisbet was taken from the gaol through the streets of Kilmarnock to the cross. The roadways were filled with folk who had come to witness the execution, and to hear the Covenanter's last words. As he was brought to the scaffold he walked upright with pride. On the scaffold Nisbet prayed and sang a Psalm, before handing his Bible to his uncle, who stood by his side. He was then surprised to discover that the soldiers were willing to allow him to address the crowd, which he did. He spoke eloquently, until some of the soldiers decided that they had heard enough and began to create a disturbance. Accordingly he was pushed from the scaffold and within minutes he was dead.[2]

Nisbet's body was taken from the cross and transferred to the Laigh parish kirkyard where a grave was hastily dug and his corpse interred. This was not the end, however, for Torrance had the body dug up, claiming that as Nisbet was a 'rebel' he had no right to lie there. Instead, the body was buried 'where evil-doers be.'[3]

1. NS 465434. Gravestone in Fenwick churchyard.
2. NS 429380. Memorial at Burns Mall shopping centre marks site of execution.
3. NS 427380. Gravestone in Laigh kirkyard, Kilmarnock.

21

GRISELL HUME'S
MIDNIGHT TRYST

The church of Polwarth stands in the Berwickshire countryside, four miles south west of Duns, and one mile from the village itself. The site is an ancient one, and the present church dates from 1703.[1]

At the time of the Covenant the local laird was Sir Patrick Hume of Redbraes Castle, the site of which is now occupied by Marchmont House. Hume was one of few lairds who wholly subscribed to the Covenant, for which most were let off with fines. He, however, was imprisoned a number of times, in 1674 and 1678, for 'remonstrating against the tyranny of the Duke of Lauderdale's administration.' In 1683 a further warrant for his arrest was issued, for it was thought he had sheltered Robert Baillie of Jerviswood, causing him to flee the castle and find shelter elsewhere. Baillie had been arrested for his part in the Rye House plot and following trial was hanged in Edinburgh on 23 December 1684 at the age of 47. His body was drawn and quartered, the head hung on the Netherbow Port and the quarters on the tolbooths of Ayr, Glasgow, Jedburgh and Lanark.

For one month in 1684 Hume came as close to his home as he dared, the parish kirk. He opened up the family burial vault and there spent the next four weeks, in total darkness and solitude. His hiding place was known only to three folk, his wife, daughter, and a faithful servant, Jamie Winter.

Grisell Hume, Sir Patrick's daughter, knew that her father was back in the locality, and wished to play her part. She was only 18 years of age, being born on Christmas Day, 1665. Each night, on the stroke of midnight, she collected food from the castle kitchen and walked the mile or so from the castle to the kirk. She passed the food through to her father, before returning back to the tower.

At Redbraes Jamie Winter and Grisell were also busy digging a hole in the ground below the floor of a cellar. Jamie made a wooden box which was laid into the hole, and the floorboards replaced. Once it was ready, Sir Patrick was secretly brought from the kirk to the new hiding place in the castle. The box, however, lay below the water-table, and it often filled with water.

Sir Patrick was later denounced as a rebel. One day a party of dragoons was sent from Edinburgh with the intention of searching the castle. Fortunately they were met en route by a distant kinsman, Home of Halyburton, near Greenlaw. He found out whom the soldiers were after and managed to divert them for a while at his own home. He offered them ale from his brew-house which, after a long ride from Edinburgh, was enough to detain them. Meanwhile he sent a groom on horseback to Redbraes with a parcel for Lady Hume. When she opened it she only found a feather, but this was sufficient to warn her of what was happening. Lady Hume ran down to the cellar and opened up the floor. Sir Patrick and Grisell fled from the castle, the whole family eventually crossing the North Sea to Utrecht in the Netherlands. In his absence his estates were forfeited.

In the Netherlands Sir Patrick Hume became an adviser to William of Orange. In April 1685 he joined the Earl of Argyll's fleet of three ships, the Anna, David and Sophia, on his planned attack on the Crown, hoping to win the Duke of Monmouth's succession to the throne. However, the reinforcements they hoped to pick up on the way did not materialise, and the soldiers they did have absconded in Glasgow. Argyll was soon apprehended by the authorities and taken to Edinburgh, where he lost his head by the Maiden. Sir Patrick managed to make his way back to the low countries where he remained until the Glorious Revolution. When the family returned to Scotland they were given back their estates. Sir Patrick was appointed Lord Chancellor of Scotland in 1696. He was raised to the peerage as Lord Polwarth in 1690 and as Earl of Marchmont in 1697. He died in 1724 aged 83.

The midnight visits to the church to feed her father were not the only daring deeds Grisell had performed. When she was only 12 years of age she had taken a letter from her father to his good friend, Robert Baillie of Jerviswood, who was at the time in prison. Although the cell was guarded, Grisell managed to gain access to it and pass over the letter which had been concealed within her clothing. Whilst visiting Robert Baillie, she became acquainted with his son, George, whom she was to marry on 16 September 1692. Grisell described George as 'the best of husbands and delight of my life for forty-eight year, without one jar betwixt us.'

George and Grisell were responsible for building part of Mellerstain House, work on which commenced in 1725. George Baillie died in 1738, Grisell outliving him until 6 December 1746. She was buried in the Baillie aisle at Mellerstain.[2]

Grisell Hume is also remembered for her skill as a poet, and one of her songs, 'And werena my heart licht I wad dee', became very popular following Robert Burns quoting it. Only one other of her songs is known to have survived. The *Household Book* which she kept was published in 1911, and is a fascinating insight to life in a Scottish country house in the early 18th century.

1. NT 749495.
2. NT 647391.

22

CAPTAIN PATON –
THE GALLANT OFFICER

One of the most notable soldiers on the Covenanting side was Captain John Paton. He was born about the year 1615 at the farm of Meadowhead in the parish of Fenwick, Ayrshire. At the age of 16 or 18 he left home and joined the armies which were then fighting in northern Germany. He fought on the Protestant side of Gustavus Adolphus, King of Sweden, at Lutzen in 1632. At the taking of one of the northern cities, Paton so excelled that he was raised to the rank of captain.

Captain Paton returned to the British Isles where at first his parents did not recognise him. He fought at the Battle of Marston Moor on 2 July 1644 where he contracted an asthmatic disorder which was never to leave him. Nevertheless, he was still an able man, who fought in the campaigns against Montrose. He was active at the Battle of Kilsyth on 15 August 1645 where Montrose defeated the Covenanters. Captain Paton had to flee the battlefield but he again fought at the Battle of Mauchline Moor in June 1648, where he is said to have killed 18 men single-handed. Paton also fought at Dunbar, another defeat for the Covenanters, and Philiphaugh, which they won.

He was active in the invasion of England which ended in the defeat at Worcester on 3 September 1651. At this battle his heroism and courage left an indelible mark on General Tam Dalyell.

John Paton decided to return to Scotland where he settled at Meadowhead once more. He became an elder in Fenwick church and remarried after his first wife, Janet Lindsay, died soon after they wed. At Meadowhead Rev Donald Cargill baptised 26 children in a single service held in the barn.

At the Pentland Rising Paton raised a party of horse from the parishes of Fenwick and Loudoun and met with the southern Covenanters, marching with them to Edinburgh. He fought at Rullion Green, and it is said that he was one of the last to leave the battlefield. He was nearly captured by Dalyell who fired a shot at him, but this missed. Paton fired back, but Dalyell was wearing chainmail armour and the bullet was deflected. Paton then loaded his gun with a silver bullet, which had better qualities for piercing armour, but when he fired it another soldier moved in front of Dalyell, taking the bullet. Paton and two of his friends were quickly surrounded by Dalyell's men but they managed to hack their way through and escape. Dalyell tried to apprehend him once more and sent three troopers to help capture him. They caught up with him at a ditch, which was difficult for horses to leap. Paton managed it however, and turning on his adversaries, swung his sword at one soldier and cleaved his head from his body. His horse started and knocked the other two soldiers from their mounts, landing in the ditch. They feared for their lives, but Paton simply told them, 'My compliments to your master, and tell him I shall not be with him tonight.'

His part in the rising meant that Paton was now on the wanted list. He spent the next 17 years on the move, avoiding populous places. Paton attended many conventicles and he was an advocate of carrying arms for defence. During a winter conventicle at Lochgoin he and 20 others had a narrow escape when the soldiers came in their midst.

Although not at Drumclog, Paton fought at Bothwell Bridge in 1679, where he acted as a colonel, and again managed to make an escape. Indeed, Paton seems to have been something of a wizard at eluding his persecutors. On another occasion he was at the farm of Lochgoin when a troop of soldiers appeared. He fled on foot, but spotted a horse grazing in a field. He was able to mount it and ride slowly back past his pursuers, who did not recognise him, they being in pursuit of a pedestrian.

Paton was eventually captured at Robert Howie's home at Floak farm in the parish of Mearns. A party of soldiers under Cornet Lewis Lauder were on the moors and came across him. His friends were willing to fight, but Paton said no, for it would only get them into trouble. 'In any case, I am weary of life, being hunted from place to place, I am not afraid to die.' At first the soldiers did not know who their prisoner was. All they knew was that he could not satisfactorily explain his movements to them. They took Paton to Kilmarnock, but at Muir Yett a farmer inadvertently revealed his name.

The soldiers took Paton firstly to Ayr, then to Glasgow, before taking him to Edinburgh where he met his old soldier adversary, General Dalyell. He exclaimed, 'John, I am both glad and sorry to see you. If I had met you in the way before you had came hither I should have set you at liberty, but now it is too late. But be not afraid, I will write to his majesty for your life.' Paton was placed on trial on 16 April, and was sentenced to die on 23 April. On two occasions the date of execution was postponed, one of these as a result of Dalyell's plea. Bishop Paterson was later accused of holding up the pardon until after the execution had taken place. The clerk of the council noted in the documents:

John Paton, in Meadowhead, sentenced to die for rebellion, and thereafter remaining in mosses and moors to the high contempt of authority, reprieved till Friday come sen'night, and to have a room by himself, that he may prepare more conveniently for death.

Captain Paton was led out to the scaffold in the city's Grassmarket on Friday 9 May 1684. He read out his final speech in which he forgave all his persecutors. He was survived by his second wife, Janet Millar, to whom he handed his Bible, and six children. His corpse was later buried in Edinburgh's Greyfriars' kirkyard.[1]

1. NS 464434. Memorial stone in Fenwick churchyard.

23

BLESS'D JOHN, ON YONDER ROCK CONFIN'D

On the last Sunday of October 1662 Rev John Blackader was ejected from his charge at Troqueer parish church, near Dumfries.[1] He was one of many ministers who were ousted for their failure to adhere to the newly appointed bishops and to accept the new laws of patronage. The day was damp and overcast, and the congregation, though not numerous, 'were dissolved in tears, and at many parts of the discourse there were loud and involuntary bursts of sorrow.' Mid-way through the service soldiers appeared at the church, whereupon Blackader said the benediction and retired to the manse. His congregation followed, and Blackader addressed them from the stairs. He asked them not to cause any disturbance, but to 'go and fend for yourselves: the hour is come when the shepherd is smitten and the flock is scattered.' As they left through the kirkyard, the soldiers noted down all their names, for anyone not attending their own church was liable to a fine of 20 shillings Scots.

Blackader was born in December 1615 at Blairhall, near Culross in Fife, the son of John Blackader and Barbara Strang. His family were of the landed class, and in 1651, on the death of his cousin, John Blackader succeeded to the baronetcy of Tulliallan, though he never used the right to call himself Sir John. In 1646 he married the daughter of Homer Haining, a merchant and landowner from Dumfries, who also owned land near to Tulliallan. Blackader studied at Glasgow University, reading for the ministry, and graduated Master of Arts in 1650. He may have spent a few years tutoring before being ordained at Troqueer on 7 June 1653.

According to his memoirs, Blackader regarded the parishioners as 'grossly ignorant, many scandalous in conversation, and divers popishly inclined. Scandals did much abound, especially idle swearing, excessive tippling in alehouses, mocking at religion, foolish jesting, obscene expressions and promiscuous dancing, especially at marriages.' He set about to improve the morals of his flock, and soon he was held in high regard for his stand against low standards. He required to hold two services on a Sunday, and a third each Tuesday.

At the Restoration of Charles II in 1660 Blackader made his opinions clear. He told the Synod of Dumfries that the actions of the government were questionable and on three successive Sundays used the Bible to demonstrate that prelacy was unlawful and that presbyterianism was the closest form of worship to that used by the early Christians. On 4 May 1662, the very same day on which new bishops were being consecrated in Edinburgh, Blackader told his flock that, 'I as a member and minister of the Church of Scotland solemnly declare and enter my dissent in heaven against this dreadful course of defection.'

Parliament decreed that 29 May 1662 should be observed as a sacred anniversary, commemorating the birthday and restoration of Charles II. Blackader was one of many ministers in the Presbytery of Dumfries who refused to celebrate that day, with the result that 50 soldiers were sent to arrest him. Taken to Edinburgh, Blackader was called before the Privy Council a number of times, and despite being threatened with torture and banishment he refused to adhere to their wishes. Some relatives of his spoke up for him, and he was allowed to go free with a caution to watch what he said and did in the future. Within months hundreds of ministers from all over Scotland were ousted from their churches and manses, being left to fend for themselves.

John Blackader moved to Caitloch House in Glencairn, which was the home of a Fergusson relative of his. He later took his wife and six young children, one of whom was to die. Whilst Blackader's family were still living at Troqueer, a party of soldiers came to the manse searching for him. His son later recorded what happened:

> A party of the King's Life Guard of horse, called 'Blew-benders,' came from Dumfries to Troqueer to search for and apprehend my father, but found him not: for what reason I know not – whether he stayed beyond the set day for transporting himself and numerous family of small children ten miles from his parish church, or because he was of the number of those who refused to observe the 29th of May. So soon as the above party entered the close, and came into the house, with cursing, swearing, and damning, we that were the children were frightened out of our little wits, and ran upstairs, and I among them; who, when I heard them all roaring in the room, like so many breathing devils, I had the childish curiosity to get down upon my belly and peep through a hole in the floor above them, to see what monsters of creatures they were; and it seems they were monsters indeed for cruelty, for one of them perceiving what I was doing, immediately drew his sword, and forced it up with all his force where I was peeping, so that the mark of the point was scarce an inch from the hole, though no thanks to the murdering ruffian who designed to run it through my eye.

The Blackaders moved to Bardennoch, nearer Moniaive, owned by a sympathetic Lady Craigdarroch. It was at Caitloch that Blackader commenced his house meetings, but soon the building was too small to cope with the numbers attending. He moved into the hills and moors, but by 1666 a letter of the Privy Council listed him as a wanted man, for 'he had oft times convened great numbers in the parish of Glencairn and neighbouring parishes, sometimes to the number of a thousand and upwards and continues so to do every Lord's Day: at which meetings he baptises the children of all disaffected persons.' The citation was affixed to the mercat cross in Dumfries, but he ignored it.

Soldiers under Sir James Turner came to Bardennoch in the winter of 1666 searching for the minister, but he was away in Edinburgh. His wife and family had to suffer their searches. They had arrived at 2 o'clock in the morning and surrounded the house. Shouting loudly, they demanded entry to the house and, when the door was opened, they ran through it stabbing at the beds in case he was hiding within them. The soldiers broke the legs off the chairs and used them to make a fire. A Blackader boy was instructed to hold a candle so that the soldiers could inspect the minister's books, all of which they classed as 'whiggish', and which they loaded into a creel and removed. The hen house was searched and every chicken within it had its neck wrung. One of Blackader's sons ran from the house wearing only his night-shirt. He made it as far as Moniaive, where he rested on the top step of the market cross. Despite the cold, he was able to cuddle up and sleep. At five in the morning an old woman spotted him and took him into her home.

Surprisingly, considering that he was supposed to appear before the Council in Edinburgh, Blackader decided to move to that city, remaining there for 14 years. At first he lived in the Canongate, and later moved to the Cowgate. When the western Covenanters were within a few miles of Edinburgh on their ill-fated march to Rullion Green, Blackader considered joining their number, but realised that their attempt was likely to fail. He was also noted throughout Covenanting history as being against rising in arms in any case.

From 1668 to 1681 Blackader was in great demand as a preacher at conventicles. No matter where he went he was given invitations to preach at other meetings, so much so that his health broke down for 14 weeks. For six weeks each year he resorted to Newmilns in Ayrshire, which had a mineral spring, and he also held conventicles in the neighbouring parishes.

Blackader officiated at conventicles that are too numerous to list. In 1668 he preached at Anstruther in Fife and at Strathmiglo near St Andrews in 1669. He preached in St Andrews itself in 1674.

Following the display of arms at a conventicle at the Hill of Beath in Fife, Blackader was listed as a wanted man. He escaped to Berwickshire for some time, but soon was travelling round the country, holding conventicles. In 1680 he journeyed to Holland for a short period as his son, William, studied medicine at Leyden. He preached on 15 successive Sundays at Rotterdam.

Blackader was arrested in his own home in Edinburgh on 5 April 1681 and taken before the Privy Council. He was questioned by the Duke of Rothes, Sir George Mackenzie, General Dalyell and Bishop Paterson of Edinburgh. They found him guilty of preaching at field meetings and he was sent to the Bass Rock on 7 April 1681, which had been converted to a gaol in 1651. Conditions were harsh – the food was poor and the prisoners were obliged to pay for it. Water was scarce, and they were forced to drink from pools of rainwater. In winter they were delighted to be able to drink from the cleaner snow and ice. It is also recorded that the fires in their rooms were so smoky that the prisoners regularly had to stick their heads out of the windows in order to breathe clean air.

Blackader remained a prisoner on this rocky islet for four and a half years. In his final months his health began to fail and his family petitioned the Privy Council to allow him to visit Edinburgh, where he might consult doctors and be allowed to die with his family. This was granted, so long as he accepted a cell in either Dunbar or Haddington. Blackader refused, 'having weighed and laid all together, I am constrained rather to choose to take God's venture in staying where I am.' He died on Bass Rock in December 1685. His body was transferred to the mainland and interred in North Berwick kirkyard.[2]

1. NX 974750. Plaque in Troqueer church.
2. NT 554855. Gravestone in North Berwick churchyard.

24
LYONS THUS CRUELLY DEVOURED ME

A party of nine Covenanters had been apprehended in Dumfriesshire and were held in the local gaols. One may have been a minister, but this is uncertain. The others included Alexander Gordon of Kinstuir, William Grierson of Lochurr, James Welsh of Little Cluden and John MacKechnie. They were tried in a justiciary court in Dumfries in July 1684 and were sentenced to be transported to the plantations. They were to be taken to Edinburgh where they were expected to be put on board a ship bound for the Americas. Twenty-eight soldiers (half a troop) under the command of Lieutenant Patrick Mulligan were sent to collect them, and the party commenced their way towards the capital. On the night of Monday 28 July they halted at the tolbooth of New Dalgarno, or Thornhill. From there the route chosen was one which took them through the Enterkin Pass, an old hill road which today has little more than a footpath through it.

Word soon spread in the neighbourhood of the route that the soldiers and Covenanters were about to take. Plans were made to try and spring the Covenanters' release, for the folk knew that otherwise they would be unlikely to see them again. James and Thomas Harkness, farmers from Locherben and Mitchellslacks (five miles east of Thornhill), were the ringleaders in the plot to free the captives. They sent for friends of the cause to join them, and when the time came numbered between 30 to 40. Others known to have taken part included a third brother, Adam Harkness, and James MacMichael, a fowler on Maxwelton estate. They chose a spot deep in the glen, where the hills dropped steeply to the roadside, from where no escape could easily be made.

The Harkness brothers ordered the group to divide into two. They waited as the dragoons made their way to the chosen spot, before descending from the hillside at a given signal. One group took up the rear, the other blocked the way forward. Stunned at the suddenness with which the ambush surrounded them, appearing out of the mist which hung low on the hills, the leader of the dragoons inquired of the Covenanters what they wanted.

'The freedom of the prisoners,' was their reply. At first the leader of the dragoons refused, and a scuffle broke out. The soldiers fired into the mist, and the Covenanters returned their shots. The leader of the soldiers was killed in the mêlée, and others were injured, but most of the Covenanters were freed, making their escape across the hillside.

John MacKechnie, however, was unlucky. He was held onto by the soldiers and taken back out of the glen. When the soldiers realised that he was still with them, the order was given to shoot him. The bullet, however, only wounded him in the arm. He was then taken to Edinburgh and imprisoned. After 13 weeks, his gunshot wound having not been treated, MacKechnie died of gangrene.

William Grierson of Lochurr (near Glencairn) was also injured in the scuffle. He received a bullet to his face, which left him blind. The soldiers also clubbed him on the head and left him for dead on the hillside, his horse dragging him to the Dry Cleugh. He was later discovered by friends and taken to a nearby shieling at Thirstown, where he recovered. The soldiers heard of this and he was recaptured. He was taken to Edinburgh and held in gaol for a time, but it was realised that because of his blindness and wounds he would no longer pose a threat to the Government and was thus released.

One of the soldiers was shot by a bullet said to have come from MacMichael's gun. Named Sergeant Kelt, he and his horse tumbled headlong down into the deep ravine, since known as Kelt's Linn. Another named Thomas Smith was killed – some accounts reckon that three soldiers died in total.

The authorities were incensed at the success of the attack, which was said to have been one of the Covenanters' best devised martial actions. On 31 July the government ordered a public inquiry into the rescue. Orders were given that all men over fifteen years of age were to appear in arms to assist the soldiers in the search for those responsible. The ministers of the six Nithsdale parishes read out warnings from the pulpit, declaring that any person over 15 was to answer on oath any questions put to them by the soldiers. Any absentees from the church were searched for and explanations demanded. The Harknesses' old grandmother, Margaret Frizelle, told the authorities that the brothers had spent the day shedding sheep at Mitchellslacks farm. A John Forsyth claimed to have seen the skirmish from a distance; Alexander MacMath, one of the soldiers, is said to have recognised James Harkness at the attack. Many folk were arrested at this time, which saw the whole of Nithsdale reeling from the backlash.

The dragoons were sent to search out those who had been involved, and soon were able to capture three of them: Thomas Harkness, Andrew Clerk and Samuel MacEwen were discovered sleeping rough in some fields in Closeburn parish. The soldiers woke them with shots from their guns, some of which wounded them. These wounds were not treated, despite the protestations of a woman, and she too was held captive for a time, before being released. The three men were then taken prisoner to Dumfries before being transferred to Edinburgh. They were put on trial for high treason and sentenced to death. At the scaffold, which was erected in the Grassmarket on 5 August 1684, they read out their testimony before suffering by hanging.

It is said that James Harkness had also been captured but had managed to escape in September 1684. A tradition handed down in the Harkness family attributes this to a robe hidden in a cheese which was gifted to him in his Edinburgh cell. At some point in his life he was asked by the parishioners of Moffat if he could help in getting rid of their curate, Rev David Johnstone. He gathered a number of friends together and they marched on the manse. Banging at the door, they yelled to Johnstone to leave in a peaceable manner. Realising that his life might be in danger, he did so. James survived until after the Revolution, dying in 1723.

A fourth Covenanter was later apprehended in the belief that he was present at the release. Daniel MacMichael, who had been present at the reading of the Sanquhar Declaration in 1680, was attending a house meeting at Lurgfoot, a shieling near Durisdeer, when a party of 50 dragoons approached. The Covenanters made an escape, but Daniel, being too infirm to follow, was hidden in a small cave nearby. He might have escaped detection if the soldiers did not have dogs with them which found his scent. He was taken into Durisdeer where John Dalziel, son of Sir Robert Dalziel of Glenae and Kirkmichael, and Lieutenant Straiton, questioned him regarding the incident. He was unable, or unwilling, to reveal anything, but when he was eventually asked to swear the Oath of Allegiance, he refused. This was enough for the soldiers to take matters further. They tied his hands together and held him prisoner overnight in the church. Next day they began the journey towards Elvanfoot, location of a garrison, where he was to be put on trial.

On 31 January 1685 the soldiers carried MacMichael up the Dalveen Pass as far as Dalveen farm where it was realised that he was too feeble and suffering from fever to be taken any further. They were also apprehensive about suffering from another attack, so they placed MacMichael on a small green knoll and told him to prepare to die. MacMichael prayed, sang the 42nd psalm, and read from John's gospel. At a given command from Dalziel, four soldiers fired instantaneously, leaving the corpse to lie.[1] MacMichael's body was later taken back to Durisdeer, where it was buried in the kirkyard.[2]

James Harkness was also apprehended by the authorities, in

this case by John Graham of Claverhouse, placed on trial and sentenced to death. However, he and 25 others managed to break free from gaol. He fled to Ireland where he lived until the Glorious Revolution. Returning home, he stayed at Locherben for a good number of years, before dying on 6 December 1723, aged 72 years. His gravestone, which is located in Dalgarnock kirkyard, near Thornhill, notes that he endured 28 years' persecution by tyranny.[3]

1. NS 883069. Monument on site of martyrdom.
2. NS 894038. Gravestone in Durisdeer churchyard.
3. NX 876936. Gravestone in Dalgarnock churchyard.

25

BY BLOODY GRAHAM WERE TAKEN

The parish of Carsphairn is a remote one, located high amid the Galloway Hills, on the border between Ayrshire and the Stewartry of Kirkcudbright. This parish was home to a number of Covenanters and, given its remoteness, it was a popular location for field meetings and Covenanters' hideouts. Aware of this, the authorities sent soldiers to stay in the district, placing garrisons at Earlstoun and Kenmure castles. The former had been the home of William Gordon, who was killed on his way to Bothwell Bridge in 1679, after which his lands were confiscated, and the latter was the home of Alexander Gordon, 6th Viscount Kenmure.

The appointed minister, or curate, at Carsphairn church was one Peter Pearson, who was greatly disliked in the district. He was a friend of Robert Grierson of Lag, one of the most feared persecutors of the Covenanters. Lag Tower stood in Dumfriesshire, but Grierson was also connected with the farm of Garryhorn in Carsphairn parish, where he made his headquarters in the district. For many years an old oak bed in the farmhouse was pointed out as belonging to Grierson, and the kennels, where he had kept his dogs, long survived. Many Covenanters in the district were hunted down and murdered by Grierson, among them John Dempster and one named MacCroy.

John Dempster was a tailor who lived at Garyyard in the

parish of Dalry. He was known for his part at Bothwell Bridge and therefore was a wanted man. He left his home and lived rough in a cave by the side of the Black Water, a tributary of the Ken, where he managed to continue his trade. On a number of occasions he came into close contact with the dragoons, but each time managed to make an escape. His luck failed to last forever, though. One day he was spotted by the dragoons on the Craig of Knockgray, but he managed to make an escape by crossing the Water of Deugh. This was surrounded by deep bogs which were enough to lose the troopers in the gloaming. They retired to Garryhorn, but Dempster was forced to spend the night on the hill of Craighit. Next day, Grierson led his men in pursuit. Dempster was fatigued from sleeping rough, but when Lag's dogs found his scent he was still able to run two miles up the steep slopes of Meaul. He was captured at a spot 1850 feet above sea level, and shot on the spot. A rude stone marks his grave.[1]

MacCroy was a tenant farmer who lived quite near to Garryhorn. One Sunday morning Grierson and his men discovered MacCroy in his fields, tending his cattle and reading a book. On being asked which book it was he replied, 'The Bible.'

'Then your kye will need to find a new herd,' Lag replied, 'for your life is now forfeited as a rebel.' At that he withdrew his pistol and shot him on the spot.

In the later summer of 1684 Grierson held court in the kirk of Carsphairn to which all the parishioners were summoned. Each was asked to swear an oath which entreated them to reveal to him the whereabouts of any Covenanters in the district, or who may be harbouring them. Pearson was present at the court, and he was able to testify whether or not the witness was in regular attendance at his church. When the court was finished, Pearson gave Grierson a list of names of those parishioners who failed to attend Lag's summons.

The list of names was lengthy, and Lag sent men to their homes to seek them out. A few were allowed to take the test, but most had absconded from their houses, allowing the soldiers to loot them and ill-treat their wives. A troop of soldiers under Lieutenant Livingston, and others under Claverhouse, were soon to appear in the parish, searching for adherents of the Covenant. The pillaging and cruelty got worse. An old woman of 73 was mistreated and her home destroyed simply because her son had not appeared before Lag's court. The soldiers appeared at her home a second time and, as the son was absent again, took her prisoner to Dumfries. There she was offered the Oath of Allegiance, but on her refusal she was fined 200 merks and scourged through the town centre on market day.

The menfolk of the district decided that Pearson's actions were too much. They met in secret at the farm of Marbrack, which stands just over two miles to the east of Carsphairn. Present were James MacMichael, a fowler in the employment of Sir Robert Laurie of Maxwelton, Roger Padzen of Sanquhar, Robert Mitchell of New Cumnock, William Herron of Glencairn, a man surnamed Watson, and a few others. They decided to send a deputation to Pearson's manse to confront him and they also drew up a paper that requested Pearson to allow the parishioners to worship as they pleased.

MacMichael, Herron, Mitchell and others made up the party which travelled to Carsphairn under the cover of darkness. They banged loudly on the door of the manse, the sound of the thuds echoing in the eery gloom. The curate was frightened by the sound, so he armed himself with a broad-sword and pistol before opening the door. Most of the Covenanters remained outside when the leaders went in to present their petition.

Pearson flew into a rage at the audacity of the Covenanters and he barred the door while threatening the men with his gun. The Covenanters screamed for assistance from their friends outside, and James MacMichael was first to force his way in. He was a rather hot-headed character, one who had already fought and survived Airds Moss and who had taken part in the rescue at Enterkin Pass. When he saw what Pearson was up to he raised his gun, took aim and fired. The minister took the force of the shot at point-blank range and dropped to the ground, stone dead. But the Covenanters were shocked at MacMichael's action, for they had planned no bloodshed.

The Societies distanced themselves from the actions of the men, and refused them membership. It was of little use, however, for the Covenanters as a whole were blamed for the murder, and it was used as justification for further actions by the likes of Grierson and Claverhouse.

Two of those present at the Marbrack meeting turned out to be either turncoats or spies. The man surnamed Watson joined the side of the persecutors, and some reckon that he was always in their employ, supplying them with information. Roger Padzen was to join the troop of dragoons under the command of Strachan. He may have always been one of their number, sent to infiltrate the Covenanters and find out where their meetings were. These two may have warned Pearson of the impending visit. Either way, he armed himself.

James MacMichael fled to the hills for his protection, afraid to appear in the populated parts of the county. Graham of Claverhouse was sent to track him, eventually coming upon him and a few friends in a remote spot in the valley of the Water of Dee, about five miles south-west of New Galloway on 18 December 1684.

Eight men had been gathered together at a spot known as Auchencloy. When Claverhouse's men discovered them, so sudden was their appearance that they were taken by surprise and thrown into confusion. Two of their number managed to make an escape, however, finding refuge in a nearby shieling. Claverhouse himself came into close combat with MacMichael. At first MacMichael had the upper hand, his swordmanship being superior, and a few blows of his blade had actually struck the soldier's steel helmet. Claverhouse called out for assistance, to which MacMichael retorted, 'You dare not abide the issue of a single combat; and had your helmet been like mine, a soft bonnet, your body would have long-since found a bed on the heather.' One of Claverhouse's dragoons came on horseback and swung his axe in mid-air. It landed on MacMichael's skull, rending it in two.

The soldiers were quick to overpower Robert Ferguson, John Grierson and Robert Stewart. There was no need to try them, for their action in fighting was sufficient to allow the dragoons to shoot them on the spot. It is thought that Stewart was known to Claverhouse, for he is said to have announced, 'Stewart's soul in heaven doth sing!' He was the son of Major Robert Stewart of Ardoch (2 miles north of St John's Town of Dalry). At first the bodies of John Grierson and Robert Stewart were laid to rest in the graves of their ancestors at Dalry, but when the authorities heard of their decent burial, orders were issued for their disinterment. The corpses were then taken to the northern side of the kirk and buried there, a place traditionally reserved for thieves and other malcontents.[2] There is said to be another unmarked Covenanter's grave at Dalry to one whose name is unknown, but some folk think that this may be the resting place of James MacMichael. Robert Ferguson (or Ferguis as he appears on his headstone) was buried on the site of his martyrdom, at Auchencloy. He probably belonged to Fore Mulligan farm.[3]

Two others were caught and taken prisoner. They were William Hunter and Robert Smith. Tied on to the back of a pony they were transported to Kirkcudbright. Their trial was unfair, and when they tried to deliver a speech at their execution the soldiers beat their drums so loudly that the crowds were unable to hear them. The pair were hanged and later beheaded. Hunter belonged to Auchenhastning farm; Smith was from Glencairn.[4]

The two men who managed to escape to the shieling then journeyed further away. Claverhouse's men made a return journey to the vicinity, and questioned those who were at the shieling at the time. Failing to get any useful information from the occupants, they took them prisoner and set the house on fire.

Two of the Covenanters present at Carsphairn manse are the subjects of two other chapters. William Herron was to die at Lochenkit, in the Stewartry of Kirkcudbright, and Robert Mitchell at Ingliston, Glencairn, Dumfriesshire.

1. NX 501918. Plaque on site of martyrdom.
2. NX 618812. Gravestone in St John's Town of Dalry churchyard.
3. NX 603709. Gravestone on site of martyrdom; also monument to all martyrs captured here.
4. NX 691511. Gravestone in Kirkcudbright cemetery.

26

DONALD CARGILL

The village of Rattray is located on the opposite side of the River Ericht from the larger and better known town of Blairgowrie. Donald Cargill was born at Hatton of Rattray in or around the year 1610.[1] His father, Laurence Cargill, was an upstanding citizen in the town, a notary and a heritor of the parish. Being comparatively well off he was able to send Donald to Aberdeen University for an education. A large period in Cargill's life is thereafter unknown. It has been suggested he spent most of these years working either as a merchant or farmer, but there is no evidence for either. At any rate he decided to enrol at St Salvator's College, St Andrews, in 1645.

Cargill commenced a course in philosophy but all the time his father was keen that he become a minister. Donald was less than willing, claiming that he was too weak a man to withstand the burden of the ministry. However, after some time, he seems to have changed his mind and enrolled in divinity classes. He was licensed by St Andrews Presbytery in April 1653, and during his time at St Andrews signed the Solemn League and Covenant

In 1655 Donald Cargill was called to be the minister of the Barony Church in Glasgow, which at that time met in the crypt of the cathedral. This was to be his first and only charge. He married Margaret Brown, the widow of Andrew Bethune of Blebo, near St

Andrews, but she died a year later and Cargill never remarried.

The government had decreed that 29 May 1662 should be celebrated as a day of thanksgiving for the king's restoration. Although it was a week day, a service was planned for the Barony church. When Cargill ascended the pulpit and saw the large congregation he began his sermon by telling them that 'We are not come here to keep this day upon the account for which others keep it. We thought once to have blessed the day when the king came home again; but now we think we shall have reason to curse it; and if any of you come here in order to the solemnising of this day, we desire you to remove.'

This act of 'treason' brought Cargill to the attention of the authorities. At a similar time he was also being ejected from his charge for refusing to accept the Middleton Act. The authorities tried to apprehend him, but when the soldiers forced their way into his church Cargill was able to escape by a back door. An Act of Council dated October 1662 officially deprived him of his charge for his non-adherence, sedition and desertion of his flock, to take effect on 1st November. This also charged him to live north of the River Tay, so he returned to his native Perthshire.

Cargill was active in attending and preaching at conventicles in the southern part of Perthshire, where there were a number of sympathisers. He is also known to have broken the bond under which he was charged, and visited Glasgow and Edinburgh on a number of occasions. The Privy Council issued a further act against him:

> Whereas Mr Donald Cargill was confined benorth Tay, October 1 1662, and that under pain of sedition, and yet he hath repaired to the city of Edinburgh and other places at his pleasure in high and proud contempt of authority, ordains the said Donald Cargill by open proclamation at the Cross of Edinburgh and Forfar to be cited to appear before the Council on the 11th of January next, otherwise he shall be denounced simpliciter.

Cargill did attend the meeting, but he was treated leniently, simply being ordered again to remain north of the Tay and keep away from both Glasgow and Edinburgh.

In 1672 the second Indulgence was passed, which allowed some ministers to return to their churches, so long as there were two of them, and they remained within their parish. The authorities appointed him as the assistant minister at Eaglesham in Renfrewshire under this act, a move which they hoped would silence him. However, Cargill refused to take them up on the offer and in 1675 his share of the stipend was given to the first minister, Rev James Hamilton. The authorities decided to apprehend him, but Cargill escaped to the Netherlands where he remained for some time.

Donald Cargill was drawn back to Scotland. His life was not easy, for he was hunted over moor and dale. Many were the tales of his escapes from pursuers. On one occasion he was preaching at a house service in the Kirk Wynd in Blairgowrie. The authorities discovered this and sent the soldiers after him. Cargill ran up Glen Ericht and was about to be captured by the dragoons when he chanced his luck and jumped from a rock across a narrow stretch of the River Ericht, landing safely and out of harms way on the other side. This spot, near to the Linn of Ericht, has been known as Cargill's Loup ever since.[2]

Cargill, Robert Hamilton and David Hackston met John Spreul, the town clerk of Glasgow, and compiled a manifesto which was adopted by the Societies at a meeting in Strathaven. The plan had been to publish it in Glasgow, but the city was too heavily guarded for this to take place, so on 29 May 1679 the 'Rutherglen Declaration' was placed on the burgh cross by between 60-80 Covenanters. This was seen as a signal for rebellion and a reward of 3,000 merks was placed on Cargill's head.

At the Battle of Bothwell Bridge on 22 June 1679 Donald Cargill was wounded and left for dead on the field. He was very much alive however, and lived for a couple of years thereafter.

Cargill was hiding at Queensferry, on the Firth of Forth, on 3 June 1680. He was in contact with Henry Hall, who was then hiding near to Bo'ness. He was laird of Haughhead at Eckford in Teviotdale and a relation of the Earl of Roxburgh. Hall was a noted Covenanter, having been captured in 1666 as he made his way to join the Pentland rising. He was imprisoned in Cessford Castle but subsequently escaped. After spending over 10 years in hiding in England he returned to Scotland where he fought at Drumclog and Bothwell Bridge. He then fled to the Netherlands but returned in 1680, spending much of his time in the Bo'ness area.

The curates of Bo'ness and Carriden told the soldiers at Blackness Castle that Cargill and Hall were in the vicinity. The governor of Blackness, Captain Middleton, spotted them at an inn in Queensferry itself. He was expecting his men to appear right behind him, but they were slow in coming. The Governor caught Hall himself, and so wounded him that he died the following day.

Hall's pockets were searched and the 'Queensferry Paper' was found on him. This was an unsigned declaration which was the most revolutionary yet. In it Charles II is described as being unfit as a king and that he should be deposed. It also claimed that the country should become a republic and stated that 'if we be pursued or troubled any further, in worshipping, rights and liberties, that we shall look on it as a declaring war, and take all the advantages that one enemy doth of another and seek to cause to perish all that shall, in a hostile measure assault us, and to maintain, relieve and right ourselves of those that have wronged us, but not to trouble or injure any but those who have injured us.'

Cargill was also injured, but not so seriously, and he was able to make an escape. He fled through Lothian to Lanarkshire, Ayrshire and Galloway, and met with Richard Cameron. Cameron was to die a week later at Airds Moss, and at a conventicle held on 25 July at Starryshaw farm, near Shotts in Lanarkshire, Cargill mentioned this, taking as his text, 1st Samuel 3, 38, 'Know ye not that there is a great man and prince fallen this day.' Starryshaw was a well known conventicle site, better known as the Deer Slunk at the time.[3]

Another large conventicle took place at Talla Linn in Peeblesshire, at which 5,000 are reputed to have attended. The singing of psalms was said to have been so loud that it drowned out the sound of the waterfall. The conventicle remained undisturbed, which was lucky, for Graham of Claverhouse was at the time only four miles away, spending the night at an inn known as The Bield. Talla Linn was used by the society members for quarterly meetings. South of here is a narrow defile known as Donald's Cleuch, named after Cargill.

In September 1680 Cargill preached at a large conventicle at Torwood, between Stirling and Falkirk. There he excommunicated Charles II and his advisers, the Duke of York, Duke of Monmouth, Duke of Lauderdale, Duke of Rothes, Sir George Mackenzie and Thomas Dalyell of the Binns.

The government issued a proclamation on 22 November denouncing Cargill as a seditious preacher and fanatical conspirator. The reward for his capture was increased to 5,000 merks. The search for him intensified, and many of Cargill's friends were captured at this time. Among these was James Skene, brother of the laird of Skene, who had claimed that it was right to kill the dragoons 'when they persecuted God's people.' Captured with Skene were John Potter, a farmer and servant of Lord Cardross, and Archibald Stewart of Bo'ness, the latter a veteran of Airds Moss. They were executed in Edinburgh on 1 December 1680.

Two female supporters of Cargill, Isobel Alison of Perth and Marion Harvey of Bo'ness were also arrested. They were still in their youth, Alison being young and unmarried, Harvey being a maid-servant of 20 years. Tam Dalyell threatened Marion with the boots and being accused of murder, she replied, 'I could never take the life of a chicken, but my heart shrinked.' Rev Archibald Riddell paid them a visit in the gaol to try and persuade them to renounce their adherence but he was unsuccessful. They were executed in Edinburgh on 26 January 1681.

One of Cargill's conventicles took place in May 1681 in the fields to the north of Maybole, in Ayrshire. He stood beside a large boulder to address the crowd, and the nearby farm was later named Cargillstone in his honour.[4] In June 1681 there was a conventicle planned for somewhere on the side of Tinto, in Clydesdale. The lady of St John's Kirk, whose land adjoined the proposed meeting place, reported that something was happening, and the soldiers came to investigate. The conventiclers, however, discovered that it was too dangerous for them to hold a meeting there, so decided to walk eight miles across the Culter Hills to Glen Holm, in Peeblesshire. Cargill, who had spent the night at a friend's house on Clydeside, was also forced to walk to the new site, at Holms Common, where he preached from Romans 11, 20.

Donald Cargill managed to elude the soldiers for 10 months after the Torwood Excommunication. A week before his eventual arrest he was hiding in the woods around Lee Castle, home of one of the main persecutors, Cromwell Lockhart. On that occasion he performed the marriage ceremony of Robert Marshall, one of three sons of Marshall of Starryshaw. The other two, Thomas and John, were banished to America as slaves for refusing to declare the battle of Bothwell Bridge as rebellion. Robert succumbed to the Privy Council's demands and was freed.

On 10 July 1681 Cargill preached at a conventicle held at Dunsyre Common in Lanarkshire. That night he travelled across the River Clyde to Covington Mill where he stayed with Andrew Fisher. James Irvine of Bonshaw was in the vicinity with a troop of dragoons from the garrison at East Kilbride and captured him. Two others were also taken, James Boig and Walter Smith, both divinity students. The three were transported to Glasgow before being taken to Edinburgh, where they appeared before the Council.[5]

The trial took place, and Cargill was sentenced to be hanged by just one vote. Otherwise he would have gone to the Bass Rock as a prisoner. On 27 July 1681 Cargill, Boig and Smith were led from the gaol to the gallows. Cargill climbed the ladder, announcing to the crowd, 'The Lord knows I go up this ladder with less fear, confusion, or perturbation of mind, than ever I entered the pulpit to preach.' After he was dead, the head of Cargill was removed and it was publicly displayed on the Netherbow Port.

1. NO 189471. Cairn on site of birthplace.
2. NO 177499.
3. NS 897608. Monument on site of conventicle.
4. NS 295110. Monument on site of conventicle.
   Part of the stone is located in Maybole (NS 299101).
5. NS 977388. Monument on site of Cargill's arrest.

27
COLONEL JAMES DOUGLAS'S KILLING YEAR

One of the principal persecutors of the western Covenanters was Colonel, later Lieutenant-General, James Douglas. He was responsible for many deaths, some of which are recounted in other chapters within this volume. Douglas was born at Sanquhar Castle, the son of 2nd Earl of Queensberry. A number of martyrs' graves note with disgust that he was the 'brother to the Duke of Queensberry'. He lived at Stenhouse, which is located near to Tynron in Dumfriesshire. At first he trained as an advocate, but in August 1684 he was appointed Colonel of Linlithgow's regiment of foot. This was a severe case of nepotism, for the Duke of Queensberry was Lord Justice-General and later Treasurer, and he had already appointed his eldest son, Lord Drumlanrig, as Lieutenant-Colonel of Claverhouse's regiment and another, Lord William, was given the command of one of Claverhouse's troop.

It is claimed that Colonel Douglas was a strict disciplinarian, insisting that his men all sported beards and haircuts of a standard length. Indeed, it was claimed that all his soldiers had to be of a similar height and build, so that his regiment appeared smarter than all others. Those who failed to meet his criteria were thrown out of the regiment and had to petition for payment of their wages. The year of 1685 was right in the middle of the 'killing time', and Douglas was active in his pursuit of those who failed to conform to the king's authority.

On 15 January 1685 James Douglas was transferred to south west Scotland, being stationed at Blairquhan Castle, near Straiton in Ayrshire, which had been taken over as a garrison.[1] From there he journeyed over the Carrick and Galloway hills, searching for hill-men and following up tip-offs given to him. His success in persecuting the rebels was limited at first, for he lost a soldier in a skirmish (the first government soldier to die in six years), and would have died himself had a gun not failed to go off. This probably intensified his resolve to spare none thereafter.

Somewhere between the rivers Fleet and Dee, in Galloway, Douglas and his party came upon a Covenanter with the surname of Mowat. He was a tailor, and as such had some lead in his possession, for this was used in his trade at that time. For no other reason than the lead being in his hands, Douglas shot him dead on the spot. Another Covenanter he killed was William Auchinleck, from the parish of Buittle, who is said to have been an associate of Viscount Kenmure. Auchinleck was a deaf man, and when Douglas put questions to him he was unable to answer. Accordingly, he ordered his men to shoot him. His body was thrown into a well at Ernespie House, in the parish of Crossmichael near Castle Douglas.

In February 1685 Douglas's party crossed the hills from Blairquhan by an old drove route known as the De'ils Elbow and arrived in the valley of the River Stinchar. At the foot of the pass was the farm of Dalwyne, which lies four miles up the glen from the village of Barr. Dalwyne was the home of a family surnamed Martin, who were known for their Covenanting adherence. George Martin, schoolmaster, notary and church elder from Old Dailly may have been a member of the family. He was tortured by Claverhouse and imprisoned in Edinburgh for four years until the authorities decided to have him executed in the Grassmarket on 22 February 1684.

In any case, at Dalwyne the soldiers discovered two men. One was Edward MacKean, who had journeyed across the Nick of the Balloch pass from Minnoch vale in Galloway. He had come in search of corn, for it had been a hard winter and his own stores were depleted. Being a stranger in the district, MacKean was unsure what to do, so tried to make a getaway. It was to be a mistake, for Douglas fired two shots through his skull. He fell to the ground, his body writhing in agony. To put him out of his misery one of the soldiers killed him outright with a third bullet.

The soldiers then turned their attention to the other man. This was David Martin, the farmer's son. He was dragged outside where the dragoons prepared to shoot him for harbouring a fugitive. However, one of the soldiers announced that this was not right in law, and reluctantly the dragoons had to agree. David Martin was allowed to go free. The shock he suffered from seeing the murder of MacKean, and the nearness of his own death, resulted in him suffering a mental illness from which he never recovered. MacKean's body was later taken to Barr where it was buried in the kirkyard.[2]

In March 1685 the authorities were concerned about the Covenanters who dared to march around Ayrshire and so on 27 March Douglas was granted a special justice's commission 'to extirpate these rebels.' This commission was to last until 20 April.

Early in April 1685 a party of soldiers returned westward from Muirkirk in Ayrshire towards the garrison at Sorn Castle. At the farm of Greenock Mains, which lies four miles west of Muirkirk, they paid a visit to the tenant, Thomas Richard, an old man of around 80 years. He was known to be a supporter of the Covenant, for in 1674 he had been selected as one of a number of possible new elders for Muirkirk church. However, the session minutes for 13 April 1674 note that:

> ...ther was sum was unwilling because of ye trubilsumes of ye times, and if they accepted, they wold only accept yt on thes termes, yt we ye present ministers remenit in ye office acording to ye actes of ye generall assembly, and did not conforme to episcopaci.

A few of the soldiers under the command of Cornet Peter Inglis deceived Richard into thinking that they were friendly and he welcomed them in. The soldiers produced Bibles, and invited the old farmer to join them in prayer. The men then asked him about the Covenanters, wondering if he knew of the whereabouts of a few wanted men. Richard replied that he did not, but told them that a few of them had spent the night at his farm a few days ago. The conversation continued, the soldiers trying to prise out information from the old man, and all the time trying to fool him into believing that they were supporters of the same cause. At one point, however, one of the soldiers swore, which Thomas Richard thought would have been unlike supporters of the Covenant. Realising his suspicions were aroused, the men revealed to Richard that they were government soldiers, and promptly arrested him.

The soldiers knew Colonel Douglas was stationed at Cumnock at the time, so they carried Richard across Airds Moss to the village. His 'confession' to the soldiers was sufficient to have him shot without trial. The execution was scheduled to take place on 5 April and traditionally took place in Cumnock Square, which at that time was the parish kirkyard.

According to a story handed down, three Episcopalian ladies went to Colonel Douglas's headquarters to plead for the old man's life, but were refused admission. A letter was later sent to them stating that Douglas could show no leniency to any supporter of the Covenant. Thomas Richard knelt to pray before facing death, but Colonel Douglas gave the order to fire whilst he did so. It is said that the bullet ricocheted after killing the martyr and lodged itself in the gable of a building which long stood on the north side of the kirkyard. As a mark of disrespect his body was buried at the village's gallows knowe.[3]

Later in April Alexander Fergusson of Kilkerran went to Blairquhan garrison where he reported a few tenants of his who had failed to attend the Episcopal curate's church services. One of the names he passed on was that of John Semple, a farmer who lived at Eldington farm with his wife and three or four children. The farm was located near to Dailly village, and was not far from Moorston House, where Fergusson lived at the time. (His old castle of Kilkerran was uninhabitable, and the present Kilkerran House was not erected until around 1730.) Semple had never carried arms against the government, but it was known that his house had been a haven for the hunted Covenanters. Fergusson directed the soldiers back to Moorston just before sundown. At his home he entertained them to supper, and they passed the time in conviviality until the midnight hour. Under the cover of pitch blackness, the soldiers made their way to Eldington. Semple was awakened by the sound of whispers outside, and realising that it was probably a party of soldiers searching for him, tried to make an escape from a narrow window. As he tried this five or six dragoons spotted him and their shots left him dead.[4]

Another martyr buried in the same spot as Semple is Thomas MacClorgan. He was killed during the hours of darkness at the house of Drumellan in 1685, but nothing more is known about him. Even less is known of two other nameless martyrs who lie in Old Dailly. The first was herding his cattle in the fields near Killoup farm when the soldiers came upon him. No doubt he refused to answer their questions satisfactorily and was shot dead. The other martyr belonged to Black Clauchrie, a remote community on the moors of Barr parish. He was struck down at his very own hearth, and some say this hearthstone was used as his gravemarker.[5]

On 10 May Colonel James Douglas arrived at the home of Adam MacWhann, a known Covenanter who spent much of his time hiding for his life in the high Galloway hills. By the side of the Curnelloch Burn, nine miles west of New Galloway, is a large boulder known as MacWhann's Stone, where Adam fashioned a secret hideout.[6] Today this boulder is passed by a forest road, but in the 17th century it was far more remote and distant from any track. MacWhann had contracted a fever and was extremely ill, so he found himself attracted to his home, which stood outside New Galloway. It was while he lay on his sick bed that Douglas barged his way into the house, pushing past his family who were caring for him. Finding the Covenanter lying there he put questions to him, but for some reason MacWhann was either unwilling or perhaps unable to answer these.

'Drag him to New Galloway,' Douglas ordered. The soldiers

in his party took the sick man into the village where he was locked up for the night. A couple of days later, on 12 May, he was taken to the centre of the village and shot. No trial had taken place. MacWhann's body was later carried to Kells churchyard (in which parish New Galloway lies) and buried secretly by friends.[7]

Colonel Douglas's dragoons were travelling across country near to the village of Tongland, which lies to the north of Kirkcudbright. It is thought that Lieutenant Livingston was also in the party, for he is named in Wodrow as being at the front of the soldiers. Livingston was a lieutenant under Douglas as captain, so it is possible that both were present. In the distance they spotted a youth of 18 years, John Hallume, as it appears on his grave, though sometimes his surname is spelled Hallam or even just Hall. Spotting the soldiers, Hallume decided to make a detour in order to avoid them. The soldiers had already seen him, and noting that he was trying to avoid them decided that this showed signs of guilt. The soldiers were ordered to chase him, and when they drew near a shot was fired which left him disabled. As he lay on the ground clutching at the open wound a dragoon came upon him and took a swipe at his head with his sword. Despite receiving two severe wounds, Hallume was still alive. The soldiers manhandled him onto a pony and tied him over its back. Being quite early in the day, Hallume was taken by the soldiers on their journey, till at length they returned to Kirkcudbright where he was imprisoned. Asked if he would take the Oath of Abjuration, Hallume refused. Douglas ordered a trial to take place, the jury comprising of the soldiers who had been in the party which captured Hallume. Not surprisingly, he was found guilty and sentenced to hang. This took place within hours. Hallume's body was later buried in the old kirkyard at Kirkcudbright.[8]

Another man to suffer death at the hands of Douglas was Robert MacWhae, who died sometime in 1685. Little is known about him, other than that he was out in his own garden, somewhere in the parish of Borgue, which lies west of Kirkcudbright. He was later buried at Kirkandrews.[9]

Not all of Douglas's prisoners were to suffer death. He captured three men in the Cumnock area, Allan Atkin, James Napier and John Peirson, who were locked up in gaol. Both Douglas and the commissioners at Cumnock sentenced them to die, but on 12 June 1685 a remission was obtained for their crime of concealing the rebels who had recently passed through the county of Ayr.

James Douglas was promoted to Lieutenant-General and Commander-in-Chief of the King's forces in 1688. They were around 3,000 strong at that time – 1,995 of foot and 841 of cavalry.

1. NS 365055.
2. NX 276941. Gravestone in Barr old churchyard.
3. NS 570203. Gravestone in Cumnock old cemetery.
4. NX 225993. Gravestone in Old Dailly churchyard.
5. NX 225993. Also buried at Old Dailliy.
6. NX 492802.
7. NX 631783. Gravestone in Kells churchyard, New Galloway.
8. NX 691511. Gravestone in Kirkcudbright old cemetery.
9. NX 601481. Gravestone in Kirkandrews churchyard.

28

BY LAG SO WICKEDLY WERE SHOT

Sir Robert Grierson of Lag Tower and Rockhall died of an apoplectic fit on 31 December 1733, aged 88, at his town house in Dumfries. From that moment on a weird set of supernatural happenings took place, which the locals reckoned were a result of his earlier years when he was an arch-persecutor of the Covenanters. The first problem his relatives and friends had was removing his corpse from his death bed. Because his body was rigid, part of the wall of his home had to be demolished in order to get it out. Once the coffin was loaded onto the hearse the horses were only able to pull it for a few hundred yards before they had to stop due to exhaustion. Sir Thomas Kirkpatrick of Closeburn sent for some of his best Spanish horses and when they were attached to the hearse they pulled it non-stop six miles to Dunscore's old kirkyard at such a rate that they died on arrival. It was also related that a black raven, a symbol of the Devil, landed on Lag's coffin at Dumfries and it took many waving mourners to frighten it away. The bird, however, followed the cortege to Dunscore and only flew away when the coffin was buried in the ground. The cost of Grierson's funeral amounted to £240 Scots, the account surviving.[1]

   The nefarious happenings at Lag's funeral are perhaps only local tales, claimed to have taken place in retribution for his part in persecuting the Covenanters. The tales associated with his suppression are still recounted, though whether he did in fact place Covenanters in empty barrels pierced with spikes and roll them down Benan Hill has no substance of proof. Sir Walter Scott used Grierson as the basis of 'Sir Robert Redgauntlet', who appears in 'Wandering Willie's Tale', an integral part of his novel, *Redgauntlet*:

> *Ye maun have heard of Sir Robert Redgauntlet of that Ilk, who lived in these parts before the dear years. The country will lang mind him; and our fathers used to draw breath thick if ever they heard him named ... He was knighted at Lonon court, wi' the King's ain sword; and being a red-hot prelatist, he came down here, rampaging like a lion, with commissions of lieutenancy, and of lunacy, for what I ken, to put down a' the Whigs and Covenanters in the country. Wild wark they made of it; for the Whigs were as dour as the Cavaliers were fierce, and it was aye which should first tire the other. Redgauntlet was aye for the strong hand: and his name is kenn'd as wide as Claverhouse's or Tam Dalyell's. Glen, nor dargle, nor mountain, nor cave, could hide the puir hill-folk when Redgauntlet was out with bugle and bloodhound after them, as if they has been sae mony deer. And troth when they fand them, they didna mak' muckle mair ceremony than a Hielandman wi' a roebuck. It was just, 'Will ye tak the Test?' – if not, 'Make ready; present; fire!' – and there lay the recusant.*

Grierson was born around 1655, the son of William Grierson of Farquhar and Margaret, a daughter of Douglas of Mousewald. According to tradition, the Griersons were a branch of the clan MacGregor, changing their surname to a more lowland spelling. In 1667 he inherited the old castle of Lag from his cousin. Grierson was also the owner of a shipping company. The *Henrietta* plied between Dumfries and Liverpool and the captain was another Robert Grierson.

Grierson was appointed the Depute Steward of Kirkcudbrightshire in 1678, the Earl of Nithsdale, hereditary Steward, being then a minor. On 8 February 1678 he drew up a bond disallowing his tenants from attending conventicles or associating with Covenanters. Grierson was unrelenting in his search for nonconformists, and was a keen administrator of the various oaths which were required to be taken by the parish-ioners. It is said that he once rounded up hundreds of folk and placed a ring of armed soldiers around them. All within were to take the Oath of Allegiance to the king, after which he dismissed them, saying, 'Now you are a fold of clean beasts, ye may go home.'

On 2 March 1685 Lag and Captain Andrew Bruce of Earlshall (deputy sheriff of Galloway) were in the eastern Galloway hills searching for Covenanters. On the low moor of Lochenkit they came upon eight Covenanters who had recently left a prayer meeting held at the Brooklands. It is said that the cry of the lapwings betrayed their presence. Four of the men were deemed sufficiently guilty for Bruce to order them to be shot where they stood. Consequently, the soldiers withdrew their guns and took aim. These four, William Herron from Glencairn, John Gordon, William Stewart and John Wallace (all Galloway), were buried where they fell.[2]

The four other Covenanters, Edward Gordon, Robert Grierson, Alexander MacCubbin and one whose name is forgotten, had to endure the sight, before Bruce ordered them to be tied up and taken five miles to the Old Bridge of Urr. At that spot Grierson was examining a number of folk who had been brought to him under suspicion of being supporters of the Covenant. Grierson was keen to have the men executed on the spot, but Bruce intervened, and insisted that they should stand trial before a jury. Lag responded angrily that, 'he would seek no assizes,' but did agree to wait until the next morning before deciding on the Covenanters' fate.

When the sun rose Edward Gordon and Alexander MacCubbin were whisked off to Kirkpatrick Irongray, where they were hanged on an oak tree which grew on a mound to the west of the church. As the hangman carried out his evil chore, he asked the men if he could be forgiven. MacCubbin responded,

'Poor man, I forgive thee, and all men: thou hast a miserable calling upon earth.'[3]

It is said that the two men were executed at Irongray in order to act as a warning to the Ferguson family, who were tenants of Hallhill farm which lies nearby and who were noted adherents of the Covenant. The farmer's daughter was present at the execution and took a scarf from her own head and tore it in two, in order to make a blindfold for the two condemned men. For her kindly act it is said that the soldiers captured her and she was sentenced to the American plantations for seven years. The ship carrying her thither was wrecked on the coast of Virginia, but fortunately she escaped. She moved to Lisbon, where she was married to a carpenter, and it is known that she was still alive in 1755.

Robert Grierson and the unknown Covenanter were also sentenced to be banished, in this case to be sold as slaves in the West Indies. Grierson survived until after the Glorious Revolution, when he was able to make his way back to Scotland and return to his wife, or 'Widow Grier' as she had become known.

On the summit of a 1632 feet high hill on the border between Dumfriesshire and the Stewartry of Kirkcudbright stands a squat memorial within circular railings. The hill is known as Allan's Cairn, for the memorial commemorates George Allan and Margaret Gracie. The monument was erected in 1857 with funds raised from a sermon preached on the spot, previously there being a cairn marking the graves.[4]

A couple of miles to the south-west of Allan's Cairn is Altry Hill, on the western edge of which is a natural depression. This was known to the Covenanters who found it to be an ideal spot for holding open-air services. The depression meant that they were difficult to see from anywhere, and the wind whistling round the hillside scattered the sound of their singing. The spot became known as the 'Whig's Hole'.[5]

A local landowner, however, became aware that the conventicle site existed, and reported this to Robert Grierson of Lag, on one of his forays into Galloway. The laird was Robert

Canning of Muirdrochwood, whose home was eight miles down the valley from the site. Not knowing when the conventicles were to be held at the hole, Grierson made a habit of searching it out each time he was in the vicinity. One day he was lucky. A group of hill-men and women had met to sing psalms and praise God. As Grierson and his troops ascended the hillside the look-out raised the alarm, and the Covenanters scattered. Grierson and Coupland pursued Allan and Gracie in an easterly direction, catching them up at the Fans of Altry, a boggy stretch of ground between the hills. Grabbing them from his horse, he threw them to the ground. He offered them the chance to swear the Oath of Allegiance to the king, but as they refused he ordered one of the troopers to execute them on the spot. The gun was drawn and two shots echoed round the hillside. The other Covenanters who had run in opposite directions winced as they heard the shots, realising what they meant.

The corpses of Allan and Gracie were left on the open moor by the dragoons, face down where they fell. Under the cover of nightfall, when the troopers were back at their garrison, the Covenanters returned to the spot and found them. They carried them to the top of the nearby hill and buried them at the junction of three parishes.

Following the Pentland Rising, Grierson spent much of his time travelling across Galloway in search of the fugitives. At St John's Town of Dalry in the Stewartry of Kirkcudbright the parish church was taken over by Lag to stable his horses. It is also recorded in Dumfries custom records that the officers of the excise were ordered, in 1685, to search ships for any Covenanters who had smuggled themselves on board in an attempt to escape the clutches of Lag.

On 11 July 1685 Lag and the Earl of Annandale were in command of a troop of heritors in the parish of Twynholm, Kirkcudbrightshire. As night fell they were riding back to their base with Annandale in the lead. At some point he came upon two Covenanters: David Halliday, who had been the farmer at Glengap in the parish, and George Short. Realising that they had no chance of escape, they gave themselves up. Annandale decided that they should be taken prisoner and face trial on the following day. However, when Lag caught up with him, he decided that the pair should be shot as they lay tied up on the ground. Annandale protested, stating that he had already promised them a trial on the following day. Lag would have none of it, claiming that they had no time, and ordered his men to shoot the two men. At first the soldiers refused, but when Lag threatened them of the consequences if he was forced to do the deed himself, they pulled out their guns and fired. The corpses were left where they fell, but were later taken to Balmaghie kirkyard where they lie in separate graves. David Halliday is buried alongside his namesake, the farmer of Miefield, who had already been martyred on 21 February 1685 at Kirkconnell Moor.[6]

At some point in the Killing Times Lag is said to have based himself at the Dunnering Inn in Maybole. Lag's work in hounding the Covenanters did not go unrecognised by the authorities, for on 28 March 1685 he was granted a Nova Scotian baronetcy plus a pension of £200. He had married Lady Henrietta Douglas, the sister of William, 1st Duke of Queensberry.

After the Glorious Revolution of 1688 Grierson was heavily fined and imprisoned three times. He was first captured in 1688 by Lord Kenmure but was released from his Edinburgh cell on payment of a large fine. He was later arrested in 1692 and 1693. In 1696 he was tried on a charge of forging coins, but was let off. Grierson was a Jacobite supporter, his two sons, William and Gilbert, being gaoled for their adherences.

1. NX 927832. Burial vault and memorial at Dunscore old churchyard.
2. NX 811752. Monument and grave on site of martyrdom.
3. NX 910797. Monument on site of execution.
4. NS 698008. Monument on site of martyrdom.
5. NS 670000.
6. NX 723663. Gravestones in Balmaghie churchyard.

29

MOST IMPIOUSLY AND CRUELLY MURTHERED

A small walled enclosure in the woods at Caldons, near the foot of Loch Trool in Galloway, marks the graves of six martyrs.[1] Within the walls is a white granite headstone, an exact copy in style and size of the original sandstone memorial, which had been erected by 'Old Mortality'. This older stone, having been damaged and repaired, is now protected within the museum at Newton Stewart.

On Sunday morning, 23 January 1685, a group of men gathered at the farmhouse of Caldons in order to hold a service of praise. It is said that the Covenanters had a few arms with them, probably little more than an odd gun and sword. The actual farmhouse where this service took place no longer exists, for it was replaced by a more modern steading, and the original building crumbled into a mound of boulders.

During the service a group of soldiers were in the district, looking for folk who were not in attendance at the parish church. Among the party was Colonel (or Lieutenant-General) James Douglas, Lieutenant Livingston and Cornet James Douglas. Another of the soldiers was Captain Urquhart, sometimes spelled Orchar, who had dreamed the previous night that he would die among the Chaldaeans. He thought little of this, for he was not aware of anywhere by that name, and were not the Chaldaeans people mentioned in the Bible? As he made his way across the rough countryside he was beginning to get angrier and angrier, and it is said that 'he wished the devil might make his ribs a broiling iron to his soul if he should not be revenged on the Whigs that day.' However, as the party headed up the Glen of Trool he heard one of the other soldiers refer to the house by its name, which caused him to startle and bring his horse to a standstill. He deliberated for some time as to whether he should continue, eventually deciding that it would be silly of him not to.

As the soldiers made their way up towards the loch they became aware of the faint sound of singing, which they soon recognised to be of psalms. They came upon the farmhouse of Caldons, which the soldiers surrounded, and took aim with their rifles. One of them made his way to the door, where he rattled the butt of his gun against it. The Covenanters quickly realised that it was no friendly party, and tried to make their escapes by various routes. As the doors and windows flew open and the Covenanters made their exit, the soldiers fired shots at them. A few volleys were returned from the windows of the house, one of which killed Captain Urquhart, toppling him from his horse. Other attempts at retaliation proved futile, and the Covenanters quickly gave up. No time was given to allow them to swear the Oath of Abjuration, for the soldiers had sufficient proof in order to carry out the death sentence. Shot as they tried to escape were James and Robert Dun (perhaps from Benquhat in Dalmellington parish), Thomas (or Robert) Stevenson, John Stevenson, James MacClive (all of Straiton), and Andrew MacCall.

The other Covenanters managed to escape death by running into the woods and up the surrounding hillsides. Although some soldiers set out in pursuit, no more Covenanters were captured or slain.

A third Dun brother was present – he managed to run like a hare into a copse and find some cover. Shots fired out around him, and he was pursued by two of the soldiers. He made his way as fast as he could towards Loch Trool where he lunged into the freezing January waters. With only his head above water, he swam into some thick reeds which were enough to conceal him. As the ripples in the loch died down his whereabouts was totally hidden. A few shots were fired into the loch, but the soldiers decided that either he had drowned, or else that he had somehow managed to effect an escape.

The Dun brother later dragged himself from the loch, his body blue with the cold. He managed to make his way to a friend's house, where his body temperature gradually returned to normal. Nevertheless, as a result of his exposure to the cold, he took the fever and was likely to die. A young woman took care of him, and gradually nursed him back to full recovery. It is recorded that the Covenanter and his nurse were to later marry.

Another who seems to have survived the attack on the Caldons was Mistress May Dunbar, the second daughter of Sir David Dunbar of Baldoon Castle. She was noted for her piety in life, and her beliefs meant that she was forced to leave the comforts of her father's castle and live in the wilds with shepherds and Covenanters. It is recorded that her rank in life often caused problems for her hosts, even although she cared nothing for her background.

1. NX 397788. Gravestone on site of martyrdom in Glen Trool. Original gravestone now located in Newton Stewart museum.

30

SHOT TO DEATH UPON KIRKCONNELL MOOR

A group of five Covenanter friends were in hiding on the moors of central Galloway. Each one had been forced into leaving their home for fear of being captured and murdered, for they had refused to adhere to the right of King Charles to claim that he was the head of the church. The men were John Bell, James Clement, David Halliday, Robert Lennox and Andrew MacRobert, and each no doubt had many tales to tell, though, apart from Bell, little is known about them.

John Bell was the farmer at Whiteside in the parish of Anwoth. He was a rather well-to-do farmer with many useful connections. Following the death of his father his mother married Viscount Kenmure. Bell was noted for his adherence to the Covenant, resulting in his home being a regular target for the soldiers. He lost much of his furniture to the raiding dragoons, and on one occasion three of his best horses were stolen.

In June 1680 Bell was named with 30 others as being accessories to the murder of Archbishop Sharp, which took place at Magus in Fife. He was also charged with having taken part in the rebellion at Bothwell Bridge and with burning the king's laws. Bell and those named were not present at the trial, which went ahead in any case, and each was found guilty. He had to leave his home after this and fend for himself on the hills of the county.

Graham of Claverhouse came to Whiteside in 1681 and made it his base for a number of weeks. He and his soldiers ate all the provisions in the house, after which he sent orders for the neighbours in the parish to send further supplies, leaving the district very destitute. When the soldiers did move on, they took with them numerous sheep, and the remaining horses. The roof timbers of Whiteside were toppled into the house and the building set on fire.

A number of traditional tales associated with Bell detail how he managed to escape on more than one occasion. At one time he was at his home when a group of soldiers came upon the house. A servant girl was busily arranging crockery into a dresser, and it was she who had the idea for Bell to disguise himself as a dealer in earthenware. Thus he carried away a basket filled with his own crockery, as though he was proceeding to the next house. The soldiers failed to notice that it was Bell who acted the salesman, and left empty handed. When the soldiers came to Whiteside on another occasion, Bell removed himself to another room, where he hid himself in a large oak kist. The soldiers searched the whole house, but for some reason missed the chest, perhaps assuming that it was simply filled with clothing.

Bell spent many nights hiding in a cave on the slopes of Cairnharrow, the steep hill above his home. A spy was sent to watch Whiteside, to see if any servants carried provisions to him, and thus reveal his hideout. Naturally enough some did, and next day a group of soldiers made their way to the spot, expecting to find the fugitive. Bell, however, was not in the cave at the time, but was nearby and was spotted by one of the soldiers. They set off in pursuit, Bell making his way westward to Cambret Moor. There a group of men were employed digging peats, and he was able to join them. When the soldiers arrived the leader of the diggers asked his men if they had seen a man running in the area, to which one replied that he had, and that the man had made his way further over the hill. Satisfied by this, the soldiers set off in pursuit of nobody.

As stated, little is known about the others. David Halliday

was a portioner in Miefield farm, which lies a mile to the west of Kirkconnell Moor. Robert Lennox was a farmer at Irelandton farm, which lies in the parish of Twynholm. A conventicle had taken place at Irelandton at which the Rev James Renwick preached. During the moonlit service a hunting dog appeared in their midst, followed by one of the Covenanters' sentries, who announced that some soldiers were coming that way. The group dispersed, some of them hiding in a pile of shorn wool in a barn – the smell of which was sufficient to mask their own smell and thus fool the dogs.

One day in the winter of 1684-5 the five Covenanters were hiding in a hollow of the low hills known as the Towers of Kirkconnell. On 21 February word reached Robert Grierson of Lag that they were in that vicinity, so he set out with a party of Claverhouse and Strachan's soldiers in pursuit. It was not too long before they came upon their place of refuge, and the soldiers quickly surrounded them.

Grierson called out to the men to give themselves up, which they were ready to do, for Douglas of Morton who was present was quite willing to take them alive. Grierson, however, was for none of it, and gave the orders for the five men to be shot where they stood.

'Can I have quarter of an hour to prepare myself for death?' pleaded Bell, but Lag would have none of it.

'What? devil! Ye've pray'd enough this long seven year on mountain and in cleugh,' he replied, pulling his gun and shooting Bell himself.

Bloody Grierson left instructions that the men were not to be buried, so they lay exposed on the ground for some time. It is said that when the soldiers later reached Kirkcudbright Viscount Kenmure remonstrated with Grierson over his cruelty to his step-son, whom he knew to be a gentleman, and for his refusal to allow burial. Lag replied, 'Tak' him if ye will, and salt him in your beef barrel.' Incensed at this reply, Kenmure drew his sword and would have killed Grierson had not Claverhouse, who was present, intervened.

Four of the martyrs were taken away by their friends and buried in different kirkyards – Bell in Anwoth,[1] Halliday in Balmaghie,[2] Lennox in Girthon[3] and MacRobert in Twynholm.[4] As James Clement was a stranger to the district, and thus unknown, he was interred on the spot where he was shot.[5] An interesting sequel to the martyrdom occurred in 1828. In that year a few men from Kirkcudbright with an interest in phrenology decided to dig up Clement's body to see if he was a religious fanatic. A screeching heron so frightened them that they ran off, leaving the grave open. One admitted his actions to a portrait painter by the name of Morrison who went to the site and reburied the corpse. The skull of Clement, however, was not returned to the grave, but was kept by Morrison until his death, when it was placed beside him in his coffin. A hole in its side confirmed Clement's death from a bullet.

1. NX 583562. Gravestone in Anwoth old churchyard.
2. NX 723663. Gravestone in Balmaghie churchyard.
3. NX 605533. Gravestone in Girthon old churchyard.
4. NX 664542. Gravestone in Twynholm churchyard.
5. NX667599. Gravestone on site of martyrdom. Obelisk to all martyrs at same site.

31

TO MURDER SAINTS WAS NO SWEET PLAY

The solid tower of Mearns Castle in Renfrewshire was appropriated as a garrison for the government troops. This old tower house dates from the 15th century and was owned by the Maxwells.[1] It had been taken over by the government as a punishment for the owner allowing conventicles to be held within it. Here 50 foot-soldiers and 12 horsemen were stationed, responsible for the whole county. One of those in charge was Major Balfour, who was responsible for a number of martyrdoms.

The Loudoun Covenanter, John Nisbet, was apprehended by Balfour in the spring of 1683 and executed at the cross of Kilmarnock on 4 April. His tale is told in the chapter entitled, 'Where pleasant Nisbet lies'. In the June of the same year Balfour was involved with the execution of the two Inchbelly martyrs, James Smith and John Wharry, mentioned in 'Sandy Smith's Rescue'.

In November 1683 Major Balfour was in Glasgow when he spotted John Richmond, the younger, of Knowe farm in the parish of Galston, which lies half a mile to the south of Darvel. Balfour thought that the man looked suspicious, perhaps from his country attire, and decided that he would apprehend him. Richmond was suspicious of anyone in the city, and when he realised that he was being chased ran away as fast as he could.

Balfour, however, managed to catch him, and questioned him. He also inflicted various forms of torture on him, even although he did not know who Richmond was. The only charge which Balfour was able to lay at Richmond's feet was that he had resisted when being apprehended. He was taken to the city prison where his feet were tied behind his back, and the rope passed round his neck. He was left bleeding overnight before the rope was removed. He was to be kept in gaol for almost five months.

In the same prison were four other Covenanters, James Johnston, John Main, Archibald Stewart, and James Winning. Johnston belonged to Cadder parish in Lanarkshire – nothing else is known about him. John Main came from West Monkland. He had been arrested for having arms on his possession in November 1683 (the day after Richmond's first arrest) in the Gorbals area of Glasgow. During his four months' term of imprisonment he tried to make an escape, but he was caught in the final throes of his bid for freedom. Archibald Stewart was a country boy of around 19 years old, from Underbank in the parish of Lesmahagow. He wrote a letter to his 'Christian Acquaintance' from the Glasgow tolbooth on 15 March. James Winning was a tailor in the city of Glasgow. He seems to have been unfortunate in his execution, for he admitted himself that he had regularly attended the church services held by the 'curates'. However, in February 1684 he was summonsed to appear before one of the city's bailies, who asked him questions concerning the death of Sharp and the battle of Bothwell Bridge. His answers were unsatisfactory in the eye of the bailie, and he was cast into gaol.

The five Covenanters were tried on 17 March. The Justiciary Commissioners in the city comprised Winram, Fleming, Turner, Buchan and Stirling, and they asked the usual leading questions concerning the king, Bothwell Bridge and Airds Moss. The trial lasted for a full day, the sentences being passed at 8 o'clock in the evening. The men were all found guilty, charged with rebellion and meeting with other rebels.

The Covenanters were all hanged at the cross of Glasgow at 2 o'clock on 19 March 1684. An order was issued that the head of

Richmond be cut off from his body and taken to the city tolbooth where it was to be displayed on a pike as a warning to other supposed rebels. The bodies of the martyrs were later taken to the cathedral burying ground where they were laid to rest.[2]

On 11 May 1685 Major Balfour and Captain Maitland were in that part of Lanarkshire known as the Loan of Polmadie, not far from Rutherglen Bridge. They were searching for three men, Thomas Cook, Robert Thom and John Urie, who had been reported as possible Covenanters. Cook and Urie were both seized as they worked at their looms, Thom, a labourer, shortly after. The men were questioned about their allegiances, and whether they were willing to pray for King James VII. They replied that they were willing to pray for all within the election of grace.

'Do you question the king's election?' asked Balfour.

'Sometimes we question our own,' was the reply.

This was deemed sufficient grounds to have them shot. Accordingly, Major Balfour ordered three of his musketeers to take aim. The men were given cravats to tie over their eyes, but they were allowed no time to pray. Balfour gave the order to his men to shoot, and they were left for dead on the ground. The corpses were later buried in the parish kirkyard of Cathcart.[3]

Archibald MacAulay was the chief of a clan which had its homelands on the southern edge of the Highlands. The clan seat was Ardencaple, a castle which stands at the west end of the later town of Helensburgh, and which today is but a fragmentary ruin. The MacAulays were a wild and turbulent clan, involved in many feuds with their near neighbours the Colquhouns, but their proximity to Glasgow and the lowland belt meant that they were absorbed into lowland life quicker than many of their more unruly counterparts.

Archibald was appointed a Commissioner of Supply for Dunbartonshire and later a Commissioner of Justiciary for the trial of the Covenanters of the county. His jurisdiction seems also to have extended to the county of Renfrew, for in 1685 MacAulay was to be found leading a party of dragoons and highlanders across the moors of Eaglesham parish. It had been reported that a conventicle had recently taken place somewhere on these moors and he and his soldiers were on the lookout for Covenanters making their way home from worship.

On 1 May 1685, at a farm known as Cowplie or Cowplaw, which lay below Melowther Hill, three miles south-west of Eaglesham, two Covenanters were spotted. The soldiers made a dash towards them and caught the first, Gabriel Thomson, of whom nothing is known. He was shot for his Covenanting adherences.

The second Covenanter, Robert Lockhart, had managed to make his escape but the soldiers were quick to pursue him. He was caught a mile further to the south-west, at another farm known as Sparrow Hall, where he too was summarily killed. Their corpses were later taken under darkness to Eaglesham, where they were laid to rest in the kirkyard. The grave was quickly dug during the night, and to reduce the size of lair required to be excavated, the two men were buried 'heids and thraws' in the old Scots parlance, that is side by side but head to foot.[4]

Two miles to the south-east of Eaglesham are the farms of Enoch, High Craig and Stonebyres, which were the homes of the Young family. Andrew and William Young were both persecuted for their Covenanting adherences. The soldiers from Mearns arrived at Enoch one day and finding the brothers absent set fire to the house and stole the cattle. On another occasion Andrew was ploughing with his nephew when the soldiers apprehended him. Just as he was being bound to prevent his escape William appeared. Spotting what was happening he came to the soldiers with his loaded musket and demanded that his brother be set free. William told his son to loosen the ropes whilst he watched for any false moves from the soldiers. The lad was a bit apprehensive at first, but his father said, 'Loose him, and let me see them dare to touch a hair of your head.'

Naturally, William and Andrew had to go into exile after this. They spent six months hiding in a peat stack, to which food was taken for them. William fought at Bothwell but survived, and it is known that he managed to escape from the clutches of the soldiers at least once after that. Both brothers were listed on a roll of fugitives, but only Andrew was captured. He was taken to gaol in Glasgow from where he and some others managed to escape, but unluckily he was caught again and this time banished to Virginia. After the Glorious Revolution he was sailing home but died en route. William survived the persecutions and was later to be buried in Eaglesham churchyard.

Another Eaglesham Covenanter was John Watt. He was attending a prayer meeting when it was disturbed by a party of soldiers. In the mêlée shots were fired, but all the Covenanters managed to escape. Watt, however, had long hair and one side of it was pulled from the roots in a struggle. He later had to shave his head, for new hair did not grow where it had been hauled out by the roots. Watt then fled to Holland where he remained for six or seven years. He did not return until a few years after the Revolution, leading his wife to believe that he was dead. One day, however, he made his way home. His wife fainted at the sight of him.

James Algie and John Park were joint-tenants of a farm on the Nether Pollok estate, which at the time was still owned by the Pollok family. This farm was at Kennishead, which in the 17th century was a small village four miles south west of Glasgow, near to Eastwood, but which is now a suburb of the city.

James Algie seems to have had no real Covenanting convictions to begin with, for he was quite happy to attend the parish church even after the minister had been ousted and a curate put in his place. John Park was of a different persuasion, however, being a staunch adherent of the Covenants. He influenced Algie to such an extent that Algie stopped attending the curate's services. Around the same time as Algie stopped going to the church both he and Park decided to relinquish the lease on their farm.

The factor, or land-agent, who had been instrumental in persuading Algie and Park to take on the lease was incensed at their giving it up, and plotted to get his own back. One way of doing this was to report the two men to the authorities for their failure to appear at church. The factor wrote a letter to the regality bailie and sent a nephew with it to the bailie's home in Paisley on Sunday 1 February. In it he accused Algie and Park 'of rebellious principles'. He claimed they disowned the king's authority and were adherents of the Apologetic Declaration. The factor concluded by saying 'that it was his business, as a judge ordinary, to notice them, as he would be answerable.'

The nephew was kept locked-up in the bailie's home until that morning's service was finished. After questioning him as to where exactly Algie and Park lived, he was allowed to go free.

A party of soldiers then set out from Paisley for Kennishead, where they came upon the two friends' house. Forcing an entry, they discovered the men were about to engage in family worship. Some dragoons grabbed them, and their hands were bound behind their backs. The men were then taken five miles west to Paisley, where they were put in cells in the town's tolbooth, a building erected at the Cross in 1610 and ornamented by the addition of a clock in 1647. On the evening of the very day they were captured questions were put to them, but the answers seem not to have pleased the authorities, so they were returned to their cells once more.

Algie and Park remained imprisoned for a couple of days. They were allowed visitors and James Hay (afterwards minister at Kilsyth) is known to have spoken to them. It is said that Hay became aware that the two men were not fanatics, and that they knew little of the background to the current troubles. Algie and Park, however, could repeat a few soundbites which they had picked up at conventicles they had attended.

The trial was set for the morning of Tuesday, 3 February 1685, when Algie and Park were hauled before the judge. However, they were refused the right of a lawyer to plead for their case. In the proceedings they were told that they would be required to take the Oath of Abjuration as well as the Test, which affirmed the king's supremacy over all matters civil and ecclesiastical. The men responded, 'If to save our lives we must take the

Test, and the Abjuration will not save us, then we will take no oaths at all.' At ten o'clock the sentence of death was therefore passed on the two men.

It seems that Algie and Park had tried to get off on a technicality by swearing the Abjuration Oath but not taking the Test. Having passed the sentence, one of the judges boasted, 'They thought to have tricked the judges, but I have tricked them.'

At two o'clock, Algie and Park were led out from the gaol to the scaffold which stood at the burgh cross. A public execution took place, the authorities using the two men as an example to anyone who felt they might ignore the laws of the land. Both wished to address the crowds in the busy town centre, but to prevent the public from hearing what they had to say the soldiers beat their drums loudly and consistenly. After the two men had died, their bodies were interred at the town's Gallow Green.[5]

The execution had taken place just four hours after the sentence had been passed. This was done for a good reason – to frighten a neighbour of the two martyrs into taking the Test Act. This man was Robert King, a miller at Pollokshaws, and he had been apprehended that day for non-conformity. He was questioned at Paisley tolbooth, but the authorities regarded his answers as being unsatisfactory. He was offered the Test, but he refused to swear it. The soldiers took him from his cell to a window, from where the two martyrs hanging from the gibbet on the outside wall were visible. King was warned that if he did not swear the act before the hour was out, when three blasts from a trumpet would sound, then he too would join them. After the second blast of the trumpet, King was so terrified for his life that he broke down and swore his allegiance to the king. Although set free, it is recorded that he regretted his decision for the rest of his life.

1. NS 552553.
2. NS 602656. Memorial in Glasgow Cathedral, located on stairway down to crypt. Richmond also commemorated at Galston churchyard (NS 500367).
3. NS 584609. Gravestone in old Cathcart churchyard.
4. NS 574519. Monument to Lockhart and Thomson in Eaglesham churchyard.
5. NS 471639. Monument behind Martyrs' Memorial Church at entrance to Woodside Cemetery, Broomlands Street.

32

SOME MUIRKIRK COVENANTERS

There are a number of tales of Covenanters who were shot in the fields simply for being in possession of a Bible. Such were the laws at the time that anyone found to be carrying a Bible, particularly on days other than the Sabbath, were assumed to be Covenanters going to or returning from a conventicle. Many tales recount men who were discovered in this way and shot without any form of trial.

The tale of William Adam of Muirkirk in Ayrshire is typical. He was employed as a labourer at Upper Wellwood farm, but was noted for his non-conformity. In March 1685 he was standing by the side of the Proscribe Burn, near to the farm, awaiting his fiancée, a servant lass from a neighbouring farm. Whilst he waited he took out his Bible and began to read it. So engrossed did he become that he was unaware of the approaching soldiers under the command of General Thomas Dalyell and Lieutenant Strachan (or Straiton). When the soldiers spotted that he was reading a Bible, Dalyell ordered them to shoot him. Adam was asked no questions, and he was given no time to appeal for his life. After this the soldiers began to ride back towards Muirkirk.

On the way they had to cross a wooden bridge over the infant River Ayr. Halfway across the bridge was a young woman, Adam's fiancée, who was rushing in the opposite direction. She had heard the sound of gunfire a few minutes earlier and feared for her fiancé's life. As she crossed the bridge one of the dragoons tried to push her off the deck with the flat of his sword. Such was her rage that she grabbed the sword and managed to break it into two bits, which she then threw into the water. The dragoon then made to attack the girl, but Dalyell is said to have held him back, laughing at him for being beaten by a 'mere girl'.

She then ran away towards Upper Wellwood where she found her fiancé lying in the grass, dead from a bullet wound. He was buried on the exact spot where he fell.[1]

Although William Adam was a known adherent of the Covenant, it has been surmised that he was actually killed in error for another. The owner of Upper Wellwood at the time was William Campbell, who had two sons, William and John, aged 20 and 18 respectively. All were suspected by the local authorities of being Covenanters.

In August 1684 a band of Lord Ross's troopers, under the command of James Irvine of Bonshaw, arrived at the farm, hoping to catch William Campbell. The soldiers had been divided into two, one group searching the surrounding moors, the other heading directly to the farm steading. The group on the moors actually managed to arrest the two sons, in whose pockets Bibles were found. They were taken down the hill to Upper Wellwood, where Irvine of Bonshaw was. They found him in a rage, however, for William Campbell had managed to make an escape.

The farm was plundered in full view of the two lads, and all the valuables were looted by the soldiers. Tying them to the back of two horses they were taken north to Newmilns where they were placed in gaol, where it is recorded they were savagely maltreated by their keepers. On the following Sunday they were transferred to Glasgow and placed on trial. They were asked to pray for the king as head of the church, but time and again they replied that they would pray for the king's soul, but not as head of the church, a place only fit for Jesus Christ. The trial was inconclusive, and they were kept in custody for another week.

The Campbell brothers were then transferred under the command of Lieutenant Murray to Edinburgh, where they were imprisoned in the Canongate Tolbooth. They were questioned by the Privy Council, who asked whether they had fought at Bothwell Bridge. John replied, 'At that time I was only a young lad of 13 years and had not.' It was said that the clerk to the council minuted the reply thus:

As to Bothwell, the prisoner says, 'I was young then; but had I been old enough I would have been there.'

When this statement was read back to him John refused to sign it and accused the clerk of putting words into his mouth. Despite threats from the authorities he resolutely refused to sign it and was sent back into gaol.

William Campbell the younger was questioned separately. The council used the ancient tactic of telling one that the other had already confessed when he hadn't, in the hope that the other would follow suit. In an attempt to find out whether this was true or not, John Campbell tried to smuggle a letter to his brother, the paper taken by Margaret Baird. She was caught with this letter in her possession and the authorities administered the thumbscrews in order to induce a confession from her.

On 13 August the two Campbells and 11 other Covenanters managed to break out of their prison. They used two gimlets, a chisel and a piece of iron to cut their way through the window. One of these escapees was injured as he dropped from the widow and a second, surnamed Young, was soon recaptured. The Campbells returned to Muirkirk where they hid on the moors for many months. They met their father, and another William Campbell from Middle Wellwood. They remained in hiding throughout the winter of 1684-5, building for themselves a remote shelter. Some friends brought provisions to them, but most of their food was caught in the wild. On one occasion the hideout was discovered by the soldiers but the Covenanters managed to effect an escape.

William Campbell the younger was eventually released from prison, but he died of consumption in the spring of 1686. John survived until the Glorious Revolution when he was able to raise a troop of dragoons and lead them in Lord Cardross's regiment in the service of William III. Old William survived until 1715.

1. NS 672256. Gravestone near Upper Wellwood farm, Muirkirk. Adam is also commemorated on memorials in Muirkirk cemetery (NS 696278) and Smallburn Road, Muirkirk (NS 685265).

33
SHOT AT MINNYHIVE MOSS

In the middle reaches of Glen Cairn, to the east of Moniaive in Dumfriesshire, is a long stretch of level farmland. It is known today as the Race Muir, but originally was Moniaive Moss, though with the advent of land drainage and ground improvements, this is something of a misnomer. In the midst of one of the fields is a large boulder, rounded at the corners, on which can be faintly discerned the words *W Smith W*. This boulder marks the spot where a Covenanter breathed his last.[1]

William Smith was the son of William Smith, farmer at Hill farm, which stood one mile to the east of Moniaive, near to Crawfordton House. He worked on the land with his father, and like him was a keen reader of his Bible.

On 2 March 1685, whilst Smith was labouring in the fields of Hill farm, he was surprised by the appearance of a small group of soldiers under the command of Cornet Bailie. The men came quickly towards him, and asked him the usual questions regarding whether he would swear allegiance to the king and would acknowledge him as head of the church. Smith, who was only 19 years old, refused to answer the cornet's questions. The soldier became angry with the lad, and took him prisoner. He was placed on the back of a horse and taken to Caitloch House, two miles to the west, where he was locked up in a room while the soldiers decided what should be done next.

Caitloch[2] seems to have originally been a place of refuge for the Covenanters, for it is known that Rev John Blackader fled there when he was ejected from his parish. The house was owned by William Fergusson but after he fled to Holland for his Covenanting adherence the house was taken over by the authorities and used as a garrison. Fergusson's wife, Elizabeth Hunter, died in the Netherlands. On one occasion some soldiers arrived at the house and there found Alexander Fergusson, but by means of a ruse he was able to escape their sentence. Tradition claims that there was a secret tunnel from the house down to the Dalwhat Water. The Fergusson's forfeiture was rescinded after the Restoration.

Word reached Smith's father that his son had been captured by the dragoons. He immediately set off two miles down the glen to Maxwelton House, the seat of his laird, Sir Robert Laurie. It was Smith the elder's hope that Sir Robert would be able to speak on the young lad's behalf. At Maxwelton the family were busily celebrating the wedding of one of the Laurie daughters, and the elder Smith hoped that the happy celebrations would make Sir Robert more inclined to help another family. He told Sir Robert what had happened to young William, and that he was currently held at Caitloch House at the command of Cornet Bailie. Sir Robert informed Smith that he would summon Bailie to a meeting the next day.

The proposed meeting between Laurie and Bailie took place on 3 March at the kirk of Glencairn, which is located in the village of Kirkland. Young Smith was brought before Laurie who asked him whether he would swear the Oath of Abjuration. Again the farm-lad refused. Laurie was annoyed at his refusal and blew into a rage. He was noted as being 'an oppressor and persecutor' and as he had been appointed as a commissioner to ensure the laws against nonconformity were put into place, he decided that the lad should die. Cornet Bailie, however, reckoned that Laurie's sentence was illegal, as there had been no trial before a jury. Laurie was incensed at the Cornet's opinions and threatened to have him reported for sparing Smith for so long.

Also present at the meeting was Douglas of Stenhouse, another small lairdship, which lies near to Tynron village. Douglas was noted for capturing Andrew Ferguson, one of his own servants. He had been listed as a fugitive and when Douglas caught him he was sent to gaol in Glasgow, where he died in 1685.

William Smith was held prisoner once more, perhaps for as long as 26 days, if the date on the gravestone is correct. At any rate, on 29 March 1685 he was taken from his prison cell and marched out to the Race Muir, near to where he was originally caught. Word had spread throughout the parish that the execution was about to take place, and a good number of folk were present to witness the event. Smith is said to have faced death with great composure, and explained to the assembled audience that he was guilty of no crime nor of rebelling, except that he had spoken to a number of Covenanters in the past and that he refused to reveal their whereabouts to the soldiers.

William Smith was forced to sit on a large boulder in the field. He was blindfolded, and the soldiers took aim with their rifles. At the command of Sir Robert they fired together, killing the young lad.

The persecution of the Covenanter did not end there, however. Sir Robert instructed that his body was not to be given a Christian burial. Instead, he informed the soldiers that the corpse was to be taken to Hill farm and buried beneath the flat stone which formed the threshold of the farmhouse, so that each time his mother and father entered or left their home they would be reminded of their son's actions. Smith's remains stayed beneath Hill farm's doorstep until after the Revolution of 1688 when his father arranged for them to be disinterred and buried with dignity in the kirkyard of Tynron. Later, a commemorative flat slab was erected over his mortal remains.[3]

1. NX 787905. Boulder with crude carving in field.
2. NX 764918.
3. NX 806930. Gravestone in Tynron churchyard.

34

A TYGER RATHER THAN A SCOT

With 11 others, James White was one of a party of Covenanters who had formed a small prayer group which met at Little Blackwood farm, in the parish of Kilmarnock, Ayrshire, in April 1685. The farm lay in open countryside near to Moscow, four miles north-east of the town. Little Blackwood was at that time tenanted by James Paton and formed part of Grougar estate. Nothing now survives of this place – it was located on the present Dykescroft farm, where a field is still known as Blackwood Park.

When James White went to Little Blackwood he had taken a firelock with him, the only member of the prayer group to do so. The gun, which was a fairly new invention at the time, was to result in his own death.

Peter (or Patrick in some accounts) Inglis was in charge of a company of troopers, based at a garrison in the 16th-century keep in the small town of Newmilns. He was the son of Captain John Inglis and one account describes him with the rank of "cornet". Peter Inglis had heard that an illegal prayer meeting was planned for Little Blackwood, so had set off with a small group of soldiers. On reaching the farm they split up and surrounded the building. Something disturbed the meeting inside – perhaps a farm dog had heard something and started to bark. In any case, the Covenanters abruptly ended their meeting, and tried to make an escape. As they stumbled about in the darkness White fired his gun, and though the priming burned, it failed to ignite the charge. But the flash was enough to light up his face, revealing his whereabouts to the dragoons who were quick to respond, and loosed a volley of shots at him. White crashed to the ground, dead.

John Gemmell and James Paton managed to escape from the house and headed for the byre. The soldiers spotted them and followed. In the byre Gemmell struggled with one of the soldiers and managed to yank off the bayonet from his gun. Using this he wounded the soldier and made his escape. Paton was less successful, being arrested by the soldiers. Some of those who fled to the innermost room in the house tried to burrow their way through the thatched roof. Only two made it to freedom; the rest were caught in the act. In all, eight Covenanters were apprehended and three managed to escape.

Peter Inglis found an axe on the farm and with it struck a blow at White's lifeless corpse. He severed his head and, grabbing it by the hair, carried it back to his horse. He tied it to the saddle, and returned with his trophy to Newmilns. The remainder of White's body was left lying on the ground and was trampled by the cattle which were stolen from the farm. His remains were later interred at Fenwick.[1]

James Paton's wife, who had a young child at her breast, pleaded with Inglis to spare their lives. It is claimed that Inglis did so because he had at one time been friendly with Mrs Paton when she lived at her father's home of Darwhilling, which had been garrisoned by the soldiers.

The Covenanters were made to leave the inner room one at a time, crawling on their hands and knees. When David Findlay came out first one of the soldiers wounded him with his bayonet, for which he received a cursing from Inglis. The other Covenanters crawled out without being touched. They were arrested and taken to the garrison at Newmilns. On the way to the tower Findlay was creating some bother for the soldiers due to his wound. Inglis decided that it would be better to have him shot, and ordered one of the soldiers to carry this out.

The following day word had spread throughout Loudoun that White was dead, and that his body had been decapitated. The news was shocking enough to the decent folk of the valley, but they were disgusted when Inglis appeared from the garrison, carrying the head by its hair. On the burgh green he threw it into the air and when it landed he and the soldiers kicked it around, playing a makeshift game of football.

The eight prisoners were held in the vault of Newmilns Tower for a second night. Next morning Captain John Inglis brought them out to the castle courtyard where they were blindfolded. He was about to execute them when some officials of the burgh intervened and stated that he was probably being a bit premature in his actions. They told him that the present authorities would not mind him killing them, but should there be a change in government he may be later called before the Crown for imprisoning men and executing them without trial. Inglis acquiesced, and the men were returned to their cell. He then sent Peter Inglis to Edinburgh for an order of execution, which he readily received from the Privy Council.

The parishioners of Loudoun were scheming in the background. A group of men made plans to spring their release and determined upon a night on which to do so. However, for a reason which they long afterward said they could never work out, they decided to carry out the gaol-break the night before. This was fortunate, for the execution had been arranged for the following day – Inglis now having his authority from Edinburgh. Many said that it was Divine intervention which had changed their minds.

The group of rescuers numbered around 60 and included John Browning of Lanfine. They approached the tower in silence and a group of them easily overpowered the guards. In the ensuing scramble two of the soldiers were shot. Using large hammers which they had borrowed from the local smithy they battered the gate which locked the men in. All were able to escape, the only casualty in the mêlée being John Law, one of the rescuers, who was shot by a soldier from an upper window in the tower. He was buried where he fell, in the castle yard.[2]

It is said that Peter Inglis was so frightened by the mob which had attacked the tower that he ran from the keep to the house where he had been put up whilst staying in Newmilns and promptly hid beneath the bed! Some accounts claim that he was later dismissed from his post for allowing the attack to succeed.

Next morning the soldiers were searching the district in order to try and recapture the prisoners. They arrested Jasper Tough, an apothecary, who had given assistance to the Covenanters who were wounded in the attack on the castle. He was taken to Dean Castle and held prisoner for some time.

Another party arrived at Wee or East Threepwood farm, also known as Croonan, which stood near to the Burn Anne, south of Galston. This was the home of James Smith, who had given the prisoners some food. He seems to have tried to escape and was wounded by the soldiers at his front door. They took him to Mauchline where Lieutenant-General William Drummond of Cromlix was based. He was held in Mauchline Castle for some time but was to die later of his wounds.[3]

1. NS 465434. Gravestone in Fenwick churchyard.
2. NS 537373. Memorial stone at Newmilns Tower, a second at Newmilns church, and also commemorated on Newmilns Covenanters' monument.
3. NS 498272. Gravestone in Mauchline churchyard. Memorial cairn on Gallow Law, near Galston (NS 532354).

35

BY BLOODY DRUMMOND THEY WERE SHOT

Lieutenant-General (later Sir) William Drummond of Cromlix and Strathallan was a friend of Dalyell of the Binns. They had both fought in Europe where they were described as having 'acted like bandits'; and Drummond was later charged with promoting rebellion and imprisoned for a time. Later, he returned to favour and was given the command of some government troops. In 1661 he is known to have corresponded with Archbishop Sharp of St Andrews. Drummond fought for the government at Rullion Green in 1666 – the martyrs' grave in Ayr refers to him as 'Herod' Drummond.

William Drummond was given a commission on 21 April 1685, succeeding James Douglas, 'for pursueing, suppressing, and utterly destroying all such fugitive rebels as resist and disturb the peace and quiet of his majesties government.' He was 'to do everything for securing peace,' which included shooting, hanging, fining and torturing, and Drummond was keen to make his mark. For a time he made his headquarters the old tower of Mauchline Castle and five martyrs were executed on Mauchline Loan at his command on 6 May 1685 (See Chapter 6). It is recorded that he collected the fines exacted on the landowners of the county of Ayr and he was also infamous for fining the poorer classes.

Soon after his appointment, Drummond and his men were

crossing the heathery moors in the south of Ayrshire. In those days there were no real roads across this part of the country, and the route taken by travellers often varied. On this occasion the soldiers had followed the Duisk River as far as Loch Duisk before striking south, heading for the height of Craig Airie Fell, the highest point in Wigtownshire.

In the distance the soldiers spotted a group of lapwings wheeling and gyrating in the sky. They kept darting into the air before circling back down towards the same spot before rising up again. At first no real notice was taken of their movement, but suddenly one of the party realised that lapwings, or peesweeps as they were known locally, were wont to do this when something or someone was near to their nests. When it dawned on them that this might be a Covenanter they decided to take a closer look.

Crossing the tussocky ground towards Craigmoddie Fell the soldiers became aware of a figure in the distance. They altered their route to circle round behind him, and thus take him by surprise. As the soldiers came upon the figure they discovered it was Alexander Linn, about whom little is known. It is said that he was a shepherd at Laris farm, which lies in the parish of New Luce. It is worth remembering that Rev Alexander Peden was for a time the minister there, and as such Linn would have been one of his congregation. Linn was out on the moors of Derry tending his flock of sheep when he decided to take a rest in the heather and look at his small pocket Bible. When the soldiers appeared from the rear he was suddenly startled and jumped upright. The fact that he was out on the moors with a Bible was sufficient to give the soldiers the right to shoot him, which they did at once. Some later time Linn's body was discovered and buried on the exact spot where he was martyred.[1]

Later that day Drummond and his dragoons met with the laird of Bellimore-on-Tig. The laird knew of a Covenanter's hideout and he was taking the soldiers to it. As they approached the site they spotted two men on a low hill above the village of Barrhill. They were Daniel MacIlwrick (or Meiklewrick), tenant in Altercannoch farm, and his friend John Murchie from the village of Barr. The two Covenanters spied the soldiers in the distance as they came towards them and tried to make an escape. They headed for Altercannoch farm, but the soldiers on horseback were quicker than them and they were soon caught. Drummond questioned the two men, and the soldiers gave them a quick body search which revealed bibles concealed beneath their clothes – again enough for the soldiers to execute them on the spot.

The two men were told to prepare for death. They sat on the ground and prayed. Drummond gave the command to fire. Gunshots resounded over the valley and the two martyrs were left where they fell. It is said that MacIlwrick's fiancée was one of those who buried his corpse. That night Drummond's men returned to Kildonan House where they threw the two Covenanters' bibles into the fire, stirring up the burning pages with the tips of their swords.[2]

The MacAdam family were the proprietors of the parish of Carsphairn in Galloway, having as their seats the ancient castles of Waterhead and Lagwyne. They are said to be descended from the MacGregor clan, but of this there is now no proof.

In the second half of the 17th century the head of the family was William MacAdam, who was married to Bessie Fullarton. Their eldest son was Gilbert MacAdam, who was noted for his Covenanting adherences. He was known for sheltering some of the persecuted men, as well as for holding prayer-meetings in his house. In 1682 he was reported to the authorities for not attending the church services held by the curate and therefore arrested. He was taken to Dumfries where he was tried and later released on his father-in-law, James Dun of Benquhat, giving the security of £400 for his appearance when required. MacAdam, however, refused to attend the meeting to which he was summoned, so his father-in-law lost the money.

The soldiers seized him again, and this time took him to Glasgow. There he was offered the chance of swearing the Oath of Allegiance but this MacAdam refused to do. The authorities then sentenced him to be banished to the American plantations. He was transported there on a boat belonging to Bailie Gibson, but on his arrival he managed to purchase his freedom with £20 his father had given him prior to embarkation. He was therefore able to return to Scotland in 1685.

In the June or July of that year, MacAdam was in attendance at a prayer meeting which was being held in Hugh Campbell's home, which stood in the grounds of Kirkmichael House. A group of soldiers led by Sir Archibald Kennedy of Culzean Castle and John Reid of Ballochmyle were in the vicinity, having been told of the meeting. They surrounded the house and on forcing an entry those inside tried to make an escape, but MacAdam was shot in the process.[3]

In the vicinity of Blairquhan Mill, near Straiton, William MacKergue[4] was executed for his covenanting adherences in 1685; Sir Archibald Kennedy being responsible for this death. Another Carrick martyr was John MacClorgan. He was visiting Drummellan farm when a party of soldiers arrived during the darkness. In the attack he was killed, but it is not known by whom.[5]

John MacLymont was the farmer at Auchalton farm, near Crosshill in Ayrshire. This was only three miles from the garrison at Blairquhan and he was targetted by the soldiers for many years. His home was often searched and on one occasion burned to the ground. He and his family were forced to live rough on Glenalla Moor and though the soldiers continued to search for them they were lucky and escaped detection. When the times of peace arrived at the Revolution they were able to return to the farm, MacLymont surviving until 1 November 1714, aged 69. He was interred at Maybole. Many years after his death, when the thatched roof of the farm was being replaced, an old sword was discovered hidden in the roof. This may have been purchased at Maybole fair in November 1677, at which so many swords were sold that a report was sent to the government authorities.[6]

1. NX 244726. Gravestone on Craigmoddie Fell.
2. NX 232819. Gravestone by side of Cross Water.
3. NS 345089. Gravestone in Kirkmichael churchyard. Also commemorated on burial enclosure at Carsphairn (NX 562931).
4. NS 374053. No memorial.
5. NX 225993. Gravestone in Old Dailly churchyard.
6. NS 301099. Gravestone in Maybole collegiate churchyard.

36

BABEL'S BASTARD
HAD COMMAND

Andrew Watson and John Ferguson were sleekit men. They became acquainted with the hiding place of five Covenanters who were fugitives from the justice which prevailed in the 17th century. Over a period of time the two visited the Covenanters, winning their trust, but they were to turn their backs on them on 28 April 1685.

The five Covenanters were close friends, having to flee their homes and spend their days in hiding, avoiding the soldiers who had their names in their list of wanted men. Robert Grierson was known to have taken part in the Covenanters' successful rescue at Enterkin Pass, and thus was being searched out by the soldiers. Robert Edgar had been asked at one time to take the Oath of Abjuration but had refused, resulting in him having to leave home. The other three were John Gibson, brother of James Gibson, the heritor of Ingliston Mains farm, James Bennoch who also lived in the parish, and Robert Mitchell, who belonged to Cumnock in Ayrshire.

The five Covenanters had found a secret cave in Glen Cairn, Dumfriesshire, where they spent some time hiding. Andrew Watson and John Ferguson found this and were not long in contacting the authorities to report their discovery. Colonel James Douglas, who was the brother of the Duke of Queensberry, and Lieutenant Livingston gathered together a small group of soldiers and when they were ready asked the two informers to lead them to the cave, which was probably located somewhere on the Green Craig or Dalmacallan Hill.

The soldiers surrounded the mouth of the cave and fired shots into it, wounding one of the occupants. The five men were then easily apprehended. Under the guard of loaded rifles they were marched down to Ingliston Mains farm, where they were herded into a walled enclosure. Colonel Douglas decided that there was sufficient evidence for their execution. John Gibson's mother and sister, who lived nearby, came as fast as they could to the scene and pleaded with the soldiers to let them speak to him. Gibson told them that this was the most joyful day of his life, that they should not 'give way to grief, but to bless the Lord upon his account, who had made him willing and ready to suffer for His cause and interest.'

The men were lined up next to a thorn tree and the command was given to shoot John Gibson first. He was given time to pray, which he did 'to the admiration and conviction even of the soldiers.' After singing some verses of a Psalm and reading from the 16th chapter of John's gospel he was shot dead. The other men, despite their protestations, were given no time for prayer, Douglas and Livingston becoming impatient. In rapid succession the shots rang out across the glen. The men slumped to the ground. John Ferguson thought that one of them was not quite dead, so he withdrew a sword and thrust it into his body to make sure. Even after this the martyr was able to call out, 'Though every hair of my head were a man, I am willing to die all those deaths for Christ and His cause.'

The five martyrs were left where they fell.[1] Later the local folk came to the site of the martyrdom. Robert Grierson was recognised as having come from Balmaclellan, in the Stewartry of Kirkcudbright. Consequently, his corpse was taken back to his home village where he was laid to rest.[2] The four other martyrs were buried at Kirkland of Glencairn churchyard.[3]

1. NX 796895. Gravestone at Ingliston Mains farm.
2. NX 651791. Gravestone in churchyard.
3. NX 809905. Gravestones in Kirkland of Glencairn churchyard.

37

BUTCHERED
BY CLAVERS

On the moors north of Muirkirk in Ayrshire stands a lonely farmhouse, known as Priesthill. A long track from the Strathaven road takes one to it, a mile and a half from the public road. From here an indistinct pathway can be followed further east, for a further mile, to the side of a small stream. Here the visitor may find a memorial and flat gravestone in memory of one John Brown.[1] These stand near to where his original farmhouse stood, though this has long-since disappeared. Some old maps and references name this Priestshiel. It was excavated in the first half of the 20th century, when various domestic implements were found. In life, Brown had fewer than a score sheep and a cow.

John Brown's death is one which achieved a certain notoriety, even in Covenanting times. He was noted in the Ayrshire and Lanarkshire district as the 'Christian carrier', for he was a fit man and took parcels by packhorse across the countryside. He was a devout Christian, and it is said that he would probably have been one of the finest preachers were it not for the fact that he had a speech impediment. In 1666 he was reprimanded by Muirkirk kirk session. According to the minute book:

> *Johne Broune in Blacksyde most sinfullie, and scandalouslie upoun the Sabboth day brought ane load upon his horse out of the Dyknouck in the parish of Dalgain [Sorn] into his awin house*

upon May 1666 at ten houres of the day witness unto it Mr Johne Reid minister and Gavin Wilson in Lammontburn.

At that time he lived at Blackside, in the parish of Sorn.

In 1680 Brown was reported with Thomas Richard of Greenock Mains and Jean Weir in Darnhunch for not attending the curate's church. Although Jean managed to claim she did not attend church as 'she had no shoune', Brown's response was noted in the session minutes:

I myself [the minister] being present, gave his ressonnes: 1st. Yt I kepit cumpani with ye indulged minister. Next. I paid sesse... Ye 3 ressonne yt he gave was yt he whom he looked on as ye treu messenger of jesus christ who is now lying at Airsmose [Richard Cameron] declared and dischargit yt as they wold ansuar to god in grat day yt nun should heir any of thes indulgit persones and therfor he would not.

Thomas Richard was later to suffer martyrdom at Cumnock (see chapter 27).

Brown was known to Rev Alexander Peden, who described him as 'a clear shining light, the greatest Christian I ever conversed with.' Peden actually conducted John Brown's second wedding. The service was arranged to take place on the open moorland in 1682, and Peden blessed the matrimonial vows of Brown and Isabel Weir. In one of his famous prophetic speeches, Peden warned Isabel that her husband would be taken from her when she least expected it, and that his death would be a bloody one. He advised her to keep linen with which to make winding sheets, or grave-clothes.

In 1682 a meeting of the Societies took place at Priesthill, where they decided on one of their number to be chosen to be educated for the ministry. James Renwick was selected, and he was soon packed off to Holland where he received his training. Throughout the struggle, Priesthill was a noted place for meetings of the Covenanters, and many hill-men arrived at Brown's cottage. They were welcomed in, and many an illegal service was held there. Brown also ran a Bible class for the young boys. In the Royal Proclamation of fugitives, issued on 5 May

1684, Brown's name was listed with many others.

On 1 May 1685 Peden arrived at the Brown household. He spent the night with them, and they enjoyed his company. On the following morning, as he made his way out the door, he noticed the dank overcast mist. His countenance changed suddenly, and he turned to Isabel Brown and uttered the lines, 'Poor woman! A fearful morning – a dark misty morning.' Isabel remembered only too well his earlier prophecy.

After morning prayers with his family, John Brown and his nephew, John Browning of Lanfine, left the house to go and cut peats, to build up a store for the winter months. They had not gone long when they found themselves surrounded by soldiers, the commander being John Graham of Claverhouse. They began questioning them – Why had they not attended the curate's church? Why did the leaders of the Covenanters visit Brown? And why he would not pray for the king? Claverhouse interrogated Browning first of all. He admitted that he had taken part in the 'attake of Neumilles', when the Little Blackwood Covenanters gained their freedom and two dragoons were killed. He was also forced to reveal names of some folk from the Irvine valley who had attended recent military training events held on the far side of Cairn Table from Muirkirk. Browning was sentenced to death and ordered to pray, but before he was to be shot Clavers changed his mind. He then passed him into the care of Lieutenant General William Drummond, who was to have him hanged on Mauchline Loan on 6 May 1685.

The soldiers then asked John Brown to swear the Oath of Allegiance, but he refused. It was noted that in his answers to Claverhouse, Brown's stutter left him, and he is said to have responded with the eloquence of a preacher.

Janet Brown, the young daughter of Priesthill, had spotted the soldiers and ran to her mother to tell her. Isabel cried aloud, 'The thing I feared has come upon me. O give me grace for this hour.' Claverhouse's men were in the meantime bringing Brown back towards his cottage. In front of his wife, daughter and baby boy in arms, they threw him to the ground and told him to prepare to die. Brown, who was 58 years old, began praying earnestly, remembering his family, praying for the persecuted church and the men who adhered to its principles. Claverhouse's temper grew as the prayers went on and on. He interrupted Brown three times and bellowed that he 'gave him time to pray, not preach.'

Claverhouse ordered his men to shoot the Covenanter, but for some reason they seem to have been slow in responding, perhaps concerned that they were to perform the act in front of a woman and her children. A letter written by Claverhouse from Galston to the Marquis of Queensberry, dated 3 May 1685, notes what happened:

> May it please your Grace. On Frayday last, among the hilles betwixt Douglas and the Plellands, we perseued tuo fellous a great way throu the mosses, and in end seised them. They had no armes about them, and denayed they had any, but being asked if they would take the abjuration, the eldest of the two, called John Brown, refused it; nor would he swear not to ryse in armes against the King, but said he kneu no king; upon which, and there being found bullets and match in his house, and treasonable papers, I cause shoot him dead, which he suffered very unconcernedly... The soldiers found out a house in the hille underground that could hold a dusen of men and there were swords and pistolles in it; and this fellou declared they belonged to his uncle, and that he had lurked in that place ever since Bothwell where he was in armes.

Isabel ran to her husband, and lifted his body onto her lap. Claverhouse asked her what she thought of her husband now.

'I ay thocht muckle o' him, but now more than ever,' was the reply.

Some friends came to her aid as soon as they heard what had happened and helped Isabel bury Brown near to where he fell. It is said that Claverhouse suffered nightmares afterwards, and that the words of Brown's prayers continually haunted him.

1. NS730315. Gravestone near to site of Brown's cottage. Also commemorated on monuments at Muirkirk cemetery (NS 696278) and Smallburn Road (NS 685265).

38

WITHIN THE SEA TY'D TO A STAKE

One of the most wicked and despicable events in the troubled years of the Covenant took place outside Wigtown. The village, for it is by no means a town, stands on a low hill above the shores of Wigtown Bay, a part of the greater Solway Firth. Down by the waterside, seemingly located inland (but the waters have receded gradually over the years) is a stone memorial marking the spot where two women were martyred for their Covenanting beliefs.[1]

Margaret Milliken was a widow of some years. Her husband had been John Milliken (or Milligan in some accounts), who was a carpenter at the farm of Drumjargon, which is located between Whauphill and Kirkinner villages, in the parish of the latter.[2] Margaret's maiden name is the subject of some dispute, for although it appears as Lachlane on her gravestone in Wigtown kirkyard, other accounts spell it MacLauchlan, Lauchlison or variants of the same. When her husband was still alive, and they lived at Killeal, they seem to have been frequently called upon to put up soldiers who were in the district. John Milliken was required to pay six soldiers eight shillings Scots every day for many weeks, and he was later taken prisoner to Dumfries and fined. Widow Margaret seems to have been around 63 years of age, although again accounts vary this from 60 to 80. She is known to have had at least one daughter, Elizabeth, and a son-in-law, with whom she lived. Margaret Lachlane was a devout Christian, 'of known integrity and piety from her youth,' according to the kirk session minutes of Kirkinner.

Margaret Wilson was a young woman – again her age is subject to dispute, with some authorities putting her at 23 years, although some make her as young as 16. Her gravestone gives her age as 18, as do the kirk session records. She was the unmarried daughter of Gilbert Wilson in Glenvernoch farm, which lies nine miles north-west of Newton Stewart, in Penninghame parish.[3] Gilbert and his wife were noted as 'conformists', that is, they attended the church services run by the curate, but they may have secretly held other beliefs. Their three children, Margaret, Thomas (16 years old) and Agnes (who was 13), refused to attend the parish church, and as such were denounced as rebels. The three of them had to flee to the wilds.

The Wilson children lived in the hills and moors for some time after this, and their parents were warned that they should neither see nor harbour them. Thomas Wilson managed to survive until after the Revolution, but no further record of Agnes survives. On one occasion Margaret wrote a letter to her parents from her hide-out. In it she explains her convictions, and why she refused to save her life by taking the Oath of Abjuration. The authorities were incensed at the Wilson children's actions, and often arrived at Glenvernoch to search for them. Fines were levied on Gilbert on behalf of his family, so much so that he was left virtually penniless and had to leave his farm. He died around 1704 in 'great poverty'. His widow had to rely on the charity of her friends in order to feed and clothe herself.

In the early spring of 1685 a group of soldiers under Robert Grierson of Lag arrived at Margaret Milliken's house and forced an entry. Her name had been given to them by the curate at Kirkinner, Andrew Symson, who noted her as 'disorderly' on his list. Margaret was on her knees at prayer, but the soldiers easily lifted the old woman and carried her out to their horses, where she was tied up. She was taken immediately to prison, and accounts state that she was thereafter transferred from one gaol to another. She was allowed no light in the evening, and it is recorded that the dragoons who transferred her from Machermore Castle (which was used as a garrison) to the county tolbooth in Wigtown tortured and treated her with considerable disrespect.

The curate at Penninghame church, James Colquhoun, likewise supplied a list of 'disorderly' parishioners, among them the three Wilson children. The Wilsons had spend some months in hiding, moving each night to a new place of concealment, which resulted in them travelling as far north as the Carrick hills, and eastward to Nithsdale. In the early part of 1685 the two sisters had ventured back towards Wigtown, where they were concealed by friends.

The Wilson girls met Patrick Stuart, who was known to them, and spent some time in his company. He produced three glasses and some wine, and suggested the girls join him in toasting the king. The girls refused to take part and, realising their danger, fled from his home. Stuart alerted the authorities that they were in the vicinity and soon a party of soldiers located their hideaway. They were transported back to Wigtown where they were at first locked up in a dungeon known as the 'thieves' hole', before being transferred to the prison wherein lay Margaret Milliken.

On 13 April 1685 the three women were taken to the courtroom in Wigtown, where the Justiciary Commission was sitting. On the bench were Robert Grierson of Lag, Sheriff of Galloway David Graham, Major Winram, Captain David Strachan and Provost Coltran. A fourth woman also appeared before the court, 20 year-old Margaret Maxwell, a serving maid to the laird of Barwhanny, near Whauphill. Although she had been warned in October 1684 for her disorderly conduct, the evidence against her was deemed to be less damning. Accordingly she was sentenced to be flogged by the burgh hangman on three successive days, and to stand for one hour in the jougs. When the hangman tied Maxwell to a handcart and stripped her to the waist in order to carry out the punishment, every door and window in Wigtown was closed and shuttered, lest the villagers witness the spectacle. Accordingly the hangman was rather light in his application of the lash, and when he wished to release her early from the jougs, Margaret Maxwell told him that she was 'neither wearied nor ashamed – let the nock go on.'

The three other women were charged with taking part in the battles at Airds Moss and Bothwell Bridge, and with attending 20 field conventicles and 20 house meetings. Despite the fact that the Wilson girls would only have been 13 and eight years old at the time of Airds Moss, they were found guilty of the charges. All three were offered the chance to swear the Abjuration Oath, but refused. According to the Penninghame session minutes, 'the assize did sit and brought them in guilty and these judges sentenced them to be tyed to palisades fixed in the sand, within the flood-mark and there to stand till the flood overflowed them and drowned them.' As the sentence was read out the women were ordered to kneel, but refused. Some soldiers grabbed them and forced them down towards the floor. Execution by drowning was scheduled for a fortnight later.

In the intervening time the folk of the district were active in trying to prevent the sentences from being carried out. Gilbert Wilson journeyed to Edinburgh where he petitioned the Privy Council for the release of his daughters and Agnes was allowed to go free on the payment of £100 sterling bond, although Gilbert was to produce her any time he was ordered to do so. A similar petition was presented on behalf of Margaret Milliken, in which it stated that she was now willing to take the oath and begged some compassion as a result of her age. As she was unable to sign her name, the petition was endorsed by William Moir, notary public. It has been claimed that this was an attempt by friends at getting her free, and that she had not agreed to take the oath.

The Privy Council is known to have taken the view that the authorities in Wigtown had overstepped their mark, and on 30 April ordered the executions to be cancelled and that the Secretaries of State approach the king for a remission. What happened thereafter is uncertain. For some reason the officers in

Galloway decided to defy the Privy Council, reckoning that no repercussions would take place. Perhaps they just wanted to frighten the women into swearing the oath, not expecting them to refuse. Accordingly the executions were planned for 11 May (some say 2 May).

The two women were marched down from the tolbooth to the sands. The tide was out, the sands being so flat that the sea recedes almost two miles thereabouts. Two stakes were hammered into the ground, one nearer the sea than the other. Margaret Milliken was tied to the one nearer the sea, Margaret Wilson a few hundred yards closer to the shore. The sands were covered with small groups of spectators, many of them praying fervently for some last-minute reprieve.

The soldiers went first to Milliken, and gave her a chance to pray for the king. She refused, but offered to pray to God to forgive the king's sins. Some men were incensed at the impudence of the old woman, and one cursed and told the soldiers to, 'Let her gang to hell.' As the tidal race worked its way up the body of old Margaret, one of the town soldiers took his halberd and held it over her throat, bringing her to a quicker end.

The soldiers then turned their attention to the young Margaret. It had been planned this way, that the older woman suffered first in order to give the younger a chance to adhere to their wishes. As the waters rose up her body the girl sang out the 25th Psalm:

Consider mine enemies, how many they are:
And they bear a tyrannous hate against me.

She then read the 8th chapter of Romans before commencing a prayer. During the latter the waters virtually engulfed her. A few soldiers went to the stake and loosened the ropes, lifting her free. She was asked if she would now pray for the king, but Wilson steadfastly refused. A friend shouted, 'Margaret, Margaret, say "God save the King".'

Margaret is said to have answered, 'God save him if He will, for it is his salvation I desire.'

A few friends then called out to the soldiers, 'She has said it, she has said it.'

Robert Grierson came forward and stated that her prayers were not enough. He then ordered Major Winram to offer her the full oath but this was refused and again Margaret Wilson was thrust into the water. Again the town soldier came up with his halberd. As he pushed her body beneath the water he said, 'Tak' anither drink, hinny; clep wi' the partans.' The reference to partans, or crabs, was made as the women are said to have grasped the stakes tightly.

At a later time, when the tide had once again receded, the corpses of the two women were taken from the waters and under cover of nightfall transferred to the parish kirkyard. A grave was hastily dug, and they were laid to rest in the consecrated soil.

Gilbert Wilson was given no peace for the next three years. He was often fined, for his daughter Agnes refused to accompany him to the courts, and on many occasions parties of soldiers were billeted with him, often as many as 100, whom he was expected to feed. He was weekly summonsed to Wigtown court, which required a round trip of 26 miles, and on occasion to Edinburgh. Some folk reckoned that he lost the equivalent of 5,000 merks (about £3,350) and died in poverty.

Thomas Wilson survived the Killing Times and after the Revolution joined the army of King William. He served in Flanders and in the barracks at Edinburgh Castle. He later returned to Wigtownshire, where in 1704 he was nominated as an elder in Penninghame kirk, but turned this down. On 1 November 1719 he finally accepted and was ordained. His name appears in the session records until 1734, when he probably died, aged 65. Thomas inherited not one farthing from his parents, but by his own endeavours was able to raise enough in order to acquire the farm of Glenvernoch once more.

1. NX 437556. Monument on traditional site of drowning. Gravestones are in Wigtown old churchyard (NX 436555) and a monument to all Wigtown martyrs stands on Windy Hill (NX 430554).
2. NX 409505.
3. NX 346753.

39

THEY SOCHT THEM OUT

From 1684-6 there were a large number of conventicles held on the uplands between Peebles and Dumfries. Tweedsmuir parish was one of the strongest supporters of the Covenant, and extracts from the Kirk Session Records include: 'No public sermon, soldiers being sent to apprehend the minister, but he, receiving notification of their design, went away and retired.' Proclamations were issued against those who had attended the conventicles, one of the most important being at Talla Linn,[1] and three commissioners were appointed as justiciars for the counties of Berwick, Roxburgh, Selkirk and Peebles. One of these was Colonel James Douglas who was responsible for the area around Peebles. He was a zealous man, and went to great lengths to seek out the Covenanters and bring them to justice for their rebellious actions.

In 1685 a gathering of hill-men had been organised in upper Tweeddale, near to the clachan of Tweedsmuir. Douglas was in the vicinity and by chance came upon the men, singing and praying among the hills. The Covenanters dispersed, fleeing across the heather in all directions, making it difficult for Douglas's men to chase more than a couple. The two who they did pursue were John Hunter and one of his neighbours, James Welsh, who lived at Tweedhopefoot. Welsh was known as 'The

Bairn' or 'The Babe', but was renowned for his muscular body. The chase was intense, for Douglas's men were mounted on horseback and Hunter and Welsh were fleet of foot. They realised that their only chance of escape was if they could find some place where horses were unable to travel. There were no real marshes in the area, but instead they reckoned that the steep rocky slopes of the Devil's Beef Tub at the head of Annandale would be too dangerous for riding.

The journey was long and tiresome but at length the two men reached the great chasm. Hunter bounded down through the rocks and scree of the Straucht Steep, part of Ericstane Brae, the soldiers remaining on their horses at the top. However, being at rest, the soldiers could aim more steadily with their firearms. As John Hunter scrambled over a rock he was left exposed to their aim. A dragoon surnamed Scott fired and the gunshot resounded throughout upper Annandale as the pellets claimed another victim. The soldiers came to his body and one of them struck Hunter's head with the butt of his gun. The corpse was then thrown over the edge of the precipice.[2]

Welsh managed to make good his escape and continue fleeing. From the bottom of the Beef Tub he ascended the steep slopes of Great Hill and crossed the Falla Moss to Carterhope, in Glen Fruid. Carterhope was the home of his aunt and he asked her to conceal him. The aunt was wise and told him to pretend he was sleeping by the fireside. When the soldiers entered the farmhouse she jumped up and slapped him on the shoulders, shouting at him, 'Get up, ye lazy lout! Get oot there and haud the sodjers' horses.' After they had searched the steading the dragoons left and Welsh was free.

The body of James Hunter was left to lie where it fell. Later, when no soldiers were in the vicinity, some of his friends secretly took it back to Tweedsmuir and buried in the lower half of the kirkyard.[3]

1. NT 138203.
2. NT 061125. Memorial stone at side of Devil's Beef Tub.
3. NT101245. Obelisk at church door and grave in lower part of churchyard.

40

SHOT IN THIS PLACE

The soldiers were out in the Lowther Hills searching for Covenanters who had been in attendance at a conventicle there. At Craignorth Hill, which flanks the Crawick Water, they came across a small group of seven men. The soldiers approached them, whereupon they tried to make an escape. A couple of the men were successful, but five were captured and held prisoner. They were William Brown, David Dun, Robert Morris, Simon Paterson and John Richmond. As the soldiers were making ready to return to their garrison a freak thunderstorm erupted as if from nowhere. The bellowing thunder and lightning flashes frightened the troopers' horses, causing them to bolt. Those riding the horses were dragged off with them, those walking set off in pursuit. The Covenanters unexpectedly found that they had regained their freedom and tried to escape.

The soldiers pursued the Covenanters, eventually capturing and killing two of them. The unlucky pair were Brown and Morris, found cowering in different narrow gullies formed by burns flowing from Craignorth Hill. Since that time these gullies have been known as Brown's Cleuch and Morris Cleuch. Perhaps a third Covenanter was killed at a spot on the hillside south of Cogshead, which is known as the Martyr's Knowe.[1]

According to a tradition handed down in the Sanquhar

area, another two Covenanters were shot in the same vicinity, and may have been connected with this incident. They were Robert Laidlaw, killed at Tonguehouse farm, and William Crichton, shot on Conrick Moor. For many years a gravestone marked Crichton's resting place below Conrick House.

The Covenanters who escaped from Craignorth fled further west, into Galloway. James Renwick had been preaching at a conventicle somewhere in the parish of Carsphairn, in the Galloway Hills, in the summer of 1685. Some say the site of the conventicle was at Glenmuck farm, which is actually in Dalmellington parish, Ayrshire. A large crowd had gathered to hear him preach, for he was a renowned speaker, one whose wisdom and knowledge of the scriptures was well-founded, even although he was then only 23 years of age.

After the conventicle had finished the congregation dispersed, each finding their own way home, lest a large crowd should attract the attention of the soldiers who were in the district, searching for such meetings. Four Covenanters travelled to the north of Dalmellington, where on the slopes of Ben Beoch they decided to rest in a large stone enclosure known as the Tod Fauld, a place where sheep were gathered at night to protect them from foxes. However, the local farmer, who was an adherent of the Covenant himself, became aware that there was a party of soldiers in the district, looking for non-conformists. He made his way to the Tod Fauld where he warned the four men of their approach, and suggested that they travel further. Although it was nightfall, the men decided to continue, and crossed the Martyrs' Moss to the upper slopes of Carsgailoch Hill, five miles distant, where they decided to stop and rest. This hill is a low eminence to the south-west of Cumnock in Ayrshire. Although it rises to almost 1,200 feet above sea level, so slowly is the ascent that the hill is little more than a high stretch of moorland, now much afforested. Old accounts spell the name 'Crossgellioch', or 'Corsegelloch', but I have used the spelling which appears on modern maps. The Covenanters' journey had been a hard one, and though it was by now day, soon they were fast asleep in the comfort of the heather.

The party of highland soldiers was under the command of Colonel James Douglas, and they came upon the men lying in the hollow. They were rudely awakened, and one of the men jumped up with such a start that he managed to run away from the soldiers. This made the highland-men even more suspicious of the small group and they were asked to swear the Oath of Allegiance to the king, but all refused to do so. With some pressure the soldiers managed to discover that the men were returning from a conventicle. This was sufficient grounds for Colonel Douglas to order his men to shoot. After the volleys echoed over the moss three corpses were left on the ground. They were Joseph Wilson, John Jamieson and John Humphrey. Of their backgrounds nothing is known.[2]

The man who had run away, Alexander Jamieson, a brother of John, was pursued by the soldiers who were on horseback and he was soon caught up. Why they did not kill him on the spot is not known, for he was arrested and taken into Cumnock where he was locked up in the tolbooth, which at that time stood on the north side of the Square. What became of him thereafter is not known.

Two more of the Covenanters caught on the hilltop were also taken. They were David Dun and Simon Paterson. It is said that David Dun almost managed to make an escape but that his horse sank into a wet area of bog. The two men were dragged to Cumnock where they were held prisoner for a short time before being shot.[3] Tradition states that word had reached David's sister, Margaret, of his arrest. As she made her way to Cumnock to find out his fate, she too was shot.

David Dun was probably a native of Ochiltree parish, for a David Dun of Closs farm was named in a list of rebels in 1684. Of Paterson nothing is known of his origins, but he may be related to the Patersons of Dalmellington. Both seem to have left their homelands and taken themselves to the uplands on the borders of Dumfriesshire with Selkirkshire, where they hid from the soldiers who were in pursuit of them.

Near to the famous waterfall of the Grey Mare's Tail in

Dumfriesshire is a lesser fall known as Dob's Linn, associated with a Covenanter by the name of Halbert Dobson. He seems to have been another of Dun's friends, for an old tale recounts the time when they were supposedly being chased by the Devil. They tried to prevent his pursuit by laying hanks of wool in the shape of crosses before him, allowing Dobson and Dun to get round the back and attack from the rear. They held their Bibles in one hand, and with a rowan stick in the other they beat Satan. They were then able to throw him over the waterfall. An old rhyme relates that:

> Little kent the worricow
> What the Covenant could dow!
> What o' faith an' what o' fen,
> What o' might an' what o' men;
> Or he had never shown his face,
> His reikit rags and riven taes,
> To men o' mak and men o' mense,
> Men o' grace and men o' sense;
> For Hab Dob an' Davie Din,
> Dang the Deevil owre Dob's Linn.

Hugh Hutchison of Dalgig farm was near to the summit of Carsgailoch Hill when the three shootings took place. Whether or not he screamed at the sight is not known, but the soldiers became aware of his presence. A few of them gave chase, but being the farmer of this hillside he knew of the moss hags and gullies round the burns where he could effect an escape. He managed to capture his horse which was grazing in a field and when mounted escaped with greater speed.

From Dalgig he forded the River Nith towards Blackfarding farm, before travelling across the face of Whitehill and Auchingee hills down towards Riggfoot farm. There the land was low-lying and boggy, and he was forced to dismount and continue on foot. Near to the confluence of the Lane Burn with the Nith there was a coppice of trees where he managed to hide himself. Unable to find him, the soldiers gave up the chase.

Colonel Douglas then led his men across the moss of

Lanemark towards Bank, crossed the Connel Burn and dropped into the lower stretches of Glen Afton. As they did so they came upon the home of James Campbell of Dalhanna, who was a known supporter of the Covenant. Campbell managed to make a getaway, climbing up the hillside behind his home. The soldiers inquired at the house if he was in, only to be told by the servant that he was not. However, he was spotted on the hill above and yet again Douglas found himself leading the chase. Campbell was able to scramble up the steep slopes of Dalhanna Hill with greater speed than the mounted soldiers were able to follow him. He came upon a patch of hillside which was covered in thick broom, and therein he was able to hide. It is said that one of the soldiers, who were by this time dismounted, actually spotted him at close quarters, but as he was exhausted from the chase and rather unwilling to start another, just shook his head at Campbell, and trudged silently onwards.

Colonel Douglas was less compassionate, for he had already lost two men in the chase. As the party of soldiers crossed the upper slopes of The Knipe they came upon two men near to Over Cairn farm. George Corson and John Hair were local farmers from the parish of Kirkconnel, Hair's family having tenanted Glenwharrie for many years. Douglas's men discovered that the pair were reading their Bibles, so this was sufficient grounds for him to order them to be executed on the spot. They were buried where they fell, and a later memorial stone on a low eminence commemorates them. Afterwards, Hair's family were ejected from their farm and the tenancy forfeited.[4]

Hugh Hutchison, in the meantime, returned to his farm. He obtained the services of a few friends and they returned to Carsgailoch to bury the martyrs on the spot of their execution. Word was to reach him that Alexander Jamieson was held in Cumnock's tolbooth, so he decided to chance his neck and pay him a visit. Whilst he was speaking to Jamieson through the barred window, the authorities became aware of him and gave chase. Hutchison, however, was too quick, and he managed to lose them. He fled towards Dalmellington where he met with

John Paterson, with whom he stayed a few nights. They thought that to stay at Pennyvenie was too risky, so they decided to return to Dalgig. However, they came across some highland soldiers in the vicinity. When questioned by these men, Hutchison and Paterson were able to convince them that they were but simple farm workers, busily looking after the cattle. Hugh Hutchison was to survive the Killing Times, dying in 1740.

Many years later, in 1827, when the foundations were being excavated for the present memorial stone on Carsgailoch Hill, the workmen discovered the bodies of the three martyrs in the ground, the soil over them being rather thin. The peatiness of the earth was such that it had preserved the bodies so much so that they looked as though they had only been buried a few weeks before. The woollen socks and plaid which they wore were still entire, and a local farmer, Ivie Campbell of Dalgig, was able to cut a small lock of hair from one of the martyrs, and a piece of clothing from another. These fragments were long preserved by the Campbell family until they were lodged for safekeeping in the Baird Institute Museum in Cumnock, along with a piece of the original 'Old Mortality' gravestone.

1. NS 810162. Brown's Cleuch. NS 811157 Morris Cleuch. NS 835127 Martyr's Knowe.
2. NS 548146. Monument at site of martyrdom.
3. NS 570203. Gravestone in Cumnock old cemetery.
4. NS 663129. Monument at Meikle Waistland, New Cumnock.

41

JOHN PATERSON OF PENNYVENIE

John Paterson of Pennyvenie, mentioned in the previous chapter, was a notable Covenanter who survived the years of persecution. Pennyvenie[1] was at that time owned by John Craufurd of Camlarg who, by the laws of the time, had to ensure that his tenants attended church and adhered to the king. Paterson arrived at Camlarg to pay his rent and let it slip that he had been at Mayfield Hill to attend a conventicle. Craufurd told Paterson that he must either give up attending conventicles or else be evicted from his farm. However, Paterson decided to remain at home but made arrangements to create a secret exit from his house. This was required sooner than he'd expected, for a group of soldiers arrived at the farmhouse in search of Covenanters. Paterson made his escape, the soldiers turning the house over and threatening his wife. At length they left, and Paterson could return to his home.

John Paterson attended a conventicle held at Fingland, at the head of the Dalwhat Water (Glen Cairn) in Dumfriesshire. Word arrived that a party of highlanders was in the vicinity so the Covenanters split up and made their way homeward. Paterson discovered that two dragoons on horseback were following him. The horses found the going difficult across the boggy moss, so Paterson managed to get ahead. However, the soldiers were beginning to catch him up as he reached Meikle Hill, on the border between Dalmellington and New Cumnock. Across the summit he found a hollow in which he hid, but the dragoons sent on their dogs to sniff him out. As they came towards him, and were about to discover his place of concealment, a fox got up and ran away down the hillside. The dogs were side-tracked and took chase, the dragoons following in error. Paterson was able to watch them descend the Cummock glen, visit his home, then continue back to the garrison at Dalmellington. John Paterson then returned home, but Craufurd of Camlarg told him the following day that he had been publicly denounced as a rebel and that a price had been put on his head.

John Paterson then found a hiding place on the lower slopes of Ben Beoch, near to the 'Tod Fauld', where a cavern in the loose rocks which had fallen from Benbeoch Craig existed.[2] He used this place on a number of occasions to hide, each time improving it and making it homely. On occasions when he was helping in his fields and word reached the locals that the soldiers were coming, neighbouring farmers would shout 'The nowt's [cattle] in the corn!' as a secret warning.

Paterson attended a conventicle at Irelandton (on the moors east of Gatehouse of Fleet) where Rev James Renwick preached under nightfall. The look-out, who had been posted to watch for signs of danger, alerted the Covenanters of the approach of a group of highland soldiers. The conventicle was broken up and all searched for hiding places. Paterson went with David Halliday, John Bell, Robert Lennox, Andrew MacRobert and James Clement to the barn on the farm and hid amongst a pile of shorn wool, the smell of which threw the searching dogs. Apart from Paterson, all the Covenanters listed were subsequently martyred when Robert Grierson of Lag surprised them at a conventicle on Kirkconnell Moor in 1685.[3]

Nearer to home, Paterson attended a conventicle near Littlemill, in the parish of Dalrymple. The local lairds of Kerse and Keirs knew of his attendance and reported to Craufurd of Camlarg, who subsequently sent for him. Craufurd arranged for

Paterson to assist in the construction of a dam across the Doon, at which a number of local lairds would be in attendance, and where he could again win favour with them. When John told his wife of the plan she feared that it was a trap to capture him, but he replied that he had promised Craufurd that he would go with him, and that he doubted the laird would actually turn him in, or be responsible for his capture. On the appointed day Craufurd and Paterson arrived at the river where they worked laboriously all day. At nightfall, MacAdam of Waterhead was in the process of adding a large sod to the dam but slipped, dropping it and causing a large splash of dirty water to soak Craufurd. Tempers flared, but Paterson intervened, scolding both parties, particularly Craufurd for his use of blasphemous language. Both parties remained silent, even when Paterson took out his Bible and gave them a lesson on the rich man and Lazarus.

John Paterson survived the Killing Times, living to see the return of Presbyterianism to Scotland and a more settled and prosperous nation. He lived to be 90, dying in 1740, and was buried in the parish kirkyard. Some of his descendants still live in the parish.[4]

1. NS 492069.
2. NS 497081
3. See Chapter 30.
4. NS 480058. Memorial to all Dalmellington Covenanters (none of which is named) is in old churchyard.

42
WITHOUT
SENTENCE OF LAW

Apart from the five Covenanters martyred at Wigtown and the isolated martyrdom of Alexander Linn, there are no other martyr graves in Wigtownshire. Yet the county was a hotbed of Covenanting adherence and hundreds if not thousands of residents suffered for their beliefs. Even the Provost of Stranraer was mortally wounded by one of Claverhouse's soldiers around the year 1679. The Agnew family had been hereditary sheriffs of the county for many years, but when Sir Andrew refused to take the Test in January 1682 he was replaced by Claverhouse himself. Agnew seems to have changed his mind at a later date, for it is recorded that both he and his son, Andrew, signed it on 17 October 1684.

When landowners became responsible for ensuring that there were no Covenanters residing on their lands, Sir David Dunbar of Baldoon seems to have undertaken the job with relish. The list of residents supplied in October 1684 was extensive and hundreds were fined or banished. Of the many reported, the Duns of Stewarton farm, Kirkinner, are worth mentioning. John Dun was banished to America but died at sea. His daughter, Janet, was tortured by holding burning matches at her fingers and by forcing them into holes with wedges. She was sent to Glasgow as a prisoner.

Sir John Dalrymple, who owned the Castle Kennedy estate, is said to have laughed at Claverhouse and only charged nominal fines of his tenants. He claimed that the fines were sufficient, and that his tenants were becoming more orderly. Claverhouse responded by saying, 'Orderly! There are as many elephants and crocodiles in Galloway as orderly persons.' Dalrymple was fined £500 and he was kept imprisoned in Edinburgh Castle until it was paid. He then sought the safety of the Netherlands, where his father and other members of the family were residing.

The tolbooth at Wigtown must have been a very busy place during the Killing Times, for hundreds were held prisoner and many more were tried in the court there. William Kerr, who lived on Barnbarroch estate, had been imprisoned in the 'thieves hole' but John Henderson helped him to escape. Henderson was a tailor in the district. He was later captured and found guilty of attending conventicles, harbouring rebels, refusing the oath, in addition to assisting Kerr to escape. He was sent to Edinburgh from where he was banished.

Thomas Baillie in Ardwell estate was punished for having entertained the fugitive Gilbert MacGhie with meat and drink in his own home. When called before the court in Wigtown on 14 October 1684 he was released. Less fortunate was John Forsyth of Upper Airies who was found guilty of 'harbouring, resetting, intertaining att his oun dwelling with meat, kyndness' the Covenanting rebel, George Strachan.

Margaret Hay, nee Gordon, lived at Airyolland farm in the parish of Mochrum. She was noted for holding a number of house meetings at the farm, at which the ministers Samuel Arnot and George Barclay preached. She was captured and tried at Wigtown tolbooth court on 14 October 1684. She was found guilty and banished. The 'goodwife's' sons, John and William, were listed as rebels, all this the result of the parish curate, Henry Walker, reporting them to the soldiers.

Another Mochrum parishioner was John MacHaffie of Gargrie, which stood to the east of Mochrum Loch. He was listed as a rebel for having been at the Battle of Bothwell Bridge. He was captured and hauled before the court in Wigtown in October 1684. Refusing to take the Oath of Allegiance he was banished to America. Sheriff David Graham ordered his house to be pulled down, as were the homes of 'all rebels'.

At Whithorn lived Hugh Dunse and his wife, Janet Brown. They endured persecution for many years, but 'kept steady in the faith and a good conscience,' according to their gravestone.[1]

James Colquhoun, the curate of Penninghame parish, was a keen stickler for the laws of the time. He kept a note of all his parishioners and whether or not they had taken the Test. Those who failed to adhere to the 'unjust laws' of the times were reported to the local garrison, and the soldiers were quick in taking to the hills and moors in search of those who failed to conform.

William Johnstone was a gardener employed by the laird of Fyntalloch, which house stood by the Loch of Fyntalloch at the northern end of the parish. When he was asked to take the Test he agreed, swearing the oath before the curate of the parish. However, he later regretted this, and was so overcome with remorse that he decided not to attend the curate's church again. The curate soon noticed his absence and reported him, resulting in Johnstone having to leave his home and live in the wilds.

Johnstone met two of his neighbours who were also on the run from the dragoons. They were John Milroy, a chapman who lived at Fyntalloch, and George Walker, a servant on the farm of Kirkcalla. They spent some time in hiding, but the soldiers were hot on their trail. Tradition asserts that the trio had many close shaves.

Major George Winram was one of a number of soldiers given full justiciary powers on 3 January 1684. Although originally appointed for the counties of Dunbarton and Lanark, he seems to have been transferred to Galloway by 1685, for he was not only involved in the drowning of the two ladies at Wigtown, but also sent out a party to search for the three Penninghame men. The soldiers found them on the moors and they were quickly apprehended and bound together. The soldiers dragged them behind their horses to Wigtown, where they were locked up in the burgh gaol.

The three Covenanters were tried before Winram, but not in a proper trial with jury, just the local militia. He asked them to take the Oath of Abjuration, but they refused. He questioned them regarding their hiding places, but the men would not reveal any of them. The Major offered them the chance to attend the church services of the curate, but all three declined. He then sentenced the men to be hanged. The next day Johnstone, Milroy and Walker were taken from the gaol to the local gibbet. One by one they were taken to the platform and the trap door was opened beneath them. Their corpses were later buried in the parish kirkyard.[2]

1. NX 444403. Gravestone in Whithorn churchyard.
2. NX 436555. Gravestone in Wigtown churchyard.

43

THE DUNNOTTAR
DUNGEON

The great sandstone pile of Dunnottar Castle[1] stands on a cliff-girt headland projecting into the North Sea, a few miles south of Stonehaven, on the Kincardineshire coast. The castle was owned by the Earl Marischal and at the time of the Covenanting struggle was used as a prison. The long vaulted cellar which was used to lock up the Covenanters can still be visited, scene of some of the worst atrocities which had to be endured by the Covenanting folk. Some old accounts state that it was below ground level, but this is an error. However, the vaulting and the dank atmosphere within gives an impression that if it were subterranean, the privations would be no worse. This cellar has since become known as the Whigs' Vault.

On 24 May 1685 George Keith of Whiteridge, the sheriff-depute of the Mearns, was at Dunnottar to receive a band of Covenanters who had been captured and held prisoner. These folk had refused to take the Oath of Supremacy and were tied and gagged. They had been held in prisons throughout the south of Scotland, but when the Earl of Argyll's expedition arrived in Scotland from the Netherlands on 6 May, the authorities panicked and ordered all religious prisoners to be transported to Dunnottar. The cells in Edinburgh and Canongate tolbooths were emptied, and the prisoners were marched down to the port of Leith, where about a score more from the local tolbooth joined them. They were put on board open boats and during nightfall were taken across the Firth of Forth to Burntisland. There the prisoners were cooped up in the two small rooms of the tolbooth for another two nights, receiving little food or water.

A message was received at Burntisland from the authorities in Edinburgh, that if any of the prisoners were willing to take the Oath of Allegiance then they should be freed. Around 40 of the prisoners, weak from their treatment and lack of sustenance, decided to capitulate and swear the oath. The men and women who were left were then made to walk like driven cattle across Fife, travelling many miles northwards. At Freuchie they stopped for the night before continuing north to the ferry port. Again the prisoners were cramped into three small rooms before being ferried across the Tay to Dundee. Those with money were allowed to buy some food in the city. The march continued north to Forfar, where again they were locked up in the tolbooth, and next day reached Brechin, where they were again allowed to purchase food.

The next day's march took them to the bridge over the North Esk river, where there was no tolbooth. Instead the soldiers herded them onto the narrow bridge and positioned guards at either end. The night was a wild and stormy one, with rain and strong winds. No shelter, other than that afforded by the parapet, was to be found, and the prisoners seemed more relieved to be allowed to commence their march at three or four in the morning. They were to reach the castle later that day.

On arrival at Dunnottar the Covenanters were taken up through the castle gateway into the main courtyard, before being herded into the vault below the Earl Marischal's suite of rooms. There were 167 people in that group, 122 men and 45 women. Of the 180 who had left Burntisland, 13 had managed to escape. At first the Covenanters spread themselves around the vault, but were soon to realise that they were all being forced into the single apartment, and they had to squeeze closer together. The room only measured 54 by 15 feet, allowing each person five square feet. So cramped were the conditions that they could not sit down without leaning against each other. The floor of the vault was wet and muddy and only two windows, located at one end, allowed air into the gloom. There was no latrine and the stench which built up must have been unbearable.

The conditions meant that most of the prisoners fell victim to one disease or another, and a number of them died. The governor did allow the prisoners to purchase some food, but at exorbitant rates. A pint of ale sold for 20 pennies, five times its worth, and a peck of meal at 18 shillings. After a few days he acquiesced to their pleadings for more room and allowed the small dungeon prison below the vault to be used. This apartment was lower in height and had no windows, but it did have a small spring of fresh water and a low hole though the wall, which the prisoners took turns lying next to, in order to breathe fresh air.

Grissell Cairnes and Alison Johnston, wives of two of the prisoners, appealed to the Privy Council for an improvement in the prisoners' conditions. They referred to:

...one hundred and ten of them in one vault, where there is little or no daylight at all, and contrarie to all modestie men and women promiscuouslie together, and fourtie and two more in another roume in the same condition, and no person allowed to come near them with meat and drink, but such bread and drink as scarce any rationall creature can live upon, and yet at extraordinary rates, being twentie pennies each pynt of ale, which is not worth a plack the pint, and the pocke of dustie sandie meal is afforded to them at eighteen shillings per peck. And not so much as a drink of water allowed to be caryed to them, whereby they are not only in a starving condition but must inevitably incurr a plague or other fearful diseases.

One day the governor's wife appealed to him to allow the prisoners more room. Consequently, the women were taken from the vault and put under lock and key in another two vaults. Twelve men, the sickest of the lot, were taken to another vault, where they had the luxury of fresh air and more room.

James Forsyth was one of the prisoners in the dungeon. He

belonged to Carthat in Annandale and had been listed as a fugitive. When captured he was sent to Edinburgh tolbooth before being transferred to Dunnottar. His wife travelled north to visit him but the governor of the castle took her in and held her prisoner also. Mrs Forsyth was pregnant at the time and despite her pleas she was not allowed to leave. She died in the vault of neglect.

One day 25 of the prisoners managed to break free from the chamber. They forced their way through the window onto the top of the cliff. They began to descend but the natural cliff, which they had still to climb down to make good their escape, was steep and two men perished in a fall. One of them was James Watson, the other's name is not known. Their bodies were later found on the shore and taken to Dunnottar kirkyard for burial. Those who managed to reach the bottom of the cliff safely dispersed and hid themselves in the countryside. However, 15 of them were betrayed and recaptured. When they were brought back to the garrison they were subjected to various tortures. A number lost one or more fingers from having lit matches inserted below their fingernails. Alexander Dalgleish died as a result of the torment.

In addition to the two who died trying to escape down the cliffs, seven Covenanters died at Dunnottar. Their corpses were taken to Dunnottar kirkyard where they were interred.[2] They were James Atchison, William Brown, William Breadie, Mary Gibson, Jean Moffat, James Russell, John Stot, James Watson and John Whyte. When a headstone was erected by 'Old Mortality', the names of Breadie, Whyte and the two women were not known. Within the castle burial ground is a small headstone bearing the inscription, 'A Bairn of nyn years lyes here, 1685.' This is strongly believed to belong to a child of one of the Covenanting women held prisoner.

The prisoners were given the chance to swear their allegiance to the king sometime in mid-July, but all refused. In the third week of August they were taken from their prison and transported back to Leith, mostly on foot, but those who still had money were allowed to hire ponies. After travelling 66 miles the chance to swear to the king was given again, to which some succumbed. Others were bailed by friends who signed a bond under the penalty of 5,000 merks. Those left were transported abroad to the plantations where they worked as slaves. Were they to return to Scotland they would have suffered the death penalty. The ship, however, was afflicted by fever, and many prisoners, passengers and crew, around 60-70 in total, died. The hull twice sprang leaks, and the winds took the vessel to New Jersey instead of Jamaica. When they landed, the prisoners were invited to live in the country, and many did so.

Most of the Dunnottar prisoners' names are known. The 'Covenanter Pedlar', Patrick Walker, was captured with another four during the night and imprisoned at Linlithgow on 29 June 1684. They were transferred to Edinburgh where they were sentenced on 2 July, guilty of supporting the Covenants, attending conventicles held by Cargill and Renwick, and other 'treasonable' offences. After surviving the horrors of Dunnottar he was brought back to Leith tolbooth on 18 August from where he managed to escape. He was later to write *Six Saints of the Covenant*, published in 1732.

Robert MacLellan of Barmagachan was one of those who arrived in America alive. He had been involved in the Pentland Rising from its inception and had fought at Bothwell Bridge. In New Jersey he gained his freedom and caught a ship bound for home in June 1689. However this boat was captured by the French and he was taken to Nantz as a prisoner before being transferred to Rochefort then Toulon. On his release he travelled through Genoa and Cadiz, and on catching a boat back to Scotland, found himself in a wild storm which forced a landing at Bantry Bay in Ireland. The Irish peasantry stripped the boat of its furniture and held MacLellan for 11 days before allowing him to continue to Dublin. He eventually arrived back at Barmagachan on 31 October 1691, two and a half years after leaving America.

Rev Archibald Riddell of Kippen in Stirlingshire had been imprisoned for four years on the Bass Rock before being sent to Dunnottar. His wife died on the way. In America Riddell became the minister of Woodbridge church. Riddell and his son arrived back in Britain quicker than MacLellan, being exchanged for two Roman Catholic priests at the request of William III's government. Back in Scotland he was appointed minister at Wemyss in Fife, followed by Kirkcaldy, then to Trinity College Church in Edinburgh in 1701. He died in 1708.

Rev John Fraser, husband of Jean Moffat, was captured in London along with Alexander Shields in January 1685. They were chained together for months, until Fraser was taken to Dunnottar, while Shields was imprisoned on the Bass Rock. Fraser was banished to East New Jersey in August 1685 and returned in February 1691. Having survived the Glorious Revolution, he became the minister of Hassendean in Roxburghshire, followed by Alness parish in Ross and Cromarty.[3] Rev William Ged and Rev William Aisdale were another two ministers in the vault. Both died on the *Henry and Francis* which was taking around 100 Covenanters abroad in 1685.

William MacMillan and John Doning were two preachers held at Dunnottar. MacMillan was banished abroad, dying en route. Quintin Dick was from Dalmellington in Ayrshire. He was later to write an account of his life under persecution.

1. NO 881838. There is a plaque listing all Covenanters imprisoned in the castle.
2. NO 863852. Headstone by 'Old Mortality' in Dunnottar churchyard.
3. NH 645690. Memorial in Alness old church.

44

THE SORN GARRISON

In the central part of Ayrshire, known historically as Kyle, the authorities established their garrison at Sorn Castle, which stands high on a cliff above the River Ayr, 15 miles east of the county town.[1] The castle was at that time owned by the Campbells of Loudoun. Still preserved in the castle is an old Covenanting banner, which belongs to the parish of Sorn, as well as a drum which belonged to one of the soldiers stationed there.

At the foot of the castle cliff, passing by the mouth of the Cleugh Burn, is an old footpath, part of which is known as the 'Curate's Steps'. During the years of struggle the curate of the parish walked from the kirk (erected in 1658) to the garrison to report those who had failed to attend that Sabbath's sermon. It is said that sometime during the years of the struggle the parishioners of Sorn chased the imposed minister from the church. Armed with pitchforks, they were gaining on him when the curate leaped across the Cleugh Burn, landing safely on the other side, next to the garrison. Thereafter the spot was known as the Curate's Leap.

The garrison was governed by Lieutenant Lewis Lauder. He seems to have issued a number of 'passes' which confirmed that the holder had sworn his allegiance to the king. The contents of one of these documents is known:

God Save the King

*I, Lewis Lauder, Governour of Sorn Castle, dow heirby certifie
and decalre, viz. — Kirkwood, servitour to Arthour Campbell of
Auchmannoch, in the parish of Sorne, did compeir before me, on
solemn oath before Almightie God, did abjure and renounce the
late tratours appollogeticall declaration, in so far as it declares
war against his Mattie [Majesty], and asserts that it is lawful to
kill all such as serve his Mattie in church, state, armie, or contrie,
conform to his Majestie's late proclamation of the 30 daye of Decr.
last.*

    Given at Sorne, the aught day of February 1685 ziers.
       Lewis Lauder.

The soldiers from Sorn garrison were responsible for a
number of martyrdoms in the district, many of which have been
mentioned elsewhere. In 1685 (or July 1684, according to
Wodrow, who wrote with some authority) the soldiers from Sorn
under the command of Lauder were riding through the county,
searching for rebels. The curate from the parish of Tarbolton had
handed in the name of William Shillilaw to the soldiers. This lad,
who was only 18 years old, had not attended his church services
for some weeks, and was accused of nonconformity.

The soldiers set out in pursuit. At Woodhead, in Tarbolton
parish, they spotted him in the distance, crossing the road.
Lauder sent one of his dragoons on in front to catch him.
Shillilaw was brought back to Lauder who put the usual questions
of allegiance to the king before him. Shillilaw was unwilling to
answer, and refused to swear his allegiance to the crown. Lauder,
accordingly, ordered him to be shot right there and then. A
dragoon drew his pistol and Shillilaw was left to lie where he fell.[2]

The soldiers then rode off to Stairhead, which lay on the
other side of the River Ayr from where the martyrdom had taken
place. Shillilaw had been employed as a farm worker here, and
the soldiers were concerned that the farmer had failed to report
him for non-attendance of the church. To harbour fugitives was
also a crime punishable by death. At Stairhead the soldiers seized
the farmer and two other men. Lauder questioned them about

Shillilaw, and he decided that they too were to be executed. He ordered them to kneel on the ground and cover their faces with scarves, so that they would not see the dragoons taking aim. But the Stairhead men were to be lucky that day, for the soldiers refused to obey Lauder's orders, claiming that the taking of one Covenanter's life per day was sufficient.

1. NS 548269.
2. NS 430272. Gravestone in Tarbolton churchyard.

45

RAISED AFTER SIX WEEKS OUT OF THE GRAWF

One of the most celebrated Covenanters was Alexander Peden. He was no martyr, for he died naturally at the home of his brother, but the story of his life is one of immense struggle and privation, and one which did not end when he died.

Alexander, or Sandy, Peden was born around 1626 at the farm of Auchencloich, which lies at the north end of Sorn parish in Ayrshire; the very building where he was born is still in existence. Peden was a well-educated young man and studied at Glasgow University, before qualifying as a minister. He was then employed as a schoolmaster at Tarbolton but within a short time received a call to the ministry. His first, and only charge, was at New Luce in Wigtownshire, where he was inducted in 1660.

On 24 February 1663 Peden had to leave his church because of the Act for Presentation and Collation. As he left the pulpit for the last time he closed the small wooden door and struck it three times with his Bible. As he did this, he said, 'I arrest thee, in my Master's name, that none ever enter thee, but such as come in by the door, as I have done.' This was an allusion to the bible; the book of John, chapter 10. No curate nor indulged minister was ever to preach at New Luce, and this may have been the first of many 'prophecies' attributed to Peden.

Sandy Peden then lived rough in the hills and moors,

holding conventicles and carrying out ministerial duties to the Covenanters. Peden was summonsed to appear before the Privy Council in Edinburgh in January 1666, but he failed to attend. The letter against Peden noted that he was charged with sedition:

> *The said Mr Alexander Peden did keep a conventicle at Ralston, in the parish of Kilmarnock, about the 10th of October last, where he baptised the children of Adam Dickie, Robert Lymburner, and many others; as also kept a conventicle in Craigie parish, at the Castle-hill, where he baptised the children of William Gilmor in Kilmarnock, and Gabriel Simpson, both in the said parish, and that besides twenty-three children more; both which conventicles were kept under cloud of night, with a great deal of confusion: as also the said Mr Alexander rides up and down the country with sword and pistols, in grey clothes.*

In 1666 Peden decided to follow the Covenanters on their march towards Edinburgh, but again he had some form of premonition that the cause was lost and he left them at Lanark. The Covenanters who continued on their march were subsequently beaten at the battle of Rullion Green. On 4 March 1666 Peden was one of a number of ministers who were declared rebels, and a price of 1,000 merks was placed on his head.

Peden fled to Ireland for a time, but returned to Scotland. He seems to have travelled all over southern Scotland, and such was his fame that many place-names recall him; these often mark the site of conventicles held by him. In the Galloway Hills is Peden's Isle in the midst of Loch Riecawr and not too far from it is Peden's Cave; in the Lowther Hills is the Peden Burn, Peden's Stone and another cave; Peden's Pulpit is a crag on the summit of Ruberslaw in the Borders, and five miles to the south-east of it is Peden's Cleuch. When Peden was in the Borders he often stayed at Langside, six miles south of Hawick. Even in Northumberland is a place known as Padon Hill, which is said to be the site of one of his field meetings.

Another 'Pulpit' is located near Glenower farm, in Glen Tig, Colmonell. One day in 1666 Peden, John Welsh, and the laird of Glenower were riding across the moors when they spotted a party of dragoons. The laird fainted, thinking that they would all be shot, but Peden told him to have faith. Sandy went to the dragoons and discovered that they were lost, so he volunteered to guide them on their way. He led them to the ford across the Tig and gave them directions to where they were headed. When he returned to the laird he was asked, 'Why did you go with them, why not send the lad?'

Peden replied, 'It was safer for me to be with them, for they might have asked questions of the lad which would have discovered us.'

A few miles from Glenower is Knockdow cottage, which sits on high ground between Colmonell and Ballantrae. It was the home of Hugh Ferguson and Peden spent some time in hiding there. From here Peden wrote a couple of letters, which illustrate his use of code letters for his friends and places of concealment.

Knockdow, Carrick, May 15th 1673.

My dear friend, – I send this to you to lett you know that I have come to this place in some safety, but have no hopes of remaining long before the arch-enemy is upon me, but I pray you to remember me to those I have left toiling there, that I am in good heart, but greatly tried. Tell John to keep the monies by him until I can find some trusty friend. I am not seen abroad just now, as I have some warning that injury is intended me. 331 and 334 are well, and send you health. You will find D. means us no good, and no good quality can be expected from L.

Ever your faithful friend,
Alexr. Peden.

This letter was to fall into enemy hands, and the address was sufficient for the soldiers to track him down. In June 1673 Major William Cockburn and his troops came to Knockdow and captured both Peden and Ferguson. Peden was regarded as a great prize, and Cockburn was rewarded with £50, £25 of which was divided amongst his soldiers. Ferguson was fined 1,000 merks for having sheltered the minister.

Peden was held for a short time in Ayr tolbooth before being sent to Edinburgh tolbooth. The arrest order read as follows:

Mr Alexr Pedene & Hew Farguson, Prisoners.
Junij 20th 1673.

Thes ar requyring you to order a pairtie of six hors and on to comand them to mairch to Aire and receive ye person of Mr Alexr Pedine, a rebell, in ye tolbuth there, and bring him in saiffe custodie to the tolbuthe of Edr. And this shal be warrant to ye keeper theroff to receive him and ye person of Hew Fargusone, allso prissoner ther and to you for ye bringing of them in, daited at the paleice off Halirudus, this 17th of Junij 1673: sic subscribitur,
      Rothes.

For Major Wm Cockburn, Leivt to ye troupe of his maists home gawrd under ye comand of the Erall off Atholl thes.

After trial in Edinburgh Peden was imprisoned on the Bass Rock. He was to remain there for four years and three months. A few friends in the west collected some money for him, and in his letter of thanks to Rev Patrick Simpson of Kilmacolm he relates the conditions endured in gaol:

We are close shut up in our chambers, not permitted to converse, diet, or worship together, but conducted out by two at once in the day, to breathe in the open air, envying the birds for their freedom, provoking and calling on us to bless Him for the most common mercies – and again close shut up day and night, to hear only the sighs and groans of our fellow prisoners.

In October 1677 Alexander Peden was transferred from the Bass Rock back to Edinburgh tolbooth. On 14 November 1678 he wrote to the Privy Council requesting permission to emigrate to Ireland, but this was refused. Instead it was decided that Peden and 66 others should be banished abroad, where they were to be employed as slaves in the West Indian plantations. Accordingly he was placed on board a ship at Leith bound for America, but the other prisoners were surprised by his attitude to this. Peden told them not to worry, that they would not be leaving British waters, for 'the ship was not built that could take him there.' Again his prophecy turned out to be true. The *St Michael* left Scotland and sailed down the east coast of England to Gravesend, London, where the prisoners were to be transferred to another ship owned by Ralph Williamson. However, the journey from Leith had taken five more days than usual, and Williamson's ship had left. Alexander Peden informed the captain of the *St Michael*, Edward Johnston, that he was a minister, and that he and the other prisoners were held under the charge of not adhering to the religious laws at that time enacted in Scotland. The captain was persuaded to allow them to go free.

Following the Covenanters' defeat at Bothwell Bridge, Peden again found it necessary to escape to Ireland where he found employment as a farm labourer. He returned to Scotland once more, hiding amid the hills and managing to elude his pursuers. The accounts of his close escapes are legion. On one occasion he was conducting a small service in the Carrick hills when a party of soldiers came upon the Covenanters and surrounded them. Out of nowhere came a mist which engulfed the party, allowing the Covenanters to escape.

Alexander Peden was known to have used a number of disguises when hiding from the soldiers. An old wig and a false face he used are still in existence. In 1682 Peden conducted the wedding ceremony between John Brown, the famous martyr, and Isabel Weir. In the same year he officiated at the wedding of John Kirkland and Janet Lindsay.

Another letter of Peden's survives. It was written to the 1st Earl of Stair, a supporter of the Covenant. Lord Stair was himself imprisoned a number of times for the cause.

> *My Lord, – I have but tyme to send you this scrip to lett your Lordship know that I have not yett given up my faith in the Restoration of this Remnant, and that I have got no news of my*

persecutors except that I have to encloss for fear. And I am tauld that 200 men have been doun this way, but I write this to you to show that the Lord has still protected me. I dare not comit more to this than I have done, because I know not into whose hands itt may pass, but praying the good Lord to keep you and yours in all health, and as much happiness as may be, I remain, in all obedience in the Lord,   *Alexr. Peden.*

From my place of 16, known to your Lordship, this 13th of Nov. 1684.

For my Lord Stair, in all haste.

In his old age Peden spent much of his time hiding in a cave on the side of the Lugar Water, north of Ochiltree. The cave was near to the farm of Tenshillingside, which was part of Auchinleck estate, and which was tenanted by his brother. Peden's brother often brought him food and clothing, and kept him informed of the whereabouts of the local troops. It is known that James Renwick, the young upcoming star of the Covenant, visited Peden in his cave and was blessed by the old prophet.

A number of Covenanters are known to have hidden with Peden at different times. Captain John Campbell of Wellwood spent some time on the moors with him in 1685 and John Clark also hid in a cave with him in 1685.

Alexander Peden knew that his health was failing quickly. One night he went to his brother's farm where he died within a few days on 26 January 1686. It was known that Peden wished to be buried alongside Richard Cameron on Airds Moss, but his brother knew this to be too risky a feat for him and a few friends to accomplish. Instead, the body of the minister was transported at nightfall to the kirkyard of Auchinleck, where he was buried in the Peden burial plot.[1]

The story does not end there, however. After a period of 40 days, the dragoons from Sorn Castle heard of Peden's death. They were angry at the fact that they had failed to capture and execute him. Under the command of Murray, they marched to Auchinleck where they dug up his grave, lifting the body back out of the ground before slinging it over the back of a horse. It was taken into Cumnock, where the intention was to have Peden's remains hung up on the gallows tree, as a warning to others of what might happen should they follow Peden's way.

But word reached the local landowner, the Earl of Dumfries, of what plans were afoot. He intervened, and refused to let the soldiers carry out their plan, stating that 'the gibbet was erected for malefactors and murderers, and not for such men as Peden.' Instead they dug a hole at the foot of the gallows tree where Peden was buried 'out of contempt,' according to the gravestone.[2]

1. NS 551215. Monument to Peden and others in Auchinleck churchyard.
2. NS 570203. Monument and two earlier gravestones in Cumnock old cemetery.

46

A WAND'RER
NOW A MARTYR

The Steel family have a few notable Covenanting ancestors –
Captain John, Thomas, Isabel and David – all of whom lived on
farms in the valley of the Logan Water, a tributary of
Lanarkshire's River Nethan. In the latter part of the 17th century
they were part of Hamilton estate. Thomas Steel lived at Over
Skellyhill, which is within one mile of the confluence of the
Logan with the Nethan; David Steel lived at Nether Skellyhill, its
near neighbour; and Captain John at Waterhead, which lies just
over one mile further up the Logan.

David and Thomas were brothers, Thomas being the older
of the two and an elder in the parish church of Lesmahagow, in
which parish the farms lie. On the ousting of the local minister
and installation of a curate he failed to attend church. For this
non-attendance he was fined £300 Scots (£25 Sterling). Isabel
Steel was apprehended for her part in attending conventicles.
She was sentenced in April 1687 to be transported to Barbados.
After the Revolution she was able to return to Lanarkshire, living
for many years thereafter on Logan-side.

Captain John Steel also suffered for his Covenanting
adherence but survived the Killing Times. He was a cousin of
David and Thomas's and had been active at Bothwell Bridge
where he captained the Covenanting forces. After the defeat he

managed to escape, but his father was captured by the soldiers and shot, even although he had not taken part in the fight. His corpse was discovered by friends and interred at Strathaven.

A bounty of 1,000 merks was placed on Captain Steel's head and he had to leave his home. Within a short time the Earl of Airlie came to Waterhead with a warrant from the Crown to take possession of the lands. Steel's wife and family were ejected from their home, and their belongings poinded. Lord Airlie's tenant could find no-one in the district willing to labour for him, and so left the farm. Steel's wife returned after some time, and Captain Steel himself dared to go home on occasion. Most of the time, however, he lived in a turf shelter known as Steel's Seat. This was located in the moors of Nethan-head, four miles from his home. The site of this was long pointed out by the shepherds on the western slopes of Mannoch Hill, now afforested.

After the Glorious Revolution John Steel was able to live peaceably at Waterhead farm, which he rebuilt in 1709. A memorial tablet was built into the farmhouse at this time, inscribed, 'Praise God. J.S. 1709.' Steel received no compensation for the goods stolen from his home. When the Cameronians were formed Steel was appointed a captain in the 26th regiment. He was also placed in charge of overseeing the replacement of the parish curate with a Presbyterian minister. When he died, John Steel was buried at Lesmahagow. A flat stone was placed over his grave, but this was not inscribed.

The most notable member of the family was David Steel, who was to suffer martyrdom. Born in 1654, his wife was Mary Weir, who is said to have been the sister of John Brown of Priesthill's wife. It is known that David also took part in the Battle of Bothwell Bridge, and as a result his name was listed on the roll of fugitives in 1684. He was also a friend of James Renwick.

There is an account of a Covenanter shot in 1680 at Bello Path, near Cumnock in Ayrshire, at which David Steel was present. Lieutenant John Creichton (born in 1648) was at Leifnoreis Castle in Old Cumnock parish when General William Drummond, commander-in-chief of the government troops, sent for him to come to Edinburgh. As Creichton passed through Cumnock he received word that David Steel and a party of Covenanters were awaiting him at the Bello Path. Having just one dragoon and one drummer with him at the time, Creichton ordered the drummer to gallop to the pass and there beat out a dragoon march whilst he and the dragoon made their way by a back route. The Covenanters, assuming from the drumbeat that a strong party of soldiers was approaching made their escape. One of their number was shot, his name is not known. According to the Memoirs of Captain John Creichton, 'Either I or the dragoon (I forget which) shot one of the rebels dead, as he crossed us to get into the moss.'

The dragoons in Lanarkshire spent many weeks searching the moors for David, and Nether Skellyhill was regularly visited just in case he had come home. David, however, had fled the farmhouse, and hid himself at Steel's Seat.

In the winter of 1686 David was suffering from the severe frosts and snows which the weather had brought. He decided to risk going back to his farmhouse where he knew his wife would hide him. David was enjoying the comfort and heat of his home when, on 20 December, a farm servant informed Mary that the soldiers were coming towards the farm.

The party was led by Lieutenant John Creichton. Some of the soldiers were mounted, others, said to be highlanders, walked alongside. As they approached Nether Skellyhill one of the soldiers spotted a figure exiting by a rear window and making its way to the small glen which runs up past the farm. The alarm raised, the soldiers set off in pursuit. Steel knew the countryside like the back of his hand and, keeping himself hidden by scrub and woodland, was able to elude his pursuers for several miles. He had with him a flask of gunpowder but, before he even dared to use it, it was rendered useless when it got soaked when he crossed the Logan Water. Near to Yonderton farm the soldiers were close enough to take a pot shot at him, but the bullet missed. A little further on, near to Meadow farm, the soldiers caught up with Steel and surrounded him.

David Steel withdrew his gun and, although it was useless as a weapon, managed to keep the soldiers at a distance. Lieutenant Creichton came to the spot and asked Steel to surrender. He promised that he would be given quarter and a fair trial in Edinburgh. Steel, realising that he had little other choice, surrendered himself to the soldiers, who were quick to remove his gun and tie him up.

But the soldiers did not take Steel to Edinburgh. Instead they forced him to walk back to Skellyhill. Steel's wife had all this time been watching the pursuit from the farm and she waited with bated breath. At the front door of the farm, in full view of his wife and child, the order was given to shoot. The soldiers refused to carry this out, and rode off on their horses. However, the highlanders agreed, and a single shot resounded throughout the glen.[1]

It is said that the shot was aimed at his head, and that his brains were scattered across the farmyard. When the soldiers left Mary Weir began to collect together the remains of her husband's head and bound these together in a napkin, uttering the long-remembered words, 'The archers have shot at thee, my husband, but they could not reach thy soul; it has escaped liked a dove far away, and is at rest.'

Friends from Glen Logan came to Nether Skellyhill and took the body of David Steel to the kirkyard of Lesmahagow, where his remains were laid to rest.[2]

1. NS 789374. Monument at Skellyhill marking site of martyrdom.
2. NS 814399. Gravestone in Lesmahagow churchyard.

47

BANISHT I WAS FOR COVENANTED CAUSE

Many Covenanters were banished to the American plantations where they were to be employed as slaves. Thousands of men and women were sold into slavery in this way for their adherence to the covenants, and millions of Americans can claim their ancestors arrived in the New World at this time.

There are many cases of Covenanters who were sold into slavery being able to earn their freedom, and many returned home. Gilbert MacAdam was a well-known Covenanter who managed to do just this. He was still unlucky, however, for he was to suffer martyrdom at a later date (see Chapter 35). Another Ayrshire survivor was John Campbell, banished to America in 1683. He managed to make his way home two years later and survived until 1721, dying aged 79.[1]

Two brothers, Gilbert and William Milroy, farmed Kirkalla, on Castle Stuart estate in Wigtownshire. In 1684 both were asked to swear the Test Act, which William did, but Gilbert bribed the Sheriff-depute with £12 and got off. In 1685, when they were due to take the new oath, they decided that they could not bring themselves to do this, and with a younger brother, Patrick, decided to leave their home and flee to the hills. Within a short time the soldiers came to Kirkalla to search for the men and finding them absent decided to plunder the house. All valuables were taken, and eight horses, 80 cattle and 500 sheep were driven away. Two days later 70 horsemen returned to the farm and took anything else which they thought was of value. The Milroy wives were still at the house, and they protested that the men would have no use for women's clothes. As a result of this the soldiers placed matches between their fingers and lit them, a common form of torture at the time.

On the following day a search was made of the immediate locality; Gilbert and William Milroy and a lad of 16 years were discovered. They were taken to Minnigaff where they were questioned by the Earl of Home. He asked who had sheltered them whilst they were away from home and, despite being tortured, they refused to tell anything. The same threats were repeated for the next six days until it was decided to send the men to Barr in Ayrshire, where Major-General Drummond was staying. Here again the men were threatened with death, but their resolve was as strong as ever.

The Milroys were then taken to Edinburgh where they had their ears cut off. They were sentenced to banishment, and taken with around 190 men to a ship at Newhaven. The Covenanters were tied together in sixes and locked below decks. The ship took them to Jamaica, a voyage lasting three months with 32 of their number dying en route. At Port Royal the survivors were sold as slaves. Gilbert Milroy was one who survived, and after the Glorious Revolution in 1688 was able to return to Scotland, surviving until at least 1710.

Alexander Brown was sentenced abroad for his adherence to the Covenants. He was able to return to Scotland and when he died was buried in the kirkyard at Douglas in Lanarkshire.[2] Another resident of the village was the tailor James Gavin. He lived in a house in the Main Street and suffered the ill will of Claverhouse, who tortured him with his own shears, cutting his left ear off on 4 August 1685. Gavin was later banished to the island of Barbados, but was able to return home after the Revolution. When he rebuilt his home in 1695 he had the lintel over his door carved with a pair of shears and some cloth, the date of erection, his initials, and 'HD', those of his wife.[3]

John Mathieson was the tenant of Rosehill, near Closeburn in Dumfriesshire. He had been hiding in a cave on the farm of Kirkpatrick with three others when they were spotted by someone who was keen to inform on them. The informer went to Sir Thomas Kirkpatrick, the local laird, to ask him to send a messenger to the soldiers stationed at Ballagan, seven miles to the north-west. Kirkpatrick, who was a friend of the Covenanters, refused, and told the man to travel there himself. Whilst this was taking place he sent one of his servants to the cave to warn the men of impending capture. The servant, however, was too late. The soldiers spotted the four men and they were quickly arrested. They were held in Dumfries gaol for a time before being sent to Edinburgh where they were put on trial on 19 June 1684. Mathieson and the three other Covenanters – John Crichton in Kirkpatrick, John MacChisholm in Spittle and James MacGeachan in Dalry – were found guilty of reset and conversing with rebels and thus sentenced to be transported to the plantations.

Mathieson and around 30 others were sold into the hands of Walter and James Gibson. He was taken to Greenock and placed on board the *Carolina Merchant*, which set sail at the beginning of July. The Gibsons were keen to take as many slaves as possible, and it is recorded that Elizabeth Linning, an innocent woman who had turned up to wave goodbye to her relations, was captured and sent abroad. She was fortunate in being able to return home later.

The journey to the Americas took 19 weeks; the slaves being ill-treated during this time. Mathieson recorded that he 'received nine great blows upon my back, so that for many days I could not lift my head higher nor my breast.' Each prisoner was only allowed one pint of water per day, some porridge, a little beer, two and a half ounces of salted beef and some hard peas. Any money they had with which to buy their freedom in the New World was taken from them, and any time they wished to worship they were locked down below.

The Covenanters arrived in Carolina where they suddenly went down with fever. Most were sold into the slave trade, but by some unknown method Mathieson managed to gain his freedom and sailed through a raging storm to Virginia before travelling by foot to Pennsylvania. He did not miss out on illness, however, for he was 'near unto death with a great weighty sickness.' He was then able to travel to New Jersey and ultimately New York. In New Jersey he became sick but was looked after by a stranger. On his recovery Mathieson offered to work as their servant, in order to purchase his return fare.

In New York he made arrangements with a shipmaster to sail back to Britain, landing in London. He travelled north to Scotland once more, arriving back in Nithsdale in the autumn of 1687. The persecutions were still taking place, and he had to live on the moors during which time he attended at least one conventicle at which James Renwick preached.

On one occasion John Mathieson returned to Rosehill farm, where his wife was still living with their children. He managed to obtain work at the harvest and went into the kitchen where he was fed. One of his sons quietly whispered to his mother, 'If my father is still alive, then this is surely him!' She looked at his face for a moment before exclaiming, 'My husband!' and ran to him.

John Mathieson lived to the age of 72, witnessing the Glorious Revolution and a return to peace. He wrote his testimony which was entitled, *Nathaniel; or the Dying Testimony of John Mathieson in Closeburn unto the noble cause and truths and testimony of Christ, for which he suffered banishment unto the foreign land of America.* This was published in *A Collection of Dying Testimonies* in 1806. Mathieson died on 6 December 1723 and was buried in the kirkyard of Closeburn.[4]

James Callum was a glover who lived in Dumfries. He had been active at the taking of Sir James Turner but it was never proved whether or not he fought at Rullion Green. He had been a supporter of the Covenant for many years and was fined in 1662 and 1663 for non-attendance at the curate's kirk. He was also imprisoned for a time and in a proclamation of 9 May 1668 was listed as one of the rebels still to be dealt with following the Pentland Rising. He escaped to the East Indies, where he remained for seven years. On his return to Scotland he was apprehended by Claverhouse and held in Dumfries tolbooth for 14 months. He was then transferred to Edinburgh where he was held for a year and a half. At length it was decided to banish him to the plantations in Carolina. Callum died there and when word returned home of his death his home was ransacked and his wife and daughters were forced to live in the hills for three and a half years.

In the old kirkyard of Tinwald, near Dumfries, is a recumbent graveslab and a later obelisk in memory of a Covenanter who suffered much for the cause, but who survived his persecutions. John Corbet was born in 1643, the year in which the Solemn League and Covenant was ratified by the English Parliament. In 1684 he was captured by a party of troops under John Graham of Claverhouse and transported to Edinburgh, where he was held with other prisoners in gaol. In the Books of Council for 16 February 1685 he is listed as one of 12 who refused to take the oath, a number of the other prisoners giving in to this and being set free.

Corbet was sentenced to be banished to the plantations in North America. Some time elapsed before he was taken on board ship, however, for on 17 August he was still listed with 21 others as being held in Leith tolbooth. Soon after he was handed over to the care of George Scott of Pitlochie in Fife, who was to transport him and around 100 others to the eastern part of New Jersey. He was placed on board the ship, but remained in Leith harbour for another fortnight, before the vessel set sail on 5 September.

The hardship endured on board was horrendous. Within a few days it was discovered that the beef had been improperly cured, and had to be thrown overboard. Food rations plummeted, and as the ship passed Land's End, fever broke out. Soon three or four passengers were dying each day, and of the crew only the captain and boatswain survived. George Scott and his family all died, bringing the total number of dead to between 60 or 70.

The time of leaving Scotland had been against them also,

for the equinoctial gales pushed them well off course. Between the storms they were becalmed which further prolonged the journey. Even the hull of the ship twice sprung a leak. At length, 15 weeks after leaving Leith, the boat landed at New Jersey.

Corbet's troubles were not over, however, for George Scott's son-in-law, a man by the name of Johnstone, went to court to claim the prisoners as his slaves. It seems that Scott had sold the remnants of his Pitlochie estate and had planned emigrating to the New World in order to start a new life as a plantation owner. The court, however, found in the prisoners' favour, for they had not agreed to work for Scott, and had been sent to America against their will. The cost of the trial left the remainder of the Scott fortunes so depleted that it was seen as divine retribution for 'making merchandise of the suffering people of God'.

Most of the prisoners travelled to New England where they settled for some time, though nothing definite is known about the actions of John Corbet. All we know is that by 1687 he was sufficiently well off to afford to pay his passage back home. He survived for another nine years, dying at the age of 63.[5]

From the parish of Kirkinner in Wigtownshire, William Sprot in Clutoch farm was forced from his home sometime in 1685, in order to avoid the soldiers who were searching for him. He thought it would be wise to escape to Ireland, but at Portpatrick there were soldiers guarding the harbour. He was apprehended and two dragoons marched him back to Wigtown tolbooth. There he was laid on a cold slab of rock and manacles fixed to his arms and legs. The dragoons used knives to cut off his ears and tortured him by lighting matches between his fingers. It was then determined that he should be banished to America but he died on board the ship. His wife, who had witnessed her husband's torture, miscarried their unborn child.

1. NX 275941. Gravestone in Barr churchyard.
2. NS 836310. Gravestone in Douglas churchyard.
3. NS 835308. Memorial cairn in Main Street.
4. NX 904923 Gravestone in Closeburn churchyard.
5. NY 002816. Gravestone in Tinwald churchyard.

48

WILLIAM CLELAND

One of the most noted Covenanters was William Cleland. He was born in the parish of Douglas in 1661, where his father was the gamekeeper to the Marquis of Douglas.

Cleland was a learned boy, and enrolled at St Salvator's College, St Andrews, on 2 March 1677. He returned to Lanarkshire where he threw in his lot with the Covenanters. When the 'Highland Host' were in the South west, Cleland wrote a scathing poem about their habits:

> Nought like religion they retain,
> Of Moral Honesty, they're clean,
> In nothing they're accounted sharp,
> Except in Bagpipe, and in Harp.

On 31 March 1679 a skirmish occurred at a conventicle held at Cumberhead, in the parish of Lesmahagow. During the service the scouts reported 20 approaching soldiers, under the command of Lieutenant John Dalyell and Ensign Menzies. They had come from the garrison at Lanark. The dragoons were attacked by the Covenanters, Dalyell being fatally wounded. William Weir, servant at Bourtries, was blamed for stabbing the lieutenant with his pitchfork. A number of Covenanters were apprehended for their part in the attack, including John Williamson of Lesmahagow. According to Ensign Menzies' report, William Cleland was one of the main actors.

At the Battle of Drumclog Cleland was appointed one of the officers in charge of the Covenanters, although he was still only 18 years of age. He held the rank of captain. He was again an officer at the Battle of Bothwell Bridge. Accounts of these battles can be found in other chapters.

After the defeat of Bothwell, Cleland fled to the Netherlands, where he remained for six years. He continued his studies at the University of Utrecht where it is thought that he became acquainted with Alexander Shields, author of *A Hind Let Loose*, published in 1687.

Cleland returned to Scotland in 1685 when he took part in the rebellion by Archibald, 9th Earl of Argyll. The expedition failed, and Cleland spent some time wandering among the moors of Ayrshire and Lanarkshire until he fled to Holland again. He was to remain there until after the Revolution.

When the Cameronians were raised at Douglas in 1689[1] Cleland was appointed to the rank of Colonel. His soldiers served for the wage of sixpence per day. Following the defeat of General Mackay at Killiecrankie, Cleland's men were given the task of defending Dunkeld against the Jacobite army, which was expected to attack on its march southward. The Cameronians numbered around 800, whereas the Jacobites were six or seven times as numerous, and were spirited with their recent success.

When the lookouts brought word back that the highland force was so numerous, a deputation was sent to Cleland asking that they make a retreat whilst they could save themselves. Cleland would have none of it. 'I have been bidden to hold Dunkeld,' he said, 'and for me, I shall stay here although every man leaves me.'

The men were still concerned, and observed that, 'The officers have horses, whereas we cannot ride for it, if things turn out for the worst.'

'Then let the horses be led out, so that they can be shot,' Cleland replied. 'Then you will know that we shall stand by you, if you will stand by us.'

The men were satisfied with this response, and told Cleland that they trusted their colonel and officers.

The Cameronian soldiers arranged their outposts around the small town and then moved back into one large mass. They awaited the Jacobites charging, which was not long in coming. On 21 August they came at speed, swords in the air, but they were met by the Cameronian pikes and halberts. Again and again the Jacobites were repelled.

The Covenanters continued to resist each time the highlanders attacked, and many of them died in the onsloughts. But the Jacobite forces kept pushing the Cameronians backward, till at last all they held was the cathedral and Dunkeld House. After some time they had no bullets left, so the soldiers stripped lead from the roof of Dunkeld House and melted it down. This was then poured into makeshift moulds formed out of the clay in the ground and when it cooled it was used as ammunition. The Jacobites took most of the houses surrounding the church, from where they continued to shoot at the Cameronian forces.

A sortie was then made by some of the Cameronians who left the cathedral and made their way round the town, setting fire to many of the houses. The Jacobite soldiers who had taken these buildings were burned to death. Other valiant attacks were made from the cathedral, forcing the Jacobite soldiers to pull back. They said that 'they could fight against men, but were not fit to fight any more against devils'.

The battle raged from 7.00am until noon on 21 August 1689, when the Jacobites under Colonel Cannon decided to abandon their attack and retreat in disorder. Nevertheless, Cannon was later to claim Dunkeld as a 'victory'. The facts were: 15 dead on the Cameronian side, 300 dead highlanders.

A contemporary report on the battle relates the story:
Colonel Cannon was heard to say when he saw our men fight so bravely that his men were not able to stand before them, that he thought it better now to fly for it than to stand and fight against madmen, for such he esteemed them who fought so valiantly, being so few in number, against such a multitude of enemies. Of the

rebels we are credibly informed, there were killed about two or three
hundred, many wounded and taken: and of ours not above thirty
soldiers in all the engagements: but the greatest loss was that
Lieutenant-Colonel Cleland returning victorious, as he was
coming through the town, had the misfortune to be shot at out of a
window, of which wound he soon died.

Bullets struck both his head and body, but Cleland was still alive and ordered his men to carry him into one of the houses, 'that the Cameronians may not lose heart when they see how I am wounded.' As he was being taken to a nearby house he breathed his last and command of the soldiers passed on to Captain Munro. Afterwards, Cleland was buried in the nave of the cathedral, near to the western door, where a memorial stone marks his grave.[2]

In 1697 a volume of poems by William Cleland was published. These reveal his wide education and inquisitive mind, with interests ranging from science and religion to philosophy and nature. A number of the verses were quite humorous. Cleland's son, William (d. 1741), was the original of 'Will Honeycomb' in the Spectator. William's son, John (d. 1789), was the author of several novels.

1. NS 835311. Statue of the first colonel, Earl of Angus, on spot where the regiment was raised.
2. NO 024426. Gravestone in Dunkeld cathedral ruins.

49

JAMES RENWICK

James Renwick was born on 15 February 1662 in Knees Cottage in the Dumfriesshire village of Moniaive. His father, Andrew Renwick, was a weaver; his mother was Elizabeth Corson. Together they had lost a number of children and Elizabeth often prayed for a son who would 'not only be an heir of glory, but that might live to serve Him in his generation.' Elizabeth was later to give birth to at least two daughters.[1]

James was always interested in religion – it was said that he first took an interest in the bible at the age of two, and by six years was able to read and question its contents. His parents were able to scrimp and save to ensure James received an education, even managing to send him to school in Edinburgh. He was later able to attend Edinburgh University where he spent too much time enjoying himself to study to the best of his ability, and he began to question the existence of God, even considering atheism. He witnessed the execution of Donald Cargill in the city on 27 July 1681, which made him determined to follow his leadership. On a couple of occasions, after some Covenanters had been hanged in Edinburgh's Grassmarket, Renwick was among those who cut down their bodies. He was to graduate with an MA degree in the summer of 1681 but was concerned about this as it involved him accepting the king's authority over the church.

Renwick moved to Lanark where he at first planned to become a burgess. He became acquainted with the Covenanters, attending one of their meetings at Logan House and being present at the posting of an 'Act and Apologetic Declaration of the true Presbyterians of the Church of Scotland' (or the Lanark Declaration) by the Society People on 12 January 1682. At noon on that day 40 horsemen and 20 on foot made their way to the cross of the burgh. They defaced the stone statues and affixed the declaration to the cross. The magistrates of Lanark were later to be fined 6,000 merks for failing to disperse the 'villains'. The authorities captured a Lanark weaver, William Harvey, who had taken part in posting the declaration. He was tried by the Justiciary Court in Edinburgh on 20 February and ordered to be hanged at Lanark Cross on 2 March 1682. He was 38 years old.[2]

When Renwick later witnessed the execution of Robert Gray from Northumberland at Edinburgh on 19 May 1682, he experienced a premonition of his own hanging.

Renwick attended a number of conventicles in 1682, notably those at Priesthill and Talla Linn, as well as a couple held in Edinburgh. It was at the Talla Linn[3] conventicle, held on 11 October, that Renwick was chosen, with William Boyd, John Flint and John Nisbet, for the ministry by the United Societies to study at the University of Groningen in the Netherlands. He travelled to Rotterdam and thence Groningen, arriving early in 1683. Dr Johannes Marck, Professor of Divinity and Church History, described Renwick as a 'notable and learned young man of great hope'. Renwick missed his homeland immensely, writing in a letter, 'I think that if the Lord could be tied to any place, it is to the moors and mosses in Scotland.' In another he recorded, 'I am not a little sorrowful at the very heart that I am not in Scotland, for nothing that ever I was trysted with was such an exercise to me as my being detained out of it is.'

Renwick was ordained on 10 May 1683 at the church of Leeuwarden. Later there was some doubt about the validity of this for a minister in Scotland, but at a meeting of the Societies held at Friarminnan in January 1686 it was agreed that the church in Holland did not make him a minister of the Church of Scotland, but had ordained him as a minister of Christ.

The return journey to Scotland was hazardous and Renwick had to travel through Ireland, where he took the name of 'James Bruce'. He arrived in his homeland in September 1683, spending some time under cover in Edinburgh. On 3 October 1683 he attended a meeting of the Societies at Darmead in Lanarkshire. After a prayer he gave an account of his ordination, displayed his certificate, and was received as the Covenanters' minister. On 23 November 1683 a large conventicle was held at Darmead[4] at which he commenced his ministry, preaching to many hundreds.

The troubles meant that Renwick could not present himself in public, and had to wander from one known adherent's home to another. His close shaves with the authorities were legion. In July 1684 he was travelling with three others in the area known as Strathaven Moor. Suddenly they were spotted by a troop of dragoons and a chase ensued. Renwick galloped towards the summit of Dungavel Hill, but dismounted and hid in a hollow near the summit cairn where he remained until nightfall before he moved on.

Lady Holme was interrogated by the authorities regarding her attendance at one of Renwick's conventicles. The Earl of Queensberry writes:

> Lady Holme, solemnly sworne and interrogate, depones that about eight dayes since or therby about nyn houres at night she saw Rennick, the rebellieous preacher, with above a dozen moe went by the house where she dwelles, but knew not which way they were goeing; and farther depones that upon the Darpell Burne she heard the said Rennick lector upon the second chapter of Ezachrie from the seventh verse downward; and that there was ane chield babteized, and the preacher discharged the parent to pay the swplie; and this is trewth as she shall answer to God, and cannot wryte. The Lords order her to be sent to the plantationes.

Renwick was in great demand for baptising the Covenanters' children, for they did not wish them to be baptised by the parish curates. Within a three-month spell he baptised no fewer than 300 children – other estimates put the figure at over 600 children in one year. He was also responsible for many marriages and funerals, all held in remote farms and on the moors.

In September 1684 the Privy Council issued an edict which stated that:

> We command and charge all and sundry our lieges and subjects that they nor none of them presume, nor take upon hand to reset, supply, or intercommune with the said Mr James Renwick, rebel aforesaid; nor furnish him with meat, drink, house, harbour, victual, nor no other thing useful or comfortable to him; or to have intelligence with him by word, writ, or message, or any other manner of way whatsoever, under the pain of being esteemed art and part with him in the crimes foresaid, and pursued therefor with all rigour to the terror of others. And we hereby require all our sheriffs and other officers to apprehend and commit to prison the person of the said Mr James Renwick wherever they can find him.

Despite this act, Renwick avoided imprisonment for another three years. The soldiers pursued him all over southern Scotland, but he hid in caves and makeshift huts, always moving on before too many people knew of his whereabouts.

Renwick was one of those who took part in writing the Apologetical Declaration, which was published on 8 November 1684. It was noted that he was not very keen on its content, which was virtually a declaration of war, but in the end had to agree in order to keep the Covenanters united. Nevertheless, he was now a wanted man, described by the government as a 'pretended field-preacher and seditious villain'.

On 28 May 1685 he was at the head of 200 Covenanters who made their way into Sanquhar in Dumfriesshire and affixed the second Sanquhar Declaration on the cross, in which James VII was denounced as a murderer and idolater.[5] After this he made sure there was a lookout stationed wherever he went and at any conventicle at which he was preaching there was always a horse standing by, saddled and bridled, on which he could make a swift getaway.

On 20 July 1686 Renwick preached at a large conventicle at Greencleugh in the Lammermuir Hills, Berwickshire. He made his way to it from East Lothian, and after his sermon from Solomon 1:4 returned by way of Byrecleuch and Danskine. During the same year he spent some time in the north of England. Other conventicles were held in the Braid Hills, to the south of Edinburgh. At the end of 1687 Renwick was almost captured at Peebles once more. Another conventicle took place at Riskenhope, near St Mary's Loch in Selkirkshire, in January 1688. This was Renwick's last, and according to James Hogg, 'When he prayed that day few of his hearers' cheeks were dry. My parents were well acquainted with a woman whom he there baptized.'

In the last few months of his life Renwick wrote to Sir Robert Hamilton:

> My business was never so weighty, so multiplied, and so ill to be guided, to my apprehension, as it hath been this year; and my body was never so frail. Excessive travel, night wanderings, unseasonable sleep and diet, and frequent preaching in all seasons of weather, especially in the night, have so debilitated me that I am often incapable for any work. Sometimes I fall into fits of swooning and fainting. When I use means for my recovery, I find it sometimes effectual; but my desire to the work, and the necessity and importunity of people, prompts me to do more than my natural strength will allow, and to undertake such toilsome business as casts my body down again. I mention not this through any anxiety, quarrelling, or discontent, but to show you my condition in this respect. I may say that, under all my frailties and distempers, I find great peace and sweetness in reflecting upon the occasion thereof; it is a part of my glory and joy to bear such infirmities, contracted through my poor and small labour in my Master's vineyard.

Renwick was apprehended on 1 February 1688 on one of his secret visits to Edinburgh. He was lodging at a friend's house on the Castlehill when he was arrested. This was the home of John Luckup, who was infamous in the city for his 'free trade' with

England. On that day a group of excisemen paid a visit, under the guise of checking up on Luckup, but in reality hoping to apprehend Renwick and claim the reward. Renwick had a pistol in his hand, a scuffle broke out, and he managed to make a bid for freedom, running down the Castle Wynd. Between there and the Cowgatehead he received a number of blows from his pursuers and he fell to the ground. He was easily apprehended and taken to gaol. Patrick Graham, Captain of the Guards, looked at the 26 year old and asked, 'Is this boy the Mr Renwick that the nation hath been so much troubled with?'

Placed on trial, the witnesses for the prosecution included Claverhouse, Livingstone, Balcarres, and Tarbat. He was sentenced to die on 8 February 1688 for having pled guilty to three charges, that of refusing the king's authority, of not paying taxes to the crown, and of persuading his followers to attend conventicles bearing arms. The execution was postponed until the 17 February, during which time a stream of visitors tried to persuade him to accept at least some rule of the king, but he refused. Among those who visited were the Bishop of Edinburgh, Dr Munro of the University, and the Lord Advocate, Sir John Dalrymple. On the day he was to be executed he was allowed to see his mother and sisters, who had made their way to the city from Moniaive. His father had died in Renwick's thirteenth year.

On the scaffold Renwick attempted to address the crowd, but all the time the soldiers beat their drums in order to drown out his words. The hangman sprung the trapdoor and he dropped to his death. He was the last Covenanter to die in the city of Edinburgh. His remains were taken from the scaffold by Helen Alexander and rolled in a winding sheet before being buried in Greyfriars' kirkyard.

1. NX 771910. Monument near site of birthplace, Moniaive.
2. NS 888432. Headstone in St Kentigern's Churchyard, Lanark.
3. NT 138202.
4. NS 901553. Monument at Darmead marking site of conventicle.
5. NS 784097. Monument on site of Sanquhar cross.

50

APPEARING FOR THE RESCUE OF MR DAVID HOUSTON

Rev David Houston, an Irishman, was one of the Covenanting ministers and an associate of James Renwick. On 22 September 1686 the Societies decided at a meeting to invite him over to Scotland to preach to them. When he arrived he travelled to the upland community of Wanlockhead, in the Lowther Hills, where a secret meeting was being held on Boxing Day. David Houston so impressed the men that day they resolved he should be asked to preach among them, though not as a settled minister. Some nine months later, in June 1687, a member of the Societies was duly sent to Ireland to bring Houston's wife and family across, allowing £5 for expenses.

David Houston spent many months preaching to the Covenanters, but sometime in January 1688 he returned to Ireland where he was arrested and kept in a Dublin prison for many months, and subjected to physical abuse. At length it was arranged that he would be brought back to Scotland, and placed on trial in Edinburgh. It was anticipated that he would be executed for his part in preaching in the fields.

The Covenanters of South-west Scotland made plans to rescue Houston, but this did not take place at the expected time. However, word reached the Ayrshire men that Houston was being taken towards Edinburgh and that the party of soldiers, with their charge, would put up for the night at an inn in Cumnock known as the Blue Tower.

Word spread like wildfire that Houston was in the town and arrangements were made to make his release the following morning. The spot chosen was the Bello Path[1], a narrow gully between rocky cliffs through which the main Edinburgh road and the Bello Water pass, three miles from the town. On 20 June, the Covenanters arranged themselves up on the heights, overlooking the road, and awaited the arrival of the party.

When the soldiers escorting Houston arrived at the spot, the Covenanters discharged their muskets. The dragoons threw themselves to the ground and grabbed for their own guns. Soon shots were returned and a gunfight ensued. Several soldiers are known to have been killed and, according to a proclamation issued on 22 June, 'others were desperately wounded.' The soldiers let go of David Houston, who was mounted on a horse, but the sound of gunfire caused it to rear up and run off. Unfortunately, Houston's legs were tied firmly beneath the horse, so that he was unable to break free. As the horse galloped off, Houston's body slipped round beneath the horse and his head was battered on the ground. He took blow after blow, resulting in severe concussion. (Although he was eventually freed, Houston suffered brain damage and he never recovered his full mental faculties. He returned once more to Ireland where he was to die in 1696.)

A number of Covenanters suffered injuries, but the only fatality on the Covenanting side was a local farmer, John MacGeachan. He managed to struggle from Bello Path southwards towards his home of Meikle Auchingibbert farm. On the way he called at a cottage by the name of Stonepark, where he asked the occupant for a drink and some sustenance. Terrified of what might happen by way of reprisal, the cottar refused. Tradition states that MacGeachan cursed the occupant and warned that no crops would ever grow in his fields again. After this the cottage of Stonepark fell into ruins, and today it is but a rickle of stones in the long grass.

On reaching his own home, MacGeachan was fed. But his family also feared reprisals, for he was a known Covenanter, one who was listed in a proclamation of Charles II, dated 5 May 1684, naming all those who 'were supposed to have been under arms, or to have harboured those who were'. Instead, MacGeachan's friends built a turf hut for him, near to Stonepark, where he was able to rest. Food was taken to him daily but MacGeachan's injuries were too severe. He died on 28 July 1688, over one month after the incident at Bello Path, and was buried where his hut had stood.[2]

After the rescue at Bello Path the soldiers from the garrison at Sorn were involved in a dragnet operation to try and capture those who were known to have taken part in Houston's rescue. The soldiers arrived at Barglachan farm, in the parish of Auchinleck, where they spotted a young lad looking after the cattle. They asked him if he knew of the whereabouts of any Covenanters but the lad was unwilling to say anything. The soldiers threatened him with torture, but still the lad revealed nothing. At length they left him alone and continued towards Sorn. Whether or not the lad did know something is unknown, but a story handed down at the farm claims that there was a 'Covenanter's mark', no longer visible, carved into the barn by a hill man who had hidden there on at least one occasion.

At Tincorn Hill in Sorn parish the soldiers came upon another young lad, George Wood, who was only 16 years of age. It was night-time, and the fact that he was out in the fields was sufficient reason for Trooper John Reid to draw out his gun and shoot him dead. Reid was challenged for having shot Wood without first questioning him, or placing him on trial, but he replied, 'I knew that he was a Whig, and Whigs ought to be shot wherever they are found.' Being killed in June 1688, George Wood not only has the distinction of being the last Covenanter to die for the cause, but also the youngest.[3]

1. NS 602217. A plaque marks the approximate location of the rescue.
2. NS592194. Gravestone located in field near to the present Stonepark cottage.
3. NS550268. Memorial stone affixed to rear gable of church.

BIBLIOGRAPHY

Barr, Rev James, *The Scottish Covenanters*, John Smith, Glasgow, 1946.

Campbell, Thorbjorn, *Standing Witnesses*, Saltire Society, Edinburgh, 1996.

Cowan, Edward J, *Montrose: for Covenant and King*, Weidenfeld & Nicolson, London, 1977.

Cowan, Ian B, *The Scottish Covenanters 1660-88*, Victor Gollancz, London, 1976.

Crone, Robert WA, *Covenanters Monuments of Scotland*, Regency Press, 1984.

Dodds, James, *The Fifty Years' Struggle of the Scottish Covenanters*, Edmonston & Douglas, Edinburgh, 1860.

Gibson, James, *Tombstones of the Covenanters*, Dunn & Wright, Glasgow, nd.

Guthrie, Ellen Jane, *Tales of the Covenanters*, Hamilton, Adams & Co., London, 1880.

Hewison, James King, *The Covenanters*, 2 vols., John Smith, Glasgow, 1913. *Dalgarnoc: Its Saints and Heroes*, Courier Press, Dumfries, 1935.

Horne, Rev A Sinclair, *Torchbearers of the Truth*, Scottish Reformation Society, Edinburgh, 1968.

Howie, John, *The Scots Worthies*, William MacKenzie, London, nd.

Kerr, Rev James (ed), *The Covenants and the Covenanters*, RW Hunter, Edinburgh, 1895.

Lawson, Rev Roderick, *The Covenanters of Ayrshire*, J & R Parlane, Paisley, 1904.

Linklater, Magnus & Hesketh, Christian, *For King and Conscience*, Weidenfeld & Nicolson, London, 1989.

MacPherson, Hector, *Outlaws for Freedom*, Protestant Institute of Scotland, Edinburgh, 1956.

Purves, Jock, *Fair Sunshine*, Banner of Truth Trust, Edinburgh, 1968.

Simpson, Rev Robert, *Traditions of the Covenanters*, Gall & Inglis, Edinburgh, 1850.

Smellie, Alexander, *Men of the Covenant*, Andrew Melrose, London, 1903.

Terry, CS, *John Graham of Claverhouse*, Constable, London, 1905.

The Pentland Rising, Maclehose, Glasgow, 1905.

Thomson, Rev John H, *The Martyr Graves of Scotland*, Oliphant, Anderson & Ferrier, Edinburgh, nd.

A Cloud of Witnesses, Johnstone Hunter, Edinburgh, 1871.

Todd, Adam Brown, *Covenanting Pilgrimages and Studies*, Oliphant, Anderson & Ferrier, Edinburgh, 1911.

Whitley, Elizabeth, *The Two Kingdoms*, Scottish Reformation Society, Edinburgh, 1977.

Wodrow, Rev Robert, *History of the Sufferings of the Church of Scotland*, 4 vols., edited by Rev Robert Burns, Glasgow, 1828-36.

INDEX